John Silvester is Australia's longest-~~~~~~~~~~~~~~porter, covering the beat since 1978. He has won four Walkley Awards, the Graham Perkin Australian Journalist of the Year Award, nine Melbourne Press Club Quills, nine Victorian Law Foundation Awards, a Ned Kelly Award for true crime writing, a Ned Kelly lifetime achievement award, an ASEAN Fellowship to study crime and corruption in South East Asia, and has been elevated to the Australian Media Hall of Fame.

John narrated and co-wrote true crime documentaries produced and directed by Terry Carlyon, including the Logie-winning ABC documentary, *Conviction*, on the murder of Jill Meagher. He has written or co-authored over 30 books, including the *Chopper* and *Underbelly* series, later adapted to film and television.

John appeared in one *Underbelly* movie as himself but was asked to quietly remove himself from the set for overacting.

He writes the award-winning 'Naked City' column for *The Age*, presents the true crime podcast of the same name, and appears weekly on the top-rating 3AW breakfast program as 'Sly of the Underworld'.

John fought world champion Barry Michael to a draw in a charity boxing match which many experts still refer to as 'The Bloodbath of Blackburn'.

For more on the *Naked City* podcast,
scan the QR code below:

NAKED CITY

True Stories of Crimes,
Cock-ups, Crooks & Cops

JOHN SILVESTER

MACMILLAN
Pan Macmillan Australia

Pan Macmillan acknowledges the Traditional Custodians of Country throughout Australia and their connections to lands, waters and communities. We pay our respect to Elders past and present and extend that respect to all Aboriginal and Torres Strait Islander peoples today. We honour more than sixty thousand years of storytelling, art and culture.

Some of the people in this book have had their names changed to protect their identities.

First published 2023 in Macmillan by Pan Macmillan Australia Pty Ltd
1 Market Street, Sydney, New South Wales, Australia, 2000

Copyright © John Silvester 2023

The moral right of the author to be identified as the author of this work has been asserted.

All rights reserved. No part of this book may be reproduced or transmitted by any person or entity (including Google, Amazon or similar organisations), in any form or by any means, electronic or mechanical, including photocopying, recording, scanning or by any information storage and retrieval system, without prior permission in writing from the publisher.

A catalogue record for this book is available from the National Library of Australia

Typeset in 12/16 pt Adobe Garamond Pro by Midland Typesetters, Australia

Printed by IVE

The author and the publisher have made every effort to contact copyright holders for material used in this book. Any person or organisation that may have been overlooked should contact the publisher.

The paper in this book is FSC® certified. FSC® promotes environmentally responsible, socially beneficial and economically viable management of the world's forests.

*To the Hounds from Police Rounds
who introduced me to the world of crime.*

*And to The Kat and Nine Lives
who always kept me grounded.*

10680–45444

CONTENTS

What the critics say	xi
Foreword	xiii
Introduction	xvii

PART 1 THE CROOKS

Copper finally comes a cropper	5
Williams no criminal mastermind	11
Inside the minds of murderers	16
Dangerous liaisons	21
Mackerel or sprat?	27
A tale of two brothers divided	33
Bread, water and the Liquorice Mile	38
Danger lurking in the shadows	43
Are crooks born or made?	48
Knight condemned by his own hand	53
Did Rocco get away with Carl Williams's murder?	58
Mokbel's big gamble for freedom	63
The dirty dozen	68

PART 2   THE GOOD GUYS

The secret society of men in black	79
Judge has seen the best and worst	84
City in blue illuminates our bind to police	89
Undercover cop in Nick of time	93
Thrown into the deep end of undercover policing	98
Hurricane Howard, the judge who committed three deadly sins	103
From a young Crowe to murder	108
Judging the judge: Vincent's work was a masterpiece	113
Hasty end to twins' crime spree	118
'Ragtag' team's courage under fire	123
'Something had to be done, don't you think?'	128
Putting faces to the crimes	133
The student, the cop and the long road to justice	138
Farewell to a giant among men	143
Act of heroism all but forgotten	148
The cutting-edge science of sleuthing	153
Above and beyond the call of duty	158

PART 3   THE CHARACTERS

A very public man of mystery	167
The life of Brian: saint or sinner?	172
Have some cash? Call Mr Clean	178
When crims and lawyers collide	183
The tragic tale of a man who wanted to be a fish	188
'Machinegun under the apron': life for a gangland widow	191
The cut-throat world inside prison	196
The Attorney's school of hard knocks	201
The TV star and the interview that 'chopped' her career	206

PART 4 THE CRIMES

Murder, they wrote	215
Violent shadow lay over tiny town	220
Legal eagle's wings clipped by greed	225
Viceland: life and death in Sin City	234
The bush plot that cost a man his country	239
Terror in the heart of Frankston	244
From Russia with love	249
A million reasons to find a serial killer	254
Horrors lurk behind closed doors	260
When acquittal does not bring peace	265
DNA links new suspect to Membrey	269
Elisabeth Membrey	273

PART 5 THE IMPACT

The sergeant with nine lives	279
Life, death and finally redemption	285
Hooking one that almost got away	290
Son's fight for murdered mother	295
David's childhood in a locked box	300
The four-decade murder mystery	305
Can a leopard change its spots?	310
Victim of a flawed system	315
Finally, 'it is now over for everyone'	321
From the thin blue line to a life line	326

WHAT THE CRITICS SAY

'Dear John, may the Yuletide log fall from your fireplace and burn your house down.'
Standover man, Mark Brandon 'Chopper' Read

'You are a gutter lowlife rodent. Be a wonderful thought having you in amongst, and in the midst, of our company on this side of the fence. Real nice.'
Convicted armed robber, Christopher Dean Binse

'Sylvester [sic] in particular fancies himself as an expert in crime ... We had a nickname for him but it's not publishable here.'
Former detective and convicted murderer, Roger Rogerson

'Sometimes I feel I am at war with Silvester, that I am a soldier in the trenches with my bayonet fixed.'
Convicted murderer, Judy Moran

'Bald headed alien.'
Convicted drug trafficker, Tony Mokbel

'John Silvester's defamatory claptrap is puerile and overblown fiction.'
Convicted murderer, Hugo Rich

'I regret to inform you that by resolution of the General Committee you have been removed from the list of members.'
Royal Yacht Club of Victoria Secretary

'No journalist has done more to explain the world of crime, the justice system and the politics of law and order. Silvester has a style with echoes of Jimmy Breslin and Damon Runyon. And he never forgets the jokes.'
Australian Media Hall of Fame

'John Silvester knows his beat; he's deeply informed, can draw on a well-stocked spice cupboard of tasty anecdotes to season any yarn, and must have one of the most colourful contact books in the game.'
Walkley Awards for Excellence in Journalism

'He brings to life the characters of the good guys, the villains and the victims. All this with good humour and a noticeable lack of self-importance.'
Graham Perkin Australian Journalist of the Year Award

FOREWORD

John Leslie Silvester knows where I live. Like a mafia boss's first wife, he also knows where bodies are buried. So when he put the hard word on the usual suspect for a foreword to this collection, there was nowhere to run.

I tried selling the idea that a picture's worth a thousand words. A polaroid of us in flares and body shirts back when we had more hair than Deep Purple, maybe. But he killed that with a look that would give Putin pause for thought.

Words, he said calmly. *A thousand. By Friday.*

An offer I couldn't refuse.

We make absolutely no reference here to the astonishing bad luck of those who have crossed J. Silvester.

Example. Nazi gangster Phillip Grant 'The Iceman' Wilson was shot by persons unknown in a Punt Road car park after threatening Silvester. It seems Wilson had put a hole in his manners by vowing to throw certain people out of a light plane.

Example. A Vietnamese crook known as the Black Duc was deported, then executed, after expressing anger at a tough Silvester review.

Example. One of the many Pasquale Barbaros sued Silvester after he wrote that Barbaro was a Mafia member. The writ lapsed when he was shot dead in Queensland . . . by the Mafia.

Example. Alphonse Gangitano was homicidal when John described him as having 'the brains of a gnat and genitalia to match'. But Big Al's threats died when he was shot dead days later, in his underpants.

All total coincidences, of course. Still, it's better to be lucky than smart.

Maybe the most sinister of Silvester's unlucky enemies was the bent senior Sydney cop on the payroll of the Griffith mafiosi who'd ordered the murder of Donald Mackay.

It was the early 1980s. John's father, Fred Silvester, then director of the Australian Bureau of Criminal Intelligence, warned him that the connected and protected Sydney policeman could 'shoot you stone dead'.

That got John's attention. When summoned to Sydney to testify to a Royal Commission about his sources, he was rightly fairly nervous. When his airport taxi driver stopped the car for no obvious reason, he grabbed the poor man in a headlock. This surprised the driver, who was actually concerned about faulty brakes and wanting to pull over to call another taxi for his twitchy passenger.

The hearing didn't look good for Silvester. Corruption flourished under the teflon-coated Wran government. It was the era of Roger Rogerson and Murray Farquar, Lionel Murphy and his 'little mate' Morgan Ryan, and the bad guys had almost rigged the game. That was right up until the dangerously bent policeman, the one Silvester had nailed in print, was exposed by a sharp barrister who noticed that all his 'corroborating' police documents covering past activities had been signed with his recent rank – whereas, at the time those statements and diary entries had supposedly been made, he had not actually reached that rank.

That slip of the forger's pen instantly revealed every document as bogus and the cop as a cold-blooded reptile in the pocket of organised crime.

The villain resigned immediately, no longer a threat to anyone but himself. And John flew home covered in relief and glory, nursing a story that still stands out among the many he has.

Which, of course, brings us to the job at hand . . .

Truth is, it's good to write a foreword for a friend because it's like doing his eulogy without the sadness of a funeral.

I might be the only person not actually related to John that he trusts not to misspell his surname as 'Sylvester', the cartoon cat version that has been in print too often to count: in books, allegedly edited by professionals; in letters and emails; even in the former newspaper of record, *The Age*, where he has occupied a rare niche since arriving from the *Herald & Weekly Times*' grand old Flinders Street premises late last century.

That niche is purely as a police and crime writer, a thing he has made his own over decades, not least as 'Sly of the Underworld', permanent fixture on what is arguably Australia's longest-running and best daily radio show.

I first met John in 1979, soon after I started at *The Age*. It was the year after he had begun at *The Sun News-Pictorial*, the nation's dominant tabloid. He was already bolted down at Police Rounds, a set of cramped rooms under Russell Street police station.

On the surface, Silvester and I had little in common.

I was from the far end of East Gippsland. While I'd spent the 1960s riding horses around the bush, shooting, and reading every Biggles book, young John was hanging around East Preston with kids who stole bikes and hubcaps. But he, too, read Biggles books, igniting an obsession with a genre that led him to write a history of World War II . . . when he was in junior high school.

That, dear reader, is a true story, an early warning of the Napoleonic self-belief that always distinguished John from normal people. Oddly, he wondered why delinquents in the same housing commission estate wanted to bash him. He had an unerring ability to wisecrack his way into trouble, which meant he had to bluff his way out of it. Like crocodile wrestling, it's great while you get it right.

Despite the fact that the teenage Silvester looked, according to some, like the English guitar hero Peter Frampton, his unnatural knowledge of world wars and Churchill's speeches failed to impress his contemporaries. Such as his schoolmate Debbie Furness, who ignored him and rubbed it in by marrying an actor some time later. The actor was Hugh Jackman.

The old 'Currant Bun' had masthead artwork of a rooster crowing at the rising sun under the slogan 'Daily at Dawn'. When some dimwit designer killed that cocky rooster, something died in Australian journalism. Not long afterwards, Silvester switched sides.

It's proof of his native intelligence that he thrived in a very different ecosystem.

At *The Sun*, he'd been a newsbreaker who winkled exclusive stories from police contacts on the phone, in the pub and at late-night dives frequented by good crooks and bad cops.

Back then, a savvy *Sun* reporter like Silvester could file half a dozen strong yarns a week and be all over page one, page three or five.

In his years at Police Rounds, he never actually had to type stories, because through his unique combination of cunning, bluff and feigned idleness, he mastered the art of filing 'off the top' by telephone to saintly copytakers who typed as fast as anyone could speak.

Those copytakers placed Silvester behind only the legendary Laurie Oakes, of the Canberra Press Gallery, when it came to dictating fluent news copy.

But at *The Sunday Age* and its daily sister, he changed gear in his 30s to do what so few useful reporters manage: to write engaging, often witty and sometimes wise and moving feature stories and columns, all well sourced, many exclusive.

Thirty years on, he still does. The proof is between these covers.

Andrew Rule, July 2023

INTRODUCTION

I was at the reception for my father's wedding (his third) when a family friend asked me, 'What are you going to do with the rest of your life?'

It was a fair question as I was completing a university double degree in drinking beer and sleeping in.

The question was from Beverley Miller, wife of newly appointed Chief Commissioner Mick Miller who would become the best police leader Australia has seen.

I responded, 'I have no idea.' She responded, 'You should be a journalist as you have an opinion on everything.' (This was, I suspect, code for smart-arse.)

It was a light-bulb moment as I grasped this as the perfect solution. I would apply to be a reporter – get knocked back – and return to my chosen vocation of drinking beer and sleeping in.

I sent off a couple of letters to the big mastheads offering them the opportunity to recruit someone of unlimited potential and immense talent – modesty is vastly overrated.

The Age suggested I sit their exam. I suggested they stick it.

The *Herald & Weekly Times* offered me an interview. I met a slightly bored chap in an office who asked a few general questions. I managed to fake a few general answers.

To my surprise I was offered a second interview. (I can only assume because I turned up sober, had my own teeth, had no visible tattoos and did not dribble tepid tea down my chin.)

This second round was an entirely different process as I met a panel of three stern newspaper executives.

They asked me questions about newspapers. I faked some answers because, to be honest, I didn't know anything about journalism.

The stern man in the middle, Bill Hoey, asked questions about a copper called Keith Plattfuss, saying, 'He knows how to handle demonstrators doesn't he?'

It was a trick question. 'The Puss', as he was known, had led a baton charge into a group of peaceful university students, later declaring, 'They got some baton today and they'll get a lot more in the future.'

I had fluked on the quote in a uni newspaper and suggested to the panel that Plattfuss might have been more psychopath than strategist. Mr Hoey looked down and read the direct quote from his blotter. He seemed pleased with himself. I, on the other hand, was not, believing I had been singled out because my father was a cop.

Mr Hoey continued to chat. I continued to stew.

He then opined that he wanted to move the journalism course from RMIT to Melbourne University. I told him it was a bad idea as journalism was a craft rather than a profession.

He gave me a patronising smile and said, 'John, your attitude is pretty typical of someone who has never been in the workforce.' (This was entirely untrue as I had proved myself as mediocre at multiple casual jobs including retailing, pub work and fruit picking.)

I responded, 'Mr Hoey, your attitude is pretty typical of someone who has never been to university and I suspect never will.'

The exec next to him was caught mid drag. His cigarette glowed red as he coughed, blowing ash over himself. I later realised he was pissing himself laughing.

I left the interview convinced a brilliant journalistic career had self-imploded on the launch pad.

Two weeks later the phone rang. It was Mr Hoey. 'We are offering you a job. Where would you like to work, *The Herald* or *The Sun*?'

'*The Herald*, Mr Hoey.'

'You start at *The Sun* on Monday.'

He added, 'I didn't think I would live to see the day when we had a Silvester on the payroll.'

Many years earlier, my father, then a gaming squad detective, wanted to prosecute *The Herald,* believing its promotion 'Wealth Words' was an illegal lottery.

The opinion from a senior government solicitor was that it was legal, quoting a judge's opinion from an appeal case. It was a crap opinion based on a deliberate selective quote. Turns out it was from the dissenting opinion, meaning the promotion was illegal but the fix was in and the prosecution was not authorised.

The solicitor was eventually promoted to a high government office.

Truth is, Mr Hoey and the others must have seen something that I didn't know existed and I will always be in their debt.

On a Monday morning in January 1978, I walked into the HWT building in Flinders Street, Melbourne. Trucks with *The Herald*'s first edition raced onto the street, the place rumbled from the printing presses and you could smell the ink and lead.

I went to the floor where the reporters worked to be introduced to my first editor, John Morgan. From the pocket of my skin-tight flared polyester trousers, the top of the gold pen presented to me for my 21st birthday was visible.

'Leave the pen at home son,' Mr Morgan said. 'It will be stolen here.'

I thought these were the mutterings of a cynical old man. Two days later it was stolen.

I asked Mr Morgan if he would be kind enough to direct me to my office. He laughed, sweeping an arm towards the newsroom where you grabbed a chair near a typewriter and hung on until someone important told you to move.

I tried to pretend I knew what I was doing, finding quickly I was mediocre at most tasks I was given. I was on a 12-month graduate cadetship and was coming to the conclusion that would be about it.

Then it became my turn to be moved to Police Rounds, the office at the Russell Street Police Headquarters, where reporters filed crime stories over the phone to typists who took them to subeditors to trim for the front page. (According to the style book it took 15 slips of copy paper, each containing one paragraph, to fill a 38-cm news column.)

When I walked in I saw a group of young guys (exclusively male despite the fact the best police reporter at the time was Edna Buchanan from the *Miami Herald*).

I thought they were a great group of blokes. They thought I was an arrogant prick. Turns out we were all pretty good judges of character. There was chief police reporter, the dapperly dressed Geoff Wilkinson (OAM) who drilled into us, 'Be right and assume nothing'; nightshift genius Graeme 'Bear' Walker, who consumed scoops and pizzas in equal measure; Peter William Robinson, whose scowl concealed a wicked sense of humour (he would regularly ring subeditors late at night threatening to come to the main office to murder them if his story was not on page one); and Big Jim Tennison, who avoided early morning breathalysers by driving the office car along unused train tracks.

We once drove a detective home who insisted on firing shots out the rear passenger window. Luckily it was open.

Over in *The Age* office was Lindsay Murdoch (OAM), as good a reporter as we have seen in 50 years; Andrew Rule, as good a writer as we have seen in 50 years; and the Hemingway-like figure Steve Ballard, who drove a sports car and reportedly carried a gun on occasion.

There were page one stories and late night visits to the City Court Hotel, Police Club, Supper Inn and the Galaxy Nightclub. The Police Rounds door would never close, with crooks and coppers wandering in on a whim.

There were no toilets (except inside the police station) which meant the night shift ABC reporter insisted on relieving himself in the electric jug, creating the occasional OH&S issue.

Eventually the police reporters ('Hounds from the Round') overcame their initial views of me and very soon I knew I would never be going back to any other form of journalism.

By the time this book is published I will have been doing it for 45 years. Not once, not ever, have I wanted to do anything else.

It is the type of journalism where you see the best and worst of humanity.

The crooks, the underworld wars, inside investigations, how cases are cracked and corruption on an industrial scale. You absorb the black humour that helps the cops (and the reporters) survive.

After 15 years, when I finally moved to the *Sunday Age*, I wasn't a bad reporter but was still banging out stories the same old way. Bruce Guthrie was the *Sunday Age* editor and he took one of my stories and rewrote just about every line. He taught me there was more to reporting than shovelling copy to subeditors.

For years I added jokes into stories and for years the subs had taken them out.

Then *The Saturday* editor Steve Foley asked Andrew Rule and me to do a crime column called 'Naked City'.

Andrew and I had teamed up together to write and publish the many books of Mark 'Chopper' Read and the *Underbelly* crime series – extremely popular, while seen by good judges as crimes against literature.

When Andrew moved on I kept going. The subs finally tired of removing the jokes and a succession of bosses allowed me to pick my own subject every week, the best of which are between these covers.

JOHN SILVESTER

I once asked Alan Howe, the energetic editor of the *Sunday Herald Sun*, 'What is the best job in journalism?'

He gave a one-word answer.

'Yours.'

I think he's right.

PART 1

THE CROOKS

The underworld has its own ecosystem. There are the sharks, the shoals that stick together and the bottom feeders. Crooks can be motivated by power, money, notoriety or dark compulsions.

We see the hitmen who will kill a stranger without hesitation and then go home for a roast dinner, the armed robbers who love the thrill of the heist and trying to outfox the cops, and the serial killers drawn to a dark world they can't even comprehend.

We ask, what makes someone evil? Why does one brother become a prison officer while the other an armed robber who rejoices in the ambush murder of two police?

What makes a man dream of killing and then follow hundreds of women for years before he strikes?

What makes a man take a gun and walk into the street to kill strangers?

Why does a hero cop turn bad and become the very type of person he swore to pursue?

Or why does the high-profile lawyer from a respectable family destroy herself and damage the justice system by becoming a police informer?

Some crooks see themselves as real-life Hollywood gangsters and only too late see that their own story will end with them dead or in jail.

We all want to know what makes them tick. Most times they don't even know themselves.

COPPER FINALLY COMES A CROPPER

For the record, I don't like former NSW Detective Sergeant Roger Rogerson and he doesn't like me.

He doesn't like me because for more than 30 years I have called him a crook and I don't like him because for more than 30 years he has been one. To say he is as rotten as a chop is to be grossly unfair to those protein-packed meaty morsels. He claims I have an obsession with corrupt NSW coppers and have treated some wonderful detectives unfairly.

He wrote: 'Sylvester [sic] in particular fancies himself as an expert in crime . . . He . . . wants to get up close to you, get right in your face and eyeball you to make sure you're not telling lies. We had a nickname for him but it's not publishable here.' Well, I have a nickname for him that is publishable: prison inmate.

To be fair, for a crooked cop, Roger had some positives. He was brave, smart, an elite investigator and – when the mood struck him – a first-class crook catcher.

The trouble was when he wasn't in the mood, he was a first-class crook. The type of cop who would race into your burning house to save a child then steal your wallet on the way out.

He was willingly seduced to the dark side, a world where he and his corrupt mates didn't just turn a blind eye to crime, they organised their own, using underworld pals to carry out armed robberies, massive burglaries and drug rip-offs. In return for a share of the profits, they protected their favourite crooks.

Those who have seen more recent images of Roger 'The Dodger' hobbling along as a 75-year-old with a dodgy hip may find it hard to imagine him as a ruthless, charismatic and dangerous detective destined for higher office. The winner of awards for bravery and devotion to duty, he was selected by an influential corrupt cell within the NSW Police as their man to eventually run the crime department.

For those who didn't live through those times it must seem inconceivable that a small but untouchable group of corrupt Sydney detectives intimidated honest cops, major crooks and elected politicians (many of whom were as bent as a Uri Geller spoon).

But make no mistake; Rogerson was brought down because he thought his Sydney influence could stretch into the heart of Melbourne, and into a major drug investigation.

Sydney Drug Squad police were chasing local heroin syndicate boss 'Jumping' Jack Richardson, the distributor Brian Hansen and the major supplier Alan Williams. The trouble was, the group was working out of Melbourne, which meant a joint NSW/Victoria operation was needed at a time when trust between the forces was short on the ground.

Eventually it was decided Victoria would provide $110,000 to buy the drugs and NSW the undercover operative, the smart and likeable Mick Drury who, along with Rogerson, had won the prestigious police Peter Mitchell Trophy.

The two controlling police were Johnny Weel from Victoria – laconic, tough, brave and as straight as a gun barrel – and Drury. The Melbourne drug sting was to be carried out in March 1982 in an Old Melbourne Hotel suite with police moving in when Drury gave the signal . . . well, that was the plan.

When Williams – stoned, distracted and suspicious – fronted in his car outside the hotel with the heroin, Drury gave the go signal by pressing a squeal button hidden under his armpit. But the arrest crew drove in too fast and the car that was supposed to block the suspect overshot by 30 metres.

It was enough to give Williams an out and he took it, driving off with the heroin. He dumped the gear and ran through Melbourne University, where he had once worked as a cleaner, and disappeared, allegedly wearing a stolen dustcoat to look like a lab technician.

Years later, Williams told me what really happened. 'I knew Brian Hansen. He said he had a drug buyer [Drury] down from Sydney.

'The deal was supposed to kick off at lunchtime, but for about nine hours I smelt a rat. I didn't want to do the business. Brian, on the other hand, was insistent, he said he had counted the money and that everything was sweet.

'Brian went into the hotel, came back with Drury and introduced him. Well, he didn't want to get into the car. [Drury wanted to control the situation and signal waiting police when he saw the heroin.]

'I smelt a rat. I showed him the gear, but there was something wrong. They were so keen to block me in that they skidded past the car. I put it in gear and just took off.'

About four months later, he was arrested in Adelaide and charged with heroin trafficking, but the committal turned into a shambles. Police who declared they could identify Williams were discredited and only Drury's evidence survived. When the Director of Public Prosecutions decided to directly present the case to a higher court, Williams believed only one man stood between him and a long jail term.

As Drury was the key witness, Williams decided to try to bribe the interstate detective to throw the case.

'I knew I needed help because the only bloke who stuck to his guns in the committal was Drury. He was unshakeable.'

He reached out through notorious hitman Christopher Dale Flannery. 'I ran into him in Melbourne and mentioned to him that

I had been pinched by an undercover copper from Sydney. I asked him if he could do anything in regard to getting him to change his evidence or slow it down.'

And that is when Rogerson became involved. 'I offered $30,000 at one stage, $50,000 at another stage, $100,000 and an open ticket in the end.'

Drury refused the offer. This tells you what Sydney was like at the time as Rogerson was happy to offer the bribe with the certain knowledge that if it was knocked back, Drury would be too frightened to report it. And he was right.

Williams met Flannery and Rogerson at a Sydney restaurant to be told it was no deal. Then Flannery the hitman suggested Plan B: 'Well, if it was me, I'd put him off [kill him].'

Williams at first said: 'That's a big step', but quickly agreed.

The agreed price was $100,000, with $50,000 down and the remainder due after the killing.

'I was a giant in the trade. I thought I was invincible, and unpinchable. But I stepped over the line with the Drury thing. It is something I will regret for the rest of my life.'

Williams sent the deposit to Flannery and then waited for the death message.

On 6 June 1984, as Drury was washing dishes at his Chatswood home, Flannery shot him twice. The NSW undercover detective, fighting for his life in hospital, made what was thought would be a dying deposition outlining Rogerson's bribery attempt.

Everyone expected him to die. He had, after all, been shot twice at point-blank range.

Flannery reassured Williams: 'He's lost a lot of blood. I don't think he'll make it.'

This time Flannery, who had more experience with gunshot wounds than most surgeons, was wrong.

'When he realised he [Drury] was going to live, Chris said not to worry about sending the other $50,000. The job hadn't been completed,' Williams said.

The attempted assassination of Drury was the tipping point. The fallout destroyed the cosy police–gangland franchises that had controlled organised crime in Sydney for decades. It led to a taskforce, integrity commissions and external reviews. No longer were bent cops like Rogerson untouchable.

The violence didn't stop there. Richardson was shot dead and, in an attempt to silence Williams, gunmen staked out his house but mistakenly killed his brother-in-law Lindsay Simpson. Flannery was also murdered, with homicide detectives convinced it was Rogerson who lured him to the ambush.

Williams went into hiding, was eventually arrested and pleaded guilty to conspiracy to murder and the attempted bribery of Drury.

'I can understand if he [Drury] was bitter to the day he died. But I just hope he is remembered as a bloke who stuck to his guns and was vindicated in what he did,' Williams, who died in 2001, told me.

Rogerson was charged and acquitted of conspiracy to murder Drury. But from the moment he was linked to the treacherous shooting, his reputation changed from colourful rogue to rat in the rank. He was sacked in 1986, two years after the attempted hit on his colleague.

Now he has been convicted with fellow ex-cop Glen McNamara of the 2014 drug rip-off murder of Jamie Gao and will die in jail. The job was so inept it shows even the baddest should know when to hang up their guns.

I ran into him when he was on the road doing crime nights with Melbourne standoverman Mark Brandon 'Chopper' Read. He was then just an old man making a modest living out of peddling dog-eared crime stories to the unsuspecting. A little like this book, really.

He was surprisingly friendly, recalling that at one show, women at the front table with an *Underbelly* book asked what he thought of me. 'He is nothing but an arsehole [he actually used another quite impossible anatomical descriptive],' Roger informed his somewhat startled female fans.

Well, that may be so, but I'm going home for tea tonight (chops, I hope). And, Roger, you never will again.

WILLIAMS NO CRIMINAL MASTERMIND

Gangland widow Roberta Williams has made many mistakes in her colourful life. One was to believe that fleeting notoriety equals lasting fame.

It is true that a certain type of crook – the ones who court publicity before they end up in court – become headline news, but rarely does it (or they) last.

There was Alphonse Gangitano, the Prince of Lygon Street, shot dead in his underpants in 1998, and Carl 'The Premier' Williams, bashed to death in Barwon Prison in 2010.

Mark Brandon 'Chopper' Read, who died of natural causes in 2013, is remembered not for his dastardly deeds but his black wit, making more money from writing and talking about crimes than committing them. He once remarked that the Old West gunslingers who were remembered were not the fastest but the ones who built media profiles when the number of headlines mattered more than the number of headstones.

Former bikie and social influencer Toby Mitchell became headline news after he survived not one but two shooting attacks. He told me that at events such as boxing bouts, his passage to his ringside seat is slowed by fans who want selfies. In a reflective mood, he said: 'You know, fame is overrated. I had to be shot seven times to become fucking famous.' The ultimate bullet point.

Which brings us back to Roberta, who became news because her husband, Carl, was a prolific drug dealer who embarked on an underworld war, hiring (and often dudding) hitmen to kill his rivals. He did so because Jason Moran, in the company of his half-brother Mark, shot Carl in his tummy at a Gladstone Park reserve back in 1999.

There were several reasons for this. One was that Roberta had left a Moran associate to shack up with Carl. In fairness, there was also a $400,000 drug debt, the disputed ownership of a pill press and quality control complaints on drug production. Carl later organised the murders of Jason and Mark.

As the bodies and headlines mounted, Carl and Roberta chose to leave the shadows and regularly engage with the media. Both their characters were dramatised in the first television series of *Underbelly*. To be frank, the talented Kat Stewart did a better Roberta than Roberta.

After Carl was sentenced in 2007 to 35 years (Roberta offered a snort of coke to the person sitting next to her in court, seemingly unaware he was a policeman's father), she tried to market her notoriety with magazine articles, public appearances and a crime tour.

Surrounded by camp followers, she didn't understand she was destined to be a filler, dragged out occasionally on slow news days.

That is, until on 11 July 2019 when an email popped up at work. I contacted the sender, who turned out to be would-be television producer Ryan Naumenko, who had planned a reality television program starring Roberta Williams.

As Roberta was keen on money but not so keen on regular employment, it was an attractive proposition. She would be paid for just being Roberta and her profile would again be on the rise. After all, she was bankrupt with assets of $2022.80 and debts of $405,759.17, including

$24,000 in school fees, $26,000 to Centrelink and $20,000 for her former husband's funeral. (At the funeral, mourners were led in the front entrance, then out the back and around again to make it appear to be a packed crowd. Meanwhile, the gold cross from the gold casket was stolen, as well as money from the priest's rectory.)

The plan was to raise $50,000 through a GoFundMe page for the reality project. Proof that Roberta was no longer a fan favourite, the page raised $840.

Naumenko says he was lured to a Collingwood production house where, over three hours, he was tied up, beaten, pistol-whipped and threatened with death until his father and sister handed over some cash.

'They told me I owed them 20 grand. They put my phone on speaker and rang my mother, father and sister to get money transferred. They made me talk to them and said: "Say anything wrong, and we'll put one in you." Roberta kept screaming that they were going to kill me and the kids.'

I assured Naumenko I would find him police he could trust and made a couple of calls. It became a Fraud and Extortion Squad investigation.

That night, Naumenko emailed: 'John, thank you. The police have been amazing – I owe you so much for putting me onto these guys. I have never been a huge supporter of the Victoria Police until today.'

The next day police raided the Collingwood studio, gathered CCTV footage and later seized phones. A few weeks later Roberta and her team of (not-so) heavies were charged.

I thought it seemed a pretty simple case; I was wrong. It would take more than three years to resolve, and shows why our justice system needs supercharging.

After Roberta was charged, I made a police statement of six paragraphs. Later I was given $10 in appearance money to attend the court where lawyers are often paid thousands. I did not have the capacity to verify what happened, and my testimony would have nothing to do with the guilt or innocence of those charged.

Come the committal hearing in November 2020 (during COVID-19 lockdown), I was instructed to be available to give evidence remotely. At the end of the first few days, I was told I would be held over. Having been released for the afternoon, I then received an urgent call that things had speeded up and I was immediately required.

I was, at this point, in a supermarket, and unless I could swear an oath on a packet of fish fingers, they would have to wait. I charged home, chucked on a shirt and gave evidence still wearing shorts.

One of the defence lawyers decided to throw in a few barbs accompanied by the appropriate eye-rolling. Did I have any more information? Was I hiding emails? Was I a Watergate burglar? Was I Vladimir Putin's secret military adviser? It was theatre without the audience.

Finally committed, the trial was listed for October 2022 for an incredible six weeks. Ronald Ryan's murder trial lasted 12 days. Again, I was told I would have to give evidence, although everyone knew it wouldn't make the slightest difference to the outcome. Here is the problem. Cases are delayed and are too complex because there is too much testimony from witnesses like me.

I first met Roberta on Sunday 14 December 2003, when she, Carl and Carl's father, George, wanted a meeting after I fingered Carl as the suspect in several murders. It was a strange time to declare Carl's feelings were hurt by being described as a killer, considering his hitmen had murdered Graham Kinniburgh outside his Kew house the day before.

Carl declared: 'I've never met him, and I've never heard a bad thing said about him. I have nothing to profit from his death. It's a mystery to me. I haven't done anything. My conscience is clear.'

To change the subject, I asked who shot him in the guts. When he failed to answer, I dared him to say: 'Jason.' Roberta laughed as if it was the height of good humour. Since then, she has soured on me big time.

Roberta Williams is no mob matriarch. Her background is tragic and her future bleak. Her father died when she was young, she was physically abused by her mother's new partners and became a street kid at the age of nine. Her first husband assaulted her and her second, Carl, was murdered. She has five children, the youngest disabled.

Roberta did a deal, pleading guilty to blackmail and recklessly causing injury on the promise she wouldn't do jail time. Judge Fiona Todd sentenced her to a two-year community corrections order, adding she would have been sent to jail for 12 months if she had been found guilty at trial. A good deal all around.

The case took over three years, from the email to sentencing. How can anyone think this is acceptable?

INSIDE THE MINDS OF MURDERERS

He didn't look much like a serial killer, the slight man sitting on a bench near a pond, surrounded by families on that early Sunday afternoon. It could have been any park in any suburb – until you looked up to see the bluestone walls that enclosed Pentridge Prison.

He agreed to meet and chat about his crimes, with no subject out of bounds – his hair swept to the left concealing the ear he had mutilated in prison years earlier.

Initially he asked for $20,000 but settled on a packet of Camel cigarettes and a cup of tea from the prison canteen. It was a 90-minute contact visit with no handcuffs, recorder or guards – designed for families, not nosy reporters.

The excellent recent Netflix series *Mindhunters*, on how two FBI investigators interviewed serial murderers as part of learning profiling techniques, took me back to the days when you could sit face-to-face with killers, not just rat through Facebook to discover personality traits.

Paul Steven Haigh is not physically imposing, not charismatic nor particularly frightening, yet he remains Australia's (equal) worst serial killer, having murdered seven times.

Stalker-killers such as Derek Ernest Percy and Peter Norris Dupas would withdraw into themselves, refusing to acknowledge their crimes, for to do so would be to acknowledge that they are monsters. Haigh and I talk of his crimes without emotion. Me because I don't want him to feel judged and withdraw, him because he seems incapable of normal feelings. (At this point, he had murdered six times. He would kill again five years later.)

He concentrates on the consequence of his actions to him, never reflecting on his victims. Which is why, perhaps, he quotes a Chinese proverb: 'When evil sees itself, it destroys itself.'

Adopted, Haigh said he was 'a neurotic youngster' who lived a sheltered life, had a 'religious upbringing' and was bullied at school. Asked why he killed, he responded: 'I don't know why. Was it my parents who tried too hard and so gave me a faulty foundation? Was it because I stubbed my toe when I was three? God knows.'

'I always was, and still am a coward . . . it takes no hero to murder. The most puny man in the world can pull a trigger. The obstacle is a psychological one.'

Aged 21, Haigh killed six people, including a nine-year-old boy, in just 11 months. He shot Evelyn Abraham at a Prahran Tattslotto agency in September 1978, and Bruno Cingolani, 45, in a Caulfield pizza parlour in December the same year.

He then killed fellow criminal Wayne Smith, Sheryle Gardner and her nine-year-old son, Danny Mitchell, then his own girlfriend, Lisa Maude Brearley, 19. He told me Gardner brought her son to a meeting as insurance, believing Haigh would not kill her in front of the boy.

'His mother I shot first. As Danny's back was to me, crying, I shot him too.'

When I ask why he stabbed Brearley 157 times, he responds: 'I lost count', before miming stabbing motions while counting out loud. He then paused to sip his tea; it was getting cold.

'The crimes I committed were atrocious, but I can't run back the clock. What is done is done.'

But Haigh wasn't done. In 1991, he helped fellow prisoner Donald George Hatherley 'suicide'. Haigh slipped the noose around his neck, pulled away the small cupboard he was standing on and then pushed down on his shoulders to make sure Hatherley couldn't survive.

Prison officers say that after Julian Knight killed seven in Hoddle Street in 1987, Haigh fretted that he was no longer Victoria's most prolific killer, so he needed another victim.

For some time, Knight wrote to me from prison, at first wanting a ghosted book, but mostly as part of a clumsy pattern of obtuse threats. Even now he writes to inmates, informing them of anything I publish about them, one assumes to curry favour with them and build antipathy to me.

Knight claims he went on his rampage after he was bullied at the army's Duntroon officers' college, where he was a failed student. But material published here for the first time would suggest he was having dangerous fantasies at least two years earlier. A fellow Melbourne High School student recalls Knight as 'bright, cheeky and funny but a bit of a weirdo. None of us anticipated he was capable of something like that [the Hoddle Street massacre].'

In 1985 Knight was in the school cadets and obsessed with weaponry. He also liked to dabble in cartooning, which gives an insight into his darkness. In one story: 'Seymour – The Six Million Dollar Mouse', a frail Seymour is shot several times while his military mates fly to his rescue. Knight's character then goes on a shooting rampage, killing 16 enemies in one frame.

That he picks an insignificant-looking mouse as the hero who exacts murderous revenge probably reflects the killer's self-image. And as an adopted child in an army family, he grew up at the Puckapunyal Base – at Seymour.

In the final drawing the once skinny hero (reflecting Knight's own slender physique) has bulked up, Rambo-style, and is pictured with a machine gun and surrounded by blood-soaked corpses.

Two years later, Knight lived out this fantasy.

Prison officers say Knight sat chain-smoking while watching reports on Martin Bryant, who in 1996 killed 35 people at Tasmania's Port Arthur. 'He couldn't take his eyes off the TV. When reports said the death toll was more than seven, he stormed off and slammed his cell door. He sulked so long he wouldn't come out for meals,' one said.

Triple killer Greg Brazel was capable of charm but would turn on a whim. 'He is cunning and sly and could never be trusted. His moods change from friendly to violent instantaneously,' police reported.

Brazel, the son of a NSW Police detective, murdered Mount Eliza shopkeeper Mildred Hanmer in 1982 and, in 1990, killed another two women – the second, police believe, when he knew he was under investigation. When arrested he smiled and said: 'I look forward to doing battle with the Homicide Squad.'

In prison he was responsible for at least 25 attacks, including stabbing three prisoners in separate incidents, breaking the noses of two prison officers, assaulting police, setting fire to his cell, cutting off the tip of his left ear, threatening to kill staff, pushing a governor's head through a plate-glass window and using jail phones to intimidate witnesses. He always seemed to have access to a phone. In the early 1990s he would often ring for a chat, always angling for a positive story.

He went on a preposterous 57-day hunger strike, with his supporters claiming he was days from death – until, that is, prison officers found a store of Mars Bars under his bed, which indicated he was in greater danger from tooth decay than malnutrition.

Unquestionably intelligent, his thirst for violence began as a teenager after a bike fall cracked his skull. A CAT scan he underwent as an adult showed damage to the left temporal lobe, the part of the brain that controls impulses. Perhaps that explains why for years Brazel was Victoria's most dangerous inmate.

Hugo Rich was another who could have been a successful businessman but became hopelessly addicted to violence. Rich was convicted of a series of armed robberies (often wearing an expensive Trussardi jacket and a silk ski mask). His defence was damaged by testimony from security guards that linked him to the bandit's guns.

Smooth but violent, he betrayed his true nature in August 1995, when in court he turned on crown prosecutor (and later County Court judge) Carolyn Douglas: 'One chance – one fucking chance. Watch your back. Every time you turn the car on . . . I'm telling you, OK. I don't care how long it takes, 25 years, bitch. I'll have a go at you. One go, that's all I want.'

A decade later he returned to armed robberies. When he pointed a gun at security guard Erwin Kastenberger at the North Blackburn Shopping Centre, the guard handed over the bag containing $162,000. Yet Rich shot and killed him, police say, to ensure Kastenberger couldn't give evidence as the guards had done a decade earlier.

Most killers act out of passion, some from dark impulses they can't control. Many of our most notorious were sexually and/or physically abused as children. But the subjects of this story all came from middle-class backgrounds and all had the brains to succeed in the straight world.

And yet they chose to kill. They share more than the same dreary cells and lack of future. It is a lack of empathy – a failure to feel for anyone else. And no crime profiler will ever be able to tell us why.

DANGEROUS LIAISONS

Welcome to the worst-kept secret in town; the identity of the witness variously known as Lawyer X, Informer 3838 and EF is, of course, criminal defence barrister Nicola Gobbo.

This ends, at least for the moment, the five-year legal battle to keep her name from the public. The police have always claimed her identity should remain secret because of fears for her life but the High Court, while acknowledging the risks, said her clients needed to know their lawyer might have dudded them so they could pursue possible retrials.

Which left us with the legal version of trying to wrestle an India-rubber man, because the violent criminals who might harm her were told her name while everyone else was kept in the dark. Except for one thing; the world wide web is like water and it will always seep through the finest crack.

Which means her name has been spread with accompanying photos and threats in the modern-day version of a 'Wanted Dead or Alive' Wild West poster. Such as this post next to a photo of Gobbo: 'Ten points for anyone who can name this person, 100 points for her current location LMFAO.'

And: 'Informer 3838 known as Lawyer X. Real identity Nicola (Rat) Gobbo.'

And: 'Dog . . . Any Rat gets it in the end cuz, goes without saying what makes her immune? . . . Rats don't last long, that I can confidently say.'

So, who is Nicola Gobbo?

Her relatives emigrated from Italy, becoming pioneers in the restaurant trade and the legal profession, with her uncle, Sir James, becoming a QC, Supreme Court judge and governor of Victoria, while her cousin, the well-respected Jeremy Gobbo, KC, has served on the Bar Ethics Committee.

Her father, Allan, died when she was in Year 12 at Genazzano College. At Melbourne University, she became editor of the student magazine *Farrago* and embraced left-wing politics while passing her law degree.

In 1993 police raided her Rathdowne Street home and seized methamphetamine valued at $82,000, half a kilo of cannabis and prohibited weapons. While two men faced more serious charges, she pleaded guilty to possession and use. No conviction was recorded, allowing her to embark on a legal career.

Certainly the arrest didn't slow her down. In fact, she was bragging to classmates within a few days of her brush with the dark side of the law. Police who dealt with her at the time believed she had just made a poor choice in boyfriends. It would not be her last.

In 1995, while still a student, she was registered as a police informer, which means from the first time she entered a court as a lawyer, she had a history of secretly talking to police. In November 1998, Gobbo became the youngest woman to be accepted at the Bar.

She was a shameless self-promoter, leaking stories to gossip columnists who referred to her as a 'hot-shot legal eagle', 'young blonde bombshell' and the 'million-dollar eagle'. Snippets included drinking rum with sailors in Bali, injuring her arm, scolding her dangerous clients in court and being picked up by police and fined $135 for not wearing a seatbelt while driving her silver Mercedes – hardly the stuff of the Law Journal.

Take this: 'Barrister Nicola Gobbo is now known in legal circles as the million-dollar eagle. Last year, she helped alleged drug boss Tony Mokbel get bail with a surety of $1 million, and this week she got murdered Jason Moran's father Lewis Moran, facing serious drug charges, out on bail with a $1 million surety.'

(It didn't do either any good. Lewis Moran was murdered while on bail while Mokbel jumped his, was caught in Greece, brought back to serve a monster jail sentence and got himself stabbed.)

Or this: 'Until recently, Ms Gobbo, niece of the former Victorian guv, was getting to be almost as big a celebrity as the gangland toughs she represented. But not anymore. She has just returned to work after a stroke that cut her down at age 31 . . . "I used to worry about my phone being bugged," she said, "or about people from the underworld watching me. Not anymore. This has changed my life."'

It certainly did. Within months, she again became a registered informer.

Her rise as a barrister coincided with the rise in underworld murders during the gangland war, which started in October 1999 when drug dealer Carl Williams was ambushed and shot in Gladstone Park.

She gathered clients for several reasons. She was smart, ruthless, available 24 hours a day and ethically loose, with many clients eventually seeing her as part of the gang. They could tell her things that would be off-limits to other lawyers and she became the keeper of dark secrets.

By 2004 she was talking informally to the Purana Taskforce and the following year registered again as an informer, given the code 3838.

A royal commission has now [2023] examined Gobbo's role as a police informer and handed down its findings. However, at the time, the High Court had already condemned the police who used her: 'Victoria Police were guilty of reprehensible conduct in knowingly encouraging [Gobbo] to do as she did and were involved in sanctioning atrocious breaches of the sworn duty of every police officer to discharge all duties imposed on them faithfully and according to law without favour or affection, malice or ill will.'

It also found she was guilty of 'fundamental and appalling breaches of obligations as counsel to her clients and of duties to the court.' And here is the sticking point. Police say that while Gobbo, now 46 and a mother of two, may have provided information that could have derailed fair process, they did not use it. They claim the information they did use came from her intimate and non-professional relationships with gangsters. Whether they are whistling in the dark remains to be seen.

She has claimed her information solved underworld murders and resulted in hundreds of convictions. Well, she would say that, wouldn't she?

In the days when real estate ads provided *The Age* with a revenue stream as big as the Nile, we had a box at the footy, which the bosses stupidly gave to the crime team for a night game. Adjoining corporate box inhabitants complained about the noise, someone kept flicking the lights off and on to replicate the atmosphere of a disco and the staff required salt tablets after cramping from running around serving copious quantities of drinks.

One of the guests was Gobbo, who in between trying (and failing) to chat up a copper in the room, made outrageous statements designed to put her at the centre of attention. She loudly named a fellow female lawyer, declaring: 'She does her best work on her knees.'

It was an insightful comment but not about the rival (who has built a reputation as hard-working and competent). It struck me that Gobbo was jealous because she had been replaced by a newer, sharper model.

Why did Gobbo become a police informer? Because she was addicted to attention and needed to be loved.

We hope the royal commission is given the time and resources to look at some broader issues, such as whether her peers should have done more to guide or discipline her when she began running too close to both her gangster clients and the police chasing them.

Or whether client–lawyer confidentiality is unbreakable. If a client told his barrister there was to be a terrorist attack on Melbourne the following day and the lawyer's children were due to visit the CBD, would he or she stay silent? Or if a lawyer told police of a plan to bring down the Rialto building, should they refuse to act because of the source of the information?

The police may have kept her role secret if they hadn't turned her from a secret informer into a public witness, persuading her to wear a wire against a former detective.

And here is where it all came crashing down. Police were desperate to solve the murder of police informer Terence Hodson and his wife, Christine, shot dead in their Kew home in May 2004.

Eventually Carl Williams told police that a former detective gave him $150,000 that he passed on to contract killer Rod Collins to murder Hodson.

It would appear police were too keen to solve the case, allowing Williams to make unreasonable demands in exchange for his evidence. He should have been told he could rot in prison unless he started telling the truth. Instead they agreed to incentives that would have added to concerns he was just telling police what they wanted to hear, including police paying his daughter's school fees and allowing him out of prison for some secret cuddle time.

This backfired on Williams. Separated from wife Roberta, he had a lovely girlfriend who turned up regularly at prison to give him a peck on the cheek and then chat about their respective days. But after the romantic time-out, she stopped coming to prison. A few months later, she returned to break off the engagement and return a very large diamond ring.

As a convicted criminal wanting a deal, Williams's statement implicating the former detective was next to useless unless a non-criminal could corroborate it.

Enter Gobbo.

The former lawyer (she had given up her ticket) eventually refused to testify because of fears for her safety. In April 2010, Williams was bashed to death in prison.

In 2018, Collins died of natural causes.

Gobbo refused to enter the witness protection program despite receiving written advice from a deputy commissioner that her life was in danger. While she now has many enemies in the underworld, most of them want her alive to testify at the royal commission. For if she helped put some of her clients in jail, her testimony may well help get them out.

MACKEREL OR SPRAT?

They are called rats, dogs, fizzes, gigs, snouts and snitches if they tell tales about you. They are called informers, protected sources or brave whistleblowers if they tell tales about someone else.

Some tell stories to save the system. Others tell stories to save themselves.

Drug dealer Dennis Allan was the master for every time his criminal enterprise sprung a leak he threw someone else overboard.

Despite being a huge drug dealer, a psychopath and the suspect in 11 murders, he kept out of jail by informing. At one point he was on bail for 60 different offences.

When he died in 1987 a death notice appeared under the names of two colourful detectives. 'Dennis the Menace with a heart so big. Sorry you're gone, you were such a good gig.'

The art of informing is a simple trade. The information you provide has to be juicy enough to absolve or, at the very least, minimise your sins. The small fish gives up the big fish.

Take Peter James Cross, former schoolteacher and son of a judge. Having read a book called *Snowblind* written by a cocaine importer, he decided it was time for a career change and persuaded a social contact, millionaire playboy and former Melbourne Lord Mayor Irvin Rockman to pay $7000 to part fund Cross's trip to Bolivia where he visited his former student Cassandra Ogden.

Flushed with the success, Cross connected with heavy gangsters (including hitman Christopher Dale Flannery) for two further trips until he was arrested.

In 1987, Cross became an informer for the National Crime Authority and it came at a terrible cost. Back in Australia, Ogden was summoned to give evidence at a secret NCA hearing and fearing she was being dragged into an underworld investigation she took her own life.

Investigators were keen to charge Rockman but the Federal Director of Public Prosecutions, Ian Temby, rightly refused because while Rockman had a higher profile, Cross's criminality was far greater than the former Lord Mayor.

It would be, he said, the equivalent of using 'a mackerel to catch a sprat'.

I was at the inquest into the death of Cassandra Ogden and became increasingly irritated that Rockman was being less than truthful in the witness box by suggesting he was not involved in any way. I had Cross's NCA testimony (which included that he and Rockman had read *Snowblind* and decided to use it as a blueprint) but it would have been a criminal offence to publish anything from the secret hearings.

So to let Irvin know I knew he was lying, I opened *Snowblind* during the court proceedings and began to read it. When the lawyer cross-examining Rockman made reference to the reporter in the court reading the book, then asked if Rockman had ever read it, the witness refused to answer questions on the grounds of self-incrimination.

Outside the court, the lawyer told me I was the worst method actor in the world because I was virtually stuffing the book in Rockman's face. Was it contempt of court? Probably. Did it work? Absolutely.

Which brings us to the most public of secret informers, Nicola Gobbo (she did a podcast for goodness sake). The former criminal barrister and police source has turned the criminal justice system upside down, put countless convictions in jeopardy and caused a Royal Commission into the use of informers.

Now, not for the first time, she is seeking a deal and according to this writer is prepared to turn on all and sundry if she is given an indemnity. (For those who may have just thawed out from the Ice Age, Gobbo was a high-profile lawyer who represented a Who's Who of gangsters while sneakily telling police their darkest secrets.)

Now, and this comes as no surprise, she says she is prepared to dump on all the coppers she curried favour from if she receives an indemnity from prosecution.

She has made a series of 'Can Say' statements. Which means if you promise not to charge me I can give up all these turkeys. A little like a test drive of a car – you can buy or send them back.

She has told the Office of the Special Examiner her actions were 'immoral', 'illegal' and a 'perversion of justice' but really it wasn't her fault.

She says she was a victim controlled by detectives who were 'alpha males calling the shots' and was 'emotionally manipulated and groomed by police and at the time was young and naive and desperately sought the approval of older male figures'.

Are you kidding me? Gobbo was a razor-smart barrister who worked on complex and high-profile criminal cases. She sought headlines, partied with the crooks and enthusiastically jumped sides to save herself when she became a person of interest in the 2004 murders of police informer Terence Hodson and his wife Christine.

She ain't no Goldilocks.

Nicola Gobbo was deeply flawed but of sound mind. She was not persuaded nor threatened. She jumped at the chance to be a secret source because she needed to be the centre of attention. When the crooks became bored with her and started using another female lawyer, one Gobbo hated, she needed to be the star to a fresh audience – the Purana Taskforce. She was two months short of her 33rd birthday when she became a gangland informer.

This was the third time she was registered as a police informer. Truth is, she rolled over more than a kelpie with an itchy tummy.

In 1995, then a law student, she turned informer to save herself from a conviction on serious drug charges that would have ruined her chances of becoming a lawyer. In July 1998, while still a young solicitor, she wanted to provide information to the drug squad about an investigation codenamed Carron. She was knocked back.

In 1999 she offered to be an informer for the Australian Federal Police and the National Crime Authority. When they wouldn't deal with her she went back to Victoria Police to tell tales about colleagues laundering money.

(Sidebar here. When Gobbo made claims against cops at the Royal Commission into police informants the names were made public. When they were made against lawyers the names were suppressed.)

In 2005 she sought out a Purana detective with many in the squad believing she was seeking a personal relationship. She was brought in from the cold and registered as Informer 3838 and was on the books for five years. It was a nightmare.

Perhaps one of the keys to the complex and deluded world Nicola Gobbo inhabited is her family background. Her grandparents immigrated from Italy and after initially failing during the Depression returned to build a restaurant business at the Queen Victoria Market.

The younger son, James, was the one designated to be the star. Private school, Melbourne then Oxford University, a world class rower, barrister, judge, knighted and the Governor of Victoria. Sir James was Nicola's uncle.

Older son Allan worked long hours serving and cleaning in the restaurant before progressing to become a well-respected Victorian public servant at the Road Traffic Authority. Allan was Nicola's father.

(Sir James was devastated by the actions of his niece – believing she had brought shame on a family that had contributed greatly to the community.)

Nicola had the famous name without the trappings of fame. She was close to her father who died when she was still at school.

From those teenage years Nicola needed to be the centre of attention, the lead in the plays, the funniest at the party and the most active in student politics and the editor (not reporter) of the university newspaper.

As a lawyer, being a solicitor working in an office was never an option. In 1998 she became a barrister (the youngest female admitted to the Bar) quickly taking on the most colourful (and headline-producing) clients.

She fed gossip columnists snippets to try and stay in the public eye.

She was hopelessly compromised and rather than just representing her clients she became part of their dark circle. Judges, magistrates and fellow barristers knew she was a ticking time bomb who would eventually detonate and while some took her aside to scold her none lodged a formal complaint.

As a secret witness, she was a diva, making ridiculous demands and going off script. When police tried to end her time as a source she wouldn't go, staying on centre stage for yet another encore even as the audience was leaving the theatre.

Should police have used Gobbo as an informer? Yes, if the information came from her running with the crooks. Should they have used information that came from her privileged client–lawyer conversations? No, and that is why many of the gangland convictions are being reviewed.

Another big sticking point. The Nettle inquiry will have to establish Gobbo and the police committed a conspiracy to pervert the course of justice and that the detectives involved knew or reasonably believed they were breaking the law.

Nicola Gobbo is no victim. She was an active participant who has been relocated more than once and received a sackful of cash in an out-of-court settlement over her $2.88 million lawsuit against police.

With her request for indemnity the authorities will have to decide, was she mackerel or sprat?

[As of June 2023, the findings of The Nettle inquiry, which recommended key figures face criminal action for their involvement in the Lawyer X scandal, went ignored by the State Government.]

A TALE OF TWO BROTHERS DIVIDED

Those who think the risk of terror attacks is new have very short memories. One straight out of the ISIS playbook is creating an incident to lure authorities to a spot where an ambush can be launched. It has been used in London, Paris and throughout Europe but more than 30 years ago the tactic was used with ruthless efficiency in quiet and leafy Walsh Street, South Yarra. It was there, just before 5 am on 12 October 1988, that police constables Steven Tynan and Damian Eyre were shot dead.

When police are killed, it is usually by an offender desperate to escape arrest. This was different. A stolen car was left in the middle of the street to lure police to the ambush. It was cold-blooded and loosely planned for months, though the final decision to act was made just hours earlier.

The red-hot suspects were a group of armed robbers who banded together through a common love of stolen money and an equal hatred of the police who pursued them. It was a time when banks were robbed at a rate of around two a week and there were at least three teams of professional bandits picking off targets.

One was the Flemington Crew led by Victor Peirce, Graeme Jensen, Peter McEvoy and Jedd Houghton. The second-tier soldiers included Victor's half-brother Trevor Pettingill, Anthony Farrell and car thief Gary Abdallah.

Most of the team came from crime families. Peter David McEvoy was different.

Far from growing up in the hard streets, he had lived in a peaceful cottage in the Botanic Gardens as his father, Stan, was chauffeur for governors Sir Dallas Brooks and Sir Rohan Delacombe.

'We met kings and queens,' McEvoy's brother, Geoff, remembers. He says they were regularly dropped at their private school in the governor's Austin Princess limousine.

Geoff says they played together because they weren't allowed friends inside the governor's grounds. Peter loved to play cowboys and Indians in the gardens. That is, until he turned rotten.

His decent, loving family tried to support him and then turned away, totally ashamed. Geoff became a policeman and then a prison officer when Peter was an inmate: 'He spent more time in Pentridge than I did.'

After police shot dead robbers Mark Militano (March 1987) and Frankie Valastro (June 1987), detectives were told the Flemington Crew had developed a so-called 'two for one' pact. If police killed another of their associates, they would kill two cops.

The intelligence was the gang would target members of the Armed Robbery Squad, following them from the crime department to their private homes. No one thought it would be a random attack.

On 11 October, three carloads of armed robbery detectives planned to arrest Jensen, the prime suspect in the murder of security guard Dominik Hefti, who was shot dead during an armed robbery at Barkly Square, Brunswick.

They considered storming Jensen's house in Narre Warren but rejected the idea because he was known to be armed.

Instead, they waited for him to leave, planning to surround him when he stopped. But there was a glitch. When he pulled up at the local shopping strip to buy a spark plug, the last unmarked police car that was to box him in arrived late and skidded through, leaving Jensen an escape route. He reversed out and was shot dead. A firearm was found in Jensen's car and detectives at the scene said he was shot in self-defence. (Jensen was found not to be Hefti's killer.)

That night Peirce and McEvoy spoke on the phone and decided to launch the ambush. Abdallah was told to steal a car that was dumped as bait. Both policemen were shot with a shotgun. Eyre, seriously wounded, was then shot with his own gun.

A police taskforce named Ty-Eyre after the two officers slain in Walsh Street was set up under the joint leadership of David Sprague and John Noonan. It was hamstrung from the beginning by a lack of computer facilities, micro-management from above, police outside of the taskforce taking unauthorised action and internal divisions.

Eventually five men – Peirce, McEvoy, Farrell, Pettingill and teenager Jason Ryan – were charged. Ryan was indemnified to give evidence against the others. Two other suspects – Houghton (17 November 1988) and Abdallah (9 April 1989) – had been shot dead by police.

The star witness was Peirce's wife, Wendy, who made detailed statements to police and was placed in witness protection. But at the 1991 trial, she flipped, refusing to give evidence. Many, including Noonan, wanted her to be declared a hostile witness and forced to testify. Instead, the jury did not hear from her. She was later jailed for perjury.

After a seven-week trial, the four men were acquitted.

Years later, Wendy confessed to me she believed they were guilty. 'It was more Jedd and Macca [McEvoy] than the others. Jedd was the trigger man; he had the shotgun. Macca took [Damian Eyre's] handgun.'

On acquittal McEvoy baited police at the court, yelling he wanted an inquiry: 'What do you think about that? . . . "I'll fix you; I'll fix you." Is that what you said? I'll be waiting. I'm not afraid to die.'

His enthusiasm for an inquiry dissolved quickly. He did jail time for stick-ups and then moved to NSW, occasionally resurfacing to say he was not involved in Walsh Street.

Behind the scenes he traded on the notoriety. A prison officer told me: 'On the day police served McEvoy with a copy of the brief of evidence, which contained a box of the evidence photos of the two slain members, McEvoy began to hold court inside the unit and distribute the evidence booklets to the gathered inmates. When McEvoy was quizzed by his audience about the shootings, he just smiled. It was a smile that exuded pure evil and at that point, I knew he was as guilty as sin.'

When he was arrested in NSW in February 2010 he taunted police, saying: 'The sweetest thing I ever heard was the police officer's last words while he was dying.' McEvoy also allegedly told the arresting police: 'I can't wait to put a shotgun to your head. Loaded up with a solid [shot] and watching your fucking head get blown up.'

Regardless, in 2012, the Coroners Court refused to reopen the inquest, saying those statements alone did not place McEvoy at the scene.

Geoff McEvoy is a year older than his brother. He says Peter was a normal kid who, when jailed for 14 days as a teenager for driving while disqualified, came home saying: 'I will never go back there again.'

By the age of 20 he was part of a gang said to be responsible for the abduction, torture and sexual abuse of up to 24 girls, mostly aged between 13 and 16. He was found guilty of two counts of rape and acquitted of several.

While inside prison he started to associate with crooks, including Victor Peirce. 'It broke Dad's heart,' says Geoff.

While working in a maximum-security division at Pentridge Geoff received a phone call from his brother. 'He said: "I hear you are giving a friend of mine a hard time." I told him it had nothing to do with him and he said: "Just remember I know where you live." If he wants to say he was not involved in Walsh Street, perhaps he shouldn't brag that he was.'

About 10 years ago, the brothers exchanged angry texts. Geoff says Peter threatened: 'You'll be lying on the ground like the second Jack [policeman] we offed [killed] saying. "No, no, don't shoot".'

'If he is going to make those sort of comments to me, then I am going to take them on board. I am certainly convinced they did it – 100 per cent.' He says he took screenshots of the threats and gave them to NSW Police but they were destroyed in a flood of a storage area.

Retired Inspector John Noonan has long thought there should be a new coronial inquest to establish the facts, though he believes the accused men ultimately suffered the consequences of their actions. Four of those alleged to have been involved are dead; Houghton and Abdallah were shot by police and Farrell died of natural causes.

In 2002 Peirce was murdered in his car in Bay Street, Port Melbourne. It was a Holden Commodore, the same type of vehicle used to lure Tynan and Eyre to Walsh Street.

'Victor Peirce died the way he should have – just a callous, callous criminal,' Noonan says. 'And he met his match at the hands of another drug dealer.'

'Jedd Houghton – I suppose you could say he was sentenced by his own hand,' Noonan adds. 'Peter McEvoy is a coward. He cringes at his own shadow now and fears what's going to come around the corner every second of the day, which is probably not a bad thing.'

BREAD, WATER AND THE LIQUORICE MILE

Prodigious armed robber and expert escapee John Killick, who turned 81 a few days ago, has a unique take on how to remain healthy in your latter years. 'In some ways, jail can preserve you. It is stressful, but it has steady hours, there is no booze and you are not running around.'

Most of the police and prison officers from four states who chased or caged him over more than 50 years are long gone, while John has just finished his fifth book and revisited Pentridge Prison, where he did six hard years from 1966 until 1972, when it was reopened by the National Trust.

Killick first arrived in Pentridge with a red-headed inmate who refused to say why he was there – for good reason. It was Keith Ryrie, who had abducted and murdered a five-year-old girl. They separated the two prisoners, farming Ryrie into a reception party of heavy crooks, who kicked him until he was nearly unconscious. 'They let the crims do it. No one liked child killers.'

Armed robber, escapee and author of the bestselling *Shantaram*, Gregory David Roberts, remembers being advised by standover man and author Mark 'Chopper' Read to prepare for the reception when he entered H Division. It was called the Liquorice Mile, where guards lined up to beat inmates as they entered.

Read told him not to run or cover his head, or it would be seen as weakness. Read, he says, strolled down, seemingly impervious to the blows hitting him on the head, chatting to his attackers as if nothing was happening.

Killick recalls his own welcome to H Division. 'I bit through my lip to stop from crying out', knowing any noise would let other inmates know he was vulnerable.

He escaped custody in three states, first from Melbourne at the Hawthorn court. Facing two armed robbery charges, he punched one of his escorts in the belly, then 'I ran down the steps – I was pretty fast then – but I got tackled by a guard. I think I was unlucky to be tackled like that in a non-rugby state.'

He was first sent to adult prison in 1960, aged 18, for housebreaking. In 1966, he pulled his first armed robbery to raise funds to travel to the United States to reunite with his girlfriend, Cathy Bishop.

The chatty ex-inmate gets a little cagey when asked how many armed robberies he pulled. 'I've been convicted of nine.'

Two were in Melbourne – a railway station for $20 ('I was drunk') and the Kensington Commonwealth Bank, where a teller (they were armed back then) fired shots: 'It just missed me.'

Killick was arrested in 1966 in Melbourne entering the Fred Astaire Dance Studio – his American girlfriend liked to get a little funky. Inside, he says, were male and female police officers masquerading as light-footed students. 'I knew there was a problem: the receptionist, her face was white. I went there to learn the tango, but they foxtrotted me out of there pretty quick.'

In 1984, while he was doing time in Brisbane's Boggo Road Prison, a woman slipped him a replica pistol when he was transferred to a local hospital. This time, he was on the run for 12 months.

His most ambitious and famous escape was in 1999, when his girlfriend, Lucy Dudko, hired a helicopter from Bankstown Airport to take a joy flight over the nearly completed Sydney Olympics site. Once in the air, she pulled a gun and demanded the pilot land at Silverwater Prison to pick up Killick. They spent 45 days on the run. It cost him a further 15 years in jail.

In 1968, he decided to escape from Pentridge – a high-risk strategy, considering previous escapee Ronald Ryan was hanged the year before after he was convicted of murdering prison officer George Hodson. Ryan's escape partner, Peter Walker, died in detention in 2022 as the government was attempting to deport him to his native Britain.

Killick used a smuggled hacksaw blade to cut through bars in E Wing, then cut through the weak part of the door to slip out of the dormitory with two others.

The plan was to jump a guard and force him to hand over the division keys. Trouble was, the patrolling prison officer was keyless. 'He went for his gun, so I hit him. He fell down and I thought I might have killed him.'

Killick and two mates ran upstairs to barricade the door in the amenities area, starting a six-hour siege. 'Eighteen carloads of police arrived. They shot out the lights,' Killick says. He knew if the prison officer had died, he would hang like Ryan: 'I considered killing myself.'

If it had escalated, it could have ended in a riot with inmates being shot. Instead, prison governor Ian Grindlay used a bullhorn to negotiate. Bellowing loud enough for every prisoner to hear, he made promises. Killick would have to do his remaining four years in H Division, but any new charges would be dealt with quietly in the magistrates' 'jail' court.

'He kept his word,' says Killick. He stepped out, fearing he would be killed. Instead, he was marched straight to the secure cell that held Ryan before he was hanged.

While the guard had blood pouring from his head, the wound was superficial and he received five stitches.

Killick gave evidence at the 1972 Board of Inquiry conducted by Kenneth Jenkinson, QC into brutality and misconduct at Pentridge.

'I was convinced by Jockey Smith [notorious armed robber James Edward Smith, shot dead by police in Creswick in 1992] to testify. It was a cover-up,' Killick says.

While no prison officers were convicted of bashings, Jenkinson's report resulted in the government loosening bail rules and banning punishments such as solitary confinement and dietary restrictions. In 1973, *The Age*, under editor Graham Perkin, called for Pentridge to be closed. Perkin was right – just 24 years early.

During his criminal career (including 30 years inside), Killick downplayed his culpability. Sure, he was a stick-up man, but he says he would never have pulled the trigger. These days, he understands the trauma he inflicted: 'I now know that robbing banks creates psychological damage. It is a heavy crime.

'I deserved to be punished, I accept that,' he adds. What still angers him was the extras: the bread-and-water punishment, being locked in a small cage ('It nearly broke me') and being beaten with batons: 'If they wanted to get you, they would get you.'

Released in 1972, Killick continued to commit armed robberies, get caught and plot escapes, culminating in the 1999 helicopter escape.

After a life of crime, Killick says: 'I know I did bad things', but he has spent his latter years counselling people heading down the same track in the hopes of paying back his debt. 'I think I've just about broken even.'

When he was finally released, he was kept on long-term parole, meaning he couldn't leave New South Wales. When it lapsed, he flew to Melbourne to revisit Pentridge, remembering the barbaric nature of D Division, where prisoners on remand were herded into open yards in the middle of winter and forced to use an open shower block. In H Division, the inmates broke rocks and had tiny exercise yards which, if they existed in a modern zoo, would create public outrage.

Pentridge is still filled with ghosts and stories. The drug trafficker and international pole vaulter who asked for a pole to practise inside; the request was refused. The prison riot where a guard broke a baton on Read's head before the bloodied inmate advised him not to do the same to the next inmate because 'He hates screws.' The infamous H Division sausage war, which resulted in bashings and stabbings after Read was accused of eating all the snags to be served for Christmas; and the 1987 Jika Jika fire, in which five inmates died.

Those who claim modern jails are soft would do well to look at Pentridge, where giant bluestone walls hid callous brutality that resulted in angry men being released back into the community. Treat people as animals, and what do you expect to get in return?

DANGER LURKING IN THE SHADOWS

There are criminals who are household names, such as Carl Williams and Tony Mokbel – the type that have appeared on page one nearly as often as a soap star during the spring carnival.

Then there are those who shun publicity, wisely reasoning that media attention is to police what berley is to fish – it tends to bring on a feeding frenzy that can take chunks out of you.

There is a third type, the ones whose names are barely known. These criminals could walk down the street without creating either curiosity or fear. But their lack of infamy does not reflect their risk factor. Sometimes anonymity can mask the greatest danger.

And so our attention is drawn to one Brendan Davies – a brilliant man with a photographic memory who can recall the tiniest incident from years in the past. Yet Davies, a loner who has never worked, is fascinated by serial killers and appears devoted to destruction.

Tragically for him, and for us, he appears impervious to punishment, rehabilitation or medical intervention, having convinced himself he possesses a unique insight into the world and that anyone who stands in his way is part of a conspiracy against him.

For reasons perhaps only he knows, Davies believes he is a victim; that his parents didn't raise him in a loving household and authorities should have saved him from his misery.

For years now, Davies has run a one-man war against anyone and anything he feels is his enemy or, more often, just for the heck of it. One of his previous (and thwarted) crime plans is so chilling, police will always consider him a long-term danger to the community.

That he hasn't killed by now can only be put down to luck, because as a serial arsonist he has set fire to occupied properties – including his family home, with his mother and two brothers inside.

Far from hiding away, he took to the internet to share his bizarre rants, often appearing hidden by a black balaclava under the alias 'Seer Travis Truman'. With his voice barely disguised, he would lecture on arson, vandalism and his other peculiar interests.

Desperate for an audience, he started his own site and would join chatrooms until he was booted out. He would not be deterred when others declared him a 'creep' or worse.

He described himself as 'a tortured victim-creation of Australian society. My society has done everything wrong in the world to me. I am a highly intelligent and deeply insightful philosopher.'

In one video he said: 'Society has created the arsonist and has victimised them terribly. The arsonist is using arson to strike and hit his society back as a form of justice, of vengeance, his own personal justice against his society that has wronged him. Arsonists have every right to attack society because society has done everything to them.'

He omitted one important point: if you want to set fire to stuff and get away with it, you should probably not post videos on arson. Police would later allege the methodology he discussed was the type he used in reality.

In 2010 a serial arsonist launched 12 attacks against buildings including schools, a nightclub, homes and commercial properties. By November, Davies – who had a prior history of arson and lived in the area as a child – had become a person of interest and the subject of a police surveillance operation.

They were able to track his car to the scene of five deliberately lit fires in January and February 2011, with targets including the unmanned Mount Waverley police station, two churches, a bakery and a childcare centre.

He was initially charged with all 17 fires, but ultimately went to trial on the five that happened while he was under electronic surveillance. The day after he set fire to the Croxley Hall Child Care Centre he was arrested.

When detectives searched his Rowville home they found hard copy and computer notes that included disturbing details on judges, police and lawyers involved in his previous cases. The material was considered so alarming that the names of the prosecution team and lead investigators were deleted from subsequent legal proceedings.

Police also found his shelves filled with books on serial killers and on his Facebook site he had 'liked' US mass murderer Charles Manson. 'It was a form of hero worship,' one source said.

Indeed, in one of his random postings, he declared: 'I am an expert on serial killers. Serial killers are tortured victim creations of their evil lie-based societies. They have every right to undertake murder acts, and society has no right to pass judgement on them.'

In the scheme of things, it should not have been a difficult trial, with the prosecution using his videos to show his tendencies to arson and tracking information to show that he was at the scene of all the fires.

Then Davies sacked his lawyers and chose to represent himself.

Every judge hates a self-represented client, as the court must then protect the accused from their own inexperience and stop them implicating themselves in a legal own-goal. One stupid comment can result in a mistrial and taint the defence's grounds for an appeal.

Judges expect these cases to hit a few speed bumps along the way, but County Court judge Gerard Mullaly could hardly have thought he would have to deal with an obstinate, argumentative, irrational and seemingly inexhaustible defender.

The case went to court 31 times before we were even close to a real hearing. It spent three years bouncing around in the Magistrates Court and a further three in the County Court. Eventually the pre-trial arguments went a staggering five months before a jury was empanelled. Then the trial went another three months over 61 sitting days. Davies challenged every witness on everything, delayed at will and launched three failed appeals to the Supreme Court.

'He was never short of a word, and a phenomenal memory and is amazingly intelligent,' one observer said.

Fairfax Media reported some of the jurors cried and cheered with relief when they returned guilty verdicts over the five fires in November 2016. But it was only in Mullaly's sentencing remarks a few months ago that you glimpse the severity of Davies's troubled past.

Since the age of 18, he had been convicted of around 40 offences, ranging from stalking to weapons possession and arson.

The most worrying was in February 2009, when his car was spotted parked outside a Blackburn brothel. When he was intercepted by police, they found a large knife and – in the boot – alternative number plates, garbage bags, plastic ties, gloves, tape, rope, handcuffs and a hammer.

Clearly he was set to commit a crime, but what? Police believe he planned to abduct, rape and murder a sex worker. The theory was supported by a notebook that included instructions: 'Look through her messages, find a client, SMS him from her phone, completely destroy the phone, strip her, put clothes in garbage bag, collect all jewellery and put in bag, cut her nails, place all 10 clipped nails in bag, remove her teeth, put into bag or leave with body, remove all ties et cetera before disposal.'

Despite the notes, he was convicted of the lesser charge of being armed with a controlled weapon with criminal intent.

Davies is a disturbed and troubled man with an autism spectrum disorder. He has effectively refused to be examined by forensic psychologists – as if he doesn't want anyone to know what is inside his head.

He claims to have had a terrible childhood yet his mother and father (who are separated) remain supportive, turning up at court often only to be abused. He is rarely paroled as he shows no signs of reform, and serves out his full term before re-offending.

In sentencing Davies, Mullaly would have considered his previous behaviour, his prison record, his failure to undertake psychological assessment, refusal to engage in rehabilitation programs and his conduct in court.

'I have formed the view based on all the evidence in these proceedings that you have a particular disdain for the justice system and a deep-set hatred of the police.

'By reason of all the evidence and the relevant factors, it is clear in my view that you are an ongoing danger to the community. The likelihood of your re-offending in the future is very high. On any realistic analysis, your prospects for reform and rehabilitation are very slim at best and most likely non-existent.'

Finally, Mullaly sentenced Davies to 14 years, six months, with a minimum tariff of 12 years and three months.

With typical judicial understatement, he added: 'I reiterate the thanks of the court to those that have worked tirelessly in respect of perhaps the most difficult case that has occurred in these courts for some time.'

ARE CROOKS BORN OR MADE?
ONE MAN'S JOURNEY FROM TEEN TERROR TO GENTLEMAN INVESTOR

For a bloke who has been shot at (a bullet creased his eyebrow), blown up and sentenced to 84 years' jail, former safebreaker Patrick Shiels remains remarkably cheerful.

At 79, dressed in his three-piece suit, spiffy kerchief, matching briefcase and shoes, he could be mistaken for a retired stockbroker out to check his investments. Indeed, these days he plays the market, making more money than he ever did as a dedicated crook.

While today we worry about juvenile offenders, Shiels is proof it is not a new problem and, even for the worst, the penny can drop (he started in pre-decimal currency days) that long stretches in prison are a waste of life.

Paddy says that in his case there is only one answer to the question of whether criminal behaviour is due to upbringing or ingrained personality traits. 'I was born a criminal,' he says with remarkable candour. 'When I was five years old someone predicted – "They'll hang you".'

And they would have gone close when, nearly 50 years ago, after shooting and wounding a policeman, he made the split-second decision not to finish the job.

Ironically he helped a man many wanted to hang – police killer William John O'Meally – escape from Pentridge Prison in what remains one of Australia's most daring jail breaks.

Shiels's road to crime was a short one – walking distance, actually – which began during World War II. He snuck out of the family home at 2 am to rob a St Kilda cafe, filling his pockets with coins (the notes had already been banked). It was 1942 and he was five years old.

His father was in the army and had neither the time nor inclination to reform his scallywag son, preferring to ship him off to an orphanage to receive a Catholic education. It worked – but only to a degree. In Year 5 he was judged third in the state for the Christian Brothers, finishing with a perfect 100 for mental arithmetic and dictation.

If he had kept his nose clean he would have been a bookkeeper, but by the age of 11 he was more interested in breaking into offices than working in one.

Inevitably there was jail time, though it failed to deter Shiels, who in 1953 escaped from the French Island Prison. After four hungry days on the lam he was caught when, in desperation, he killed a sheep.

The unimpressed judge sentenced him to 84 years, commenting: 'You are an appalling problem. For a boy of 16 your record is incredible.'

Too nimble and rebellious for juvenile reformatories, he ended up in Pentridge Prison as the second-youngest inmate ever (he was actually 15 years and five months), working in the stone yard breaking up bluestone with a sledgehammer. While it was mind- and hand-numbing, it did build muscles, which led to one of his few semi-legitimate jobs – as a male stripper.

In Pentridge he mixed with Victoria's most notorious and at the age of 18 helped organise the jail's biggest escape. Five made it out, including O'Meally, who three years earlier had murdered Constable George Howell when O'Meally was disturbed trying to steal from cars.

Shiels was not keen on the cop killer. 'I never liked him. Shooting Howell was an imbecile act. He was trying to steal from a car and would have got three months. He was a dog and was happy to try and convict others for what he had done.'

Within weeks of release from prison in 1955, Shiels broke back in to hide a shotgun and a rifle near the jail football field. From the back of a truck he jumped on the exterior wall. 'I lowered the ladder from the guard tower and put the guns under a mattress in a shed near the footy ground.

'They were supposed to go that Saturday but couldn't find the guns.' And so Shiels went back again, this time as a visitor, to tell a go-between where the guns were hidden. 'The next Saturday they were gone.' All were recaptured and O'Meally went on to become the last man legally flogged in Australia.

It wasn't the only time Shiels broke into prison, once building a homemade canoe to slip off French Island, rob a general store on the mainland and return with contraband for the inmates. 'The screws couldn't work out how we were drinking better coffee than them.'

By 1960 he graduated from factory breaker to armed robber, targeting the Toorak Drive-in. Shiels and his sidekick escaped with only £20 (the takings had been banked) and he was one twitch away from murder. 'I had my gun [a Smith and Wesson magnum] pointed at the manager. My hands were sweating and when I pulled the hammer back it nearly slipped. It would have blown his guts out.'

The victim didn't hold a grudge, for at the trial he took a dislike to the prosecutor's style, deliberately giving a description so different to the accused the jury had to acquit.

His acquittal didn't deter Shiels from crime, although he decided to improve his skills and headed to South Australia for a newish start. First stop was the Adelaide public library, where he used the reading and comprehension skills honed by the Christian Brothers to learn the intricacies of explosives. After studying *Metal Working with Explosives*, volumes one and two, he went to the sunken Liberty freighter *Eleni K* off the Ceduna coast to practise letting off charges on the deck. If you can punch a hole in a ship, you can do the same to a safe.

He started hitting supermarkets (leaving a Coles manager tied up in the office after he – not unreasonably – asked not to be dumped in the freezer).

It was December 1968 when it all went wrong in a Norwood Woolworths, because the security system had been upgraded due to a previous burglary.

'I climbed on the roof and disabled the alarm but I didn't know there was a second one,' Shiels says. As he was setting up just after 5 am, alarms were ringing at the manager's house and police headquarters.

Armed with three sticks of gelignite and a nine-millimetre Browning automatic, he was preparing to blow the safe when he heard police walking down the stairs.

He slipped over to the butchers' section only to be spotted. 'He yelled that he was going to shoot me,' and so Shiels turned and fired first, hitting the constable in the shoulder.

Cornered, he ran to the back only to find a policeman standing outside. Deciding he would rather die than go back to prison, Shiels aimed at the officer and fired through the glass door.

'I tried to shoot him. He was standing between me and freedom but the bullet deflected when it hit the glass.' The policeman dived to the footpath while Shiels fired more shots before crashing through the shattered glass.

He aimed again at the policeman, who was on the ground desperately digging at the concrete with his bare hands. 'I nearly pointed the gun up his nose and I was going to blow his head off. He looked at me and I could see he was begging for life with his eyes. I thought he couldn't hurt me so I ran.'

He was wrong, as the policeman and a third constable (the wounded one was still inside) gave chase across the car park. 'They yelled to stop or they'd shoot. I couldn't believe it; in Victoria they would have emptied their guns straight away. Then there were bullets flying everywhere. I thought they had a machinegun.'

He still believes the policeman whose life he spared was trying to shoot at his legs rather than kill him.

He was arrested a few days later after he was identified by caravan park staff where he was hiding. He was heading off to rob a bank when a detective walked up and 'stuck a gun in my ribs. He was the coolest bloke I have ever met.'

Shiels says he hoped his female companion sitting in the car with two loaded pistols would shoot his captor. 'It was her moment to be Bonnie to my Clyde but she didn't take it.'

A prison fight left him with a jaw broken in two places, which delayed the trial. 'Luckily the judge who was to hear the case had a heart attack. If he had taken the case, he would have thrown away the key and I would still be inside.'

Instead the new judge agreed to a deal where Shiels pleaded guilty to a series of offences if the attempted murder charge was dropped. Even with that stroke of luck he went back to crime, but after robbing a chemist shop in 1976 and a degree of soul searching he describes as 'spiritual', he decided to finally pack it in.

'Now I would rather cut my hand off than steal a dollar.'

KNIGHT CONDEMNED BY HIS OWN HAND

These are words you thought you would never read in a mainstream publication: mass killer Julian Knight is right. The decision to ban him from applying for parole is unjust and has left him the victim of political populism.

On Wednesday 9 August 2017, it was 30 years since Knight took three firearms to Hoddle Street on a quiet Sunday night with a plan to hunt down and kill as many innocent people as he could.

In just 38 minutes, the 19-year-old failed (and bullied) army officer candidate fired 200 rounds of high-grade ammunition, killing seven people, wounding 19 and nearly shooting a police helicopter out of the sky. When police closed in on him, he threw down his guns and surrendered, later telling detectives he intended to shoot himself but misplaced his last bullet.

Knight pleaded guilty and was sentenced to multiple life sentences. Because of his age, he was given a minimum sentence of 27 years, meaning he should have been eligible to apply for parole in 2014.

The outrage about Knight's sentence has grown over the years. Back then the headlines shouted 'Life' and there was little emphasis on the bottom end of his potential jail term. Indeed, sentencing judge Justice George Hampel made it clear Knight needed to reform to be freed, telling him the 27 years was just the minimum he could serve and not a guaranteed release date.

Many thought Knight would die in prison, either by his own hand or from the career crooks who would show him less sympathy than Justice Hampel. But Knight had the instincts of a survivor, first shown at Hoddle Street, when he meekly surrendered the moment he saw anyone who could return fire.

Slight but fit, Knight went to prison and taught himself to box, hitting the heavy bag at every opportunity and – more importantly – used the sound military tactic of developing strong allies, including some of the worst killers Australia has known.

But there were other heavyweights who didn't warm to him. In 1993 prison authorities discovered a mass escape plot involving up to 30 inmates in Pentridge's notorious H Division. The plan included attacking Knight in his cell.

While Knight was not a model prisoner (there were a few minor assaults and discipline issues) he was usually well behaved. 'He quickly learnt to fly under the radar and keep a low profile,' a veteran Pentridge officer said. 'He didn't steal anything and didn't try to stand over anyone.'

'He has a huge ego,' another prison officer said of Knight, who was once assessed as intelligent but a 'chronic underachiever'.

'He always believes he is the smartest in the room,' a prison source said.

In one conversation Knight talked of an international mass killing then added that if you wanted to create maximum casualties: 'You would just fly a plane into the MCG.'

His cell has always been maniacally ordered and he even lined up his soft drink bottles 'like little soldiers'. Sometimes uninvited guests would sneak in to rearrange his possessions. 'He would be furious,' a source said.

The military-obsessed Knight ranked inmates, referring to career criminals and murderers as 'long-termers' while those serving shorter sentences were 'shitkickers'.

By 2012 Knight started to prepare to apply for parole telling people he would 'make a mark' on release. 'He wasn't talking about crime – he just thought he was special and a natural high achiever.'

But in 2014 the then Coalition state government brought in one-off legislation shutting the cell door, effectively banning him from parole.

'This is guaranteeing that he remains in jail until he's dead, or so seriously incapacitated he's no risk to other people in Victoria or indeed in the community,' then premier Denis Napthine said.

Knight wrote in response: 'The Victorian state government changed the law to keep me in prison not because I pose a threat to the community, but because they believe I did not deserve to be given a minimum non-parole term.

'The fact is a minimum term was not opposed by the prosecution and the minimum term that was set was not appealed against. They didn't think I would survive to see the end of my 27-year minimum term and when I did they brought into law retrospective legislation that rewrote history to suit their views as to what they thought my sentence should have been.'

Knight is right. In reality he has been re-sentenced by politicians with a law designed to trump the courts entrusted with the job of setting prison terms and the parole board that should decide release dates.

Knight should be able to apply for parole in the same way as any other inmate, and if he has reformed, it should be considered.

If.

So, we know what Knight did 30 years ago, but what has he become? Let's not ask those traumatised by his actions nor look at the image Knight would like to portray.

Let us look at the real Knight – the one he shares with the killers and crims who have been his friends and allies for decades. To do so, we must reach back to an investigation that does not directly relate to Knight, but shows his actions are at odds with his claims of reformation.

In February 1992 schoolgirl Prue Bird was abducted from her Glenroy home and murdered. Her body has never been found. Police believe the 13-year-old was targeted as revenge against her grandmother's partner, who gave evidence against the men responsible for the 1986 Russell Street bombing.

One of those convicted of the bombing was Craig Minogue (a Knight ally) who is alleged to have said, while warning people not to talk: 'It would be a shame if anything happened to your sweet little Prue, wouldn't it?'

In February 2012 police charged Bega schoolgirl killer Les Camilleri with Prue's murder. Camilleri, who was already serving life with no minimum for the 1997 murders of Lauren Barry, 14, and Nichole Collins, 16, eventually pleaded guilty to the Bird murder. There was never any incentive to tell the truth as his papers have been marked never to be released. He refused to implicate anyone else in the crime and gave a clearly bogus account of what happened.

Within weeks of the charges being laid, Knight involves himself, identifying a fellow prisoner he claims was the police informer. He claims the prison source was paid $500,000 for information, an allegation that put the man's life in danger. The man Knight repeatedly claimed was the informer in the Bird case was an old enemy, one of the inmates from Pentridge who had planned to attack him in 1993 during a prison break-out.

On 19 March 2012, Knight wrote to Minogue, saying: 'I have been following the Prue Bird investigation . . . I have it on good authority who the prison source is.

'On a completely different subject, [names prisoner] is on the loose after being sentenced in a closed court. I hear he is hoping to invest $500,000.'

In another letter he tries to organise another inmate who is a Minogue associate to connect with Camilleri to compare notes, implying police will not be able to link the Russell Street bombers to the Bird murder. 'I predict no one else will get charged and the case against Les will collapse. We will wait and see.'

In a letter of support to Camilleri, he sends him media transcripts on the case before ending: 'Take care of yourself Big Boy.' In another letter he names the suspected informer, asking Camilleri to remember where he met him: 'Mate, think hard.'

In a note to triple murderer Ashley Mervyn Coulston, Knight says: 'I predict the case against Les will collapse. A jail-house informant has 500,000 reasons to make up stories. Say no more.'

There is something else in Knight's letters that is deeply concerning. This mass killer who says he is no longer violent has chosen to use as his personalised letterhead the image of two armed soldiers on patrol with the caption *Call of Duty 2*.

Knight says he has changed. In his latest plea he writes: 'Thirty years have passed since the Hoddle Street shootings and I am far from the immature disturbed, desperate teenager who committed them.' He says he wept for his victims but when it came to the murder of the innocent Prue Bird, he shows no compassion at all, preferring to use the crime to even an old score and curry favour with killers.

Knight should be able to apply for parole, and there can be no doubt the parole board would reject any such submission – not because his initial sentence was inadequate, but because he would be judged as still being too great a risk.

Julian Knight went to jail for what he did, and should remain there for what he is now. He stands condemned by his own words.

DID ROCCO GET AWAY WITH CARL WILLIAMS'S MURDER?

For a multimillionaire drug trafficker, gunman and feared gangster, Rocco Arico first came to notice as an average kidnapper – more a character out of *The Hangover* than *The Godfather*.

Yet he rose from bumbling boob to a real-life *Sopranos* figure who finally came crashing down when sentenced in the County Court this month [March 2017] to a minimum of 10 years for drug trafficking and crimes of violence.

The fact someone like Arico was able to build an empire says more about our inexhaustible desire for drugs than his talents as a master criminal.

In August 1999, Arico, Dino Dibra and a couple of other hoons kidnapped a man in the western suburbs, punching, kicking and pistol-whipping the fellow before throwing him in the boot of their car. So far, so good.

But they failed to understand that the boot could be popped from the inside, and so when they pulled up at the lights, the victim jumped out and bolted. The kidnap team gave chase then, in front of startled witnesses, beat him and dragged him back into the boot.

They then drove to Dibra's Taylors Lakes house, where they rang the victim's brother and demanded $20,000 before being haggled down to $5000.

Luckily for the victim, and sadly for Arico and his mob, the house was already filled with law enforcement bugs and video cameras. And if they needed any further evidence, when police arrived, the bashed man was still in the boot.

While the kidnapping was inept, the bugged conversation gives an insight into Arico's love of violence and explains why he is now implicated in two murders, including ordering the 2010 prison killing of drug kingpin Carl Williams.

Arico: 'Hey, if I'd have known he's only gonna get five grand, I would have put one in when he tried to jump out of the car.'

Dibra: 'You're an idiot. Listen to you.'

Arico: 'I would have just went fucking whack. Cop this slug for now. I would have slapped one in and I would have said hold on to that for a while, don't give it to anyone and jump in the coffin.'

(Having been caught out by police recordings over the botched kidnapping, Arico was always worried that he was being bugged. And so when this reporter wrote a story on his connections to Williams, he threw his phone in a bush fearing it was being intercepted in a police sting. It turned up at a second-hand store when a homeless man tried to pawn it.)

In July 2000, Arico and Dibra were driving in separate cars, returning from a nightclub, when they cut off another motorist in Taylors Lakes who was on his way to work. It was 7 am.

In the subsequent confrontation, Arico produced an automatic pistol and fired six shots, five hitting the driver before he'd even unbuckled his seatbelt. He was struck on his forearms, abdomen, right elbow and shoulder but, against the odds, he survived.

Williams hid Arico for two days then drove him to the airport, where Arico was arrested about to board a flight to Perth. He told police he was going on a three-week holiday, despite having no luggage.

He travelled light – but not that light. He had $100,000 worth of cocaine in his pocket. He was jailed for seven years, which probably saved his life. If he had been on the outside, he would have been one of Williams's favourite gunmen and would almost certainly have been shot dead like associates Dibra, Andrew Veniamin and Paul Kallipolitis.

In fact, Arico was connected with two gangland hits before the road rage took him off the market. One was the execution of Richard 'The Lionheart' Mladenich, who was shot dead in May 2000 – almost certainly on Williams's orders.

Police have been told Mladenich owed Williams $120,000 for drugs, with underworld sources saying Williams used Mladenich as a jail heavy and wanted him to reprise the role on the outside. One story goes that Mladenich rejected the job offer and joined the Morans – Williams's major enemies.

Almost certainly, Williams handed the job to two of his (then) mates, Arico and Dibra. On the night of the murder, Williams's and Arico's phones were 'pinged' together in the city. And then they were simultaneously turned off.

Shortly after 3 am on 16 May 2000, a lone gunman wearing a hoodie and dark glasses walked into room 18 of St Kilda's Esquire Hotel and shot Mladenich in front of three witnesses.

Far from hiding, Dibra turned up at the Homicide Squad to be interviewed on 15 June – the very night Mark Moran was shot dead outside his Aberfeldie home. Dibra clearly knew that Moran was about to be hit and was setting up the perfect alibi. (Dibra was later shot 14 times with .22 and 9 mm guns, so he wasn't that smart.)

And what of Arico? He chose the exact time of the Moran hit to buy a gangster-chic suit and had the documentation to prove it.

Williams was eventually charged with the murder of Mark Moran but there are some police who say he couldn't have pulled the trigger as he was recorded on CCTV in a Gisborne shop 20 minutes after the hit. When police raided his house at 4 am (less than eight hours after the murder), he was in bed and his mate Arico was asleep on the floor.

Flash forward. After doing his seven years, Arico is released about the time Williams finally pleads guilty to three murders and an attempted murder.

While Williams is becoming more desperate and despondent, Arico fills the big man's position in the drug world, reinventing himself as a 'property developer' and acquiring a $20 million fortune. One of his bayside properties, a four-level palace with a lift, rooftop garden, sauna, steam room and home cinema, sold for $2.5 million.

The house was in his mother's name. For an older lady, she is apparently extremely sprightly because judging by the size of the weights in the gym, she could bench-press 100 kilos. The framed picture from the film *Scarface* in the wine cellar probably showed where Arico's real interests lay.

At his new property on the other side of town, he offered to put security cameras on his neighbours' properties to keep the area safe.

While Arico was building a property empire, a loose end was fraying; his former mate Williams was trying to do a deal with police. He had made a statement over the 2004 murders of prosecution witness Terry Hodson and his wife, Christine, in the hope of getting a sentence discount.

By 2010, there were only two inmates with Williams in his Barwon Prison unit. One was Matthew 'The General' Johnson and the other, who still cannot be named, was a mate of Arico, so close they were seen together on the night of the Mladenich killing.

Arico received regular telephone updates from his inside man, and their recorded conversations were illuminating. The day before the murder, Arico told him: 'You haven't got, like, one friend out here. You've chosen to accept it mate, it's not good. You're not the same as you were three months ago. You put yourself in that position, keep on making weak decisions.'

It was alleged that on that afternoon, Arico's mate told Johnson that Williams was planning to kill 'The General' with pool balls in a sock – an old jail weapon of choice.

This is, of course, nonsense. Williams wanted Johnson to act as his protector. He was looking to get out of jail, not commit another murder.

A prison intelligence officer would later tell the Ombudsman: 'It's quite obvious that [Arico] was putting the word inside Barwon that the criminal world on the outside, not only being Victoria but interstate, are not happy with the word that Williams is giving information.'

On 19 April, Johnson crushed Williams's skull with eight blows using the metal stem of an exercise bike.

You can only imagine the sickening noise when a man's head is beaten beyond recognition yet Arico's mate, whose back was conveniently turned, didn't react, flinch or look. The reason is simple – he knew what was coming.

And what did the inmate do? Run? Remonstrate? Call for help? No, he rang Arico and used dialogue that would be thrown out of a dinner theatre.

He said to Arico: 'I'm shocked, mate . . . something just really terrible just happened. I think Carl's dead. I think Carl's dead mate. Matty just went crazy.'

Arico responded: 'What happened, mate?'

Inmate: 'I don't know, mate, the screws haven't come yet or nothing, so we're going to get locked in. I think he just threatened Matty. I just heard some noise and I turned over and seen Carl on the floor.'

Johnson claimed it was self-defence but was convicted of murder and sentenced to 32 years. Arico was never charged.

But he has been convicted of drug trafficking, extortion, intentionally causing injury, and firearms offences.

After serving his time, and having failed in a last-minute bid to take out Australian citizenship, he will face deportation to Italy, the country of his birth.

He will, more than likely, be stripped of his assets. But police believe he got away with murder – not once, but twice.

MOKBEL'S BIG GAMBLE FOR FREEDOM

There are two types of drug dealers: dumb ones and smart ones. The dumb ones keep going until they are caught or shot. The smart ones know when to cash their chips and move on, often to become property developers or currency traders.

The smart ones are like deep-sea divers who surface just in time to avoid the bends, while the dumb ones wait too long and are found with a belt full of precious pearls and a bellyful of salt water. Some get addicted to the game of beating the police rather than keeping their eyes on the purpose, which is to acquire obscene amounts of wealth.

If there was a degree in drug dealing, the notorious George Marrogi would be forced to repeat the unit 'Why We Traffic Drugs'.

Marrogi, 33, has had only one adult year of freedom. That hasn't stopped him running the Notorious Crime Family from inside prison.

He was serving a minimum of 27 years for murder, and that term was extended to 32 years due to his drug trafficking. If he behaves himself – which he won't – he'll be out at retirement age.

George doesn't understand that you traffic drugs to make money to buy nice stuff and eat in posh restaurants with cosmetically enhanced girlfriends.

It is highly unlikely that George will ever require a Harvey Norman online catalogue to order a flat-screen TV, leather La-Z-Boy and a shiny coffee machine for his maximum-security cell. And even if UberEats could deliver to prison, the XO prawns from Flower Drum would be cold and a little chewy by the time they had got through security.

Another who didn't understand the rules was Nik Radev. His nickname in the underworld was 'The Bulgarian', though some geographically challenged members of the media decided to change it to 'The Russian'.

Radev's ex-wife, Sylvia, says he just wanted to be a gangster. 'He had no fear and no shame. It was just a power thing for him. He wanted to be like Al Pacino in *Scarface*.'

This drug dealer from behind the Iron Curtain spent $55,000 cash to have his teeth straightened, whitened and capped. As he was shot dead soon after, the dental work proved to be the ultimate in negative gearing.

A while ago I was wandering along the footpath lost in thought when two wannabes in their high-performance hatchback roared past. One opened his window, yelled my name and poked his steroid-swollen arm towards me, fashioning his stubby fingers into the shape of a gun and pulling the trigger. Luckily for me, it wasn't loaded (although I suspect he was).

Some drug dealers become caricatures of themselves.

Which brings us to Tony Mokbel, the drug dealer who had it all – except the brains to know when to quit. Just released from hospital and returned to prison after another health scare, the one-time Mr Big is depressed, losing his mental capacity (years in jail and an attack that leaves you in a coma for three weeks will do that) and, despite years of adhering to a strict vegetarian diet, faces a shortened lifespan due to a dodgy heart.

The Court of Appeal has reduced his sentence by two years, giving him a potential parole date of 2031, but whether he ever gets to the exit gate may rely more on the skills of his doctors than his lawyers.

The former Boronia pizza shop owner built an asset base of $55 million before his 2007 arrest at an Athens seafood restaurant.

His assets in 1995 were $128,000. By 2000 he controlled 38 different companies, including fashion label LSD (Love Style and Design) and had multiple luxury cars, including one with the plates 'RUDARE' (are you there?), a tease to police following him.

He planned to build an $18 million 10-storey 'winged keel' apartment tower over Melbourne's Sydney Road with 120 apartments and townhouses, offices, restaurants and a gym with pool. When the market he owned was seized as an asset of crime, a storeholder asked officials if they wanted the rent in cash 'like Tony'.

If only he had quit while he was quite a bit ahead.

Two hitmen told police they were commissioned by Mokbel to kill rivals – Lewis Moran in 2004 and Michael Marshall in 2003. (He was acquitted of the Moran murder and the Marshall charge was dropped.)

I wandered into the court on the day he was acquitted. He turned to give me a radiant smile and a nod, as if we were pals who recently returned from a caravan holiday to Anglesea.

Over the years his charm faded, and he began to refer to me as the 'Bald-Headed Alien' – which is profoundly unfair (and probably defamatory) to extraterrestrials.

For a drug dealer, Mokbel wasn't a bad bloke and always preferred a non-violent settlement. He was generous and a big tipper, with one restaurant saying his favourite meal was a medium rare steak topped with prawns and salmon.

When he visited a friend on remand, he gave a prison officer $350 to pick up 40 gourmet pizzas and soft drinks for inmates and staff.

During the gangland war, Mokbel put on his UN hat and decided to broker a peace deal. He told police he would guarantee the murders would stop, key figures such as drug dealer Carl Williams would plead guilty to some charges, Tony would go back to selling drugs and the Purana Taskforce could concentrate on other crooks.

'Con [Heliotis, his barrister] and Paul [Coghlan, then director of public prosecutions] will be able to work out the details,' he declared. Police declined the offer.

In 2012, faced with overwhelming evidence, Mokbel pleaded guilty in the Supreme Court to drug trafficking, with a doctor giving evidence that, due to his heart condition, he would be lucky to last a further 24 years.

This is why Mokbel is fighting to have his convictions quashed, even though, if he did win a retrial, pleaded not guilty and lost, he could be sentenced to life. He sees it as a gamble worth taking because he's already facing dying in jail.

He argues his lawyer at the time of his original conviction – disgraced barrister Nicola Gobbo – was a police informer and he didn't have a chance in court.

In August 2001, Mokbel was arrested over importing barrels of ephedrine that could have made 40 million ecstasy tablets. He spent several months in prison and when bailed went straight back to manufacturing drugs. If he had pulled up then, even if convicted, he would have done 15 years and been released, no doubt with a fortune hidden away.

He thought he could beat the system and now is a shadow of his former self.

In a massive misjudgement, police wrote in his criminal file in the early days that he 'lacked financial acumen'. Nothing could have been further from the truth.

If Tony had stuck to his pizza shop in Boronia, he would have built a small chain and invested in several properties, driven a nice car and lived in a nice house.

He might not have been able to buy the ocean-going yacht he used to escape Australia but he could have owned a speedboat on the Eildon

Lake, near where he hid at Bonnie Doon when he jumped bail, eating freshly caught trout rather than farmed salmon.

No one but his friends, family and customers would have ever heard of him. But he would be free.

So it is true, at least for Tony, that crime doesn't pay.

THE DIRTY DOZEN

Before drugs made every second street dealer strut around like Al Capone, gangsters were home-grown, white and local. And back then police produced a super-secret annual report, which was their Football Record on crooks.

It was the early 1970s, when police were expected to recognise major criminals on sight, with the freshly arrested paraded each morning before detectives like livestock at an agricultural show.

It was a time when a crook's nickname reflected characters such as: The Bear, The Arsey Punter, Wall Eye, Face-Ache, Evil George, Hoover Junior, Whako, Iron Bar George, Sexy Rexy, The Pom, The Boy, King Hit Louis, Saturday Afternoon Gangster, Batman, Mr Big, London John, English Johnny, The Creeper, Whiplash and Long Grass John.

Long before the BRW Rich List, the annual Australasian Criminal Register identified our top 100 crooks with insights from the police who arrested them. Here are extracts about 12 of the most notorious, taken directly from the registers of the 1970s.

1. Karl Frederick Bonnette
Gunman, standover man, procurer of prostitutes. A desperate criminal who is depraved and is strongly suspected of trafficking drugs.

One of Australia's first international criminals to see the future was drugs. Networked in Europe, Asia, the US and South America and brought senior NSW crooks together in 1972 to develop an organised crime business plan.

2. Arthur William Delaney
Thief, shoplifter, pickpocket, car thief and housebreaker. This offender has a total of 110 arrests in NSW, Victoria, Queensland and England. He is Australia's, possibly the world's, most active thief. He has been an expert in forming gangs of thieves around him, to perpetrate large-scale robberies. An international criminal well known overseas as the 'Duke'. He walks with a slight limp due to a bullet lodged in his spine.

[A key member of the infamous Kangaroo Gang international shoplifting crew that became a finishing school for a generation of Australia's professional criminals.]

3. Linus Patrick Driscoll: The Pom
Assailant, thief, gunman, house-, shop- and safebreaker. Has a record in Queensland, Victoria, NSW and England. One of the most violent criminals ever to arrive in this country. An extremely vicious human being who it is alleged has tortured other criminals to find out the whereabouts of stolen property.

He, with a group of criminals, formed a gang known as the 'Toe-Cutters'. It is alleged by members of the underworld that this gang sought out those who perpetrated the $250,000 Mayne Nickless robbery; they then attempted to gain information regarding the proceeds of the money by cutting off the toes of their victims with bolt cutters.

['The Pom' was an underworld predator who provided modified automatic guns for some of Australia's biggest armed robberies. His use of bolt cutters made him a feared adversary.]

4. Leslie Herbert Kane

Thief, gunman, standover man. A Melbourne gunman, associates with the worst of the Melbourne Painters and Dockers gunmen. He is one of the Kane brothers of Melbourne and they form one of the most notorious and dangerous families in Australia. This offender is an extremely bad criminal and would commit any type of crime using all the viciousness or violence required to achieve his ends.

[An underworld shark who bit off more than he could chew when he went after the Great Bookie Robbers, led by the brilliant Ray Bennett, who in April 1976 grabbed an estimated $2 million on settlement day at the Victorian Club. Following a fight between Les's brother, Brian, and one of the Bookie Robbers, Bennett decided to launch a pre-emptive strike. In October 1978, Bennett and two other gunmen burst into Les Kane's Wantirna home, shot him and disposed of the body. The three were charged and acquitted but the murder ignited an underworld war.]

5. Brian Kane

Thief, gunman and assailant: The offender has been arrested 38 times. He broke into a tennis pavilion at Carlton one evening and stole cigarettes and chocolates. In August he felled a man by hitting him with a crank handle.

[Brian Kane was blood loyal to his family and was never going to let the murder of his brother go unanswered. In November 1979 he calmly waited for Bennett to be led by detectives to his armed robbery committal hearing in the City Court.

Kane then shot him dead, disappearing via a carefully prepared escape route. The killing signed his own death warrant, although it would take three years for it to be delivered. In November 1982 he was shot dead by two gunmen in the Quarry Hotel, Brunswick. One became a feared contract killer now doing time for a double murder while the other lives the quiet life in Queensland.]

6. Raymond John Kane: Muscles

Thief, gunman, standover man, assailant: He has become rather notorious as a gunman and standover man. He can be most aggravating when he drinks.

[Ray 'Muscles' Kane survived his more notorious brothers but continued the family tradition, eventually being convicted of murder. He graduated to armed run-throughs on drug dealers, stealing their product and any cash he could find.

Made the mistake of threatening an Armed Robbery Squad detective who was with his pregnant wife in their private car.

As a result, detectives raided Muscles's house and 'found' a stick of gelignite wrapped in Christmas paper. Ray learnt two valuable lessons – don't keep explosives at home and don't threaten armed robbery detectives. Muscles died in 2016 of natural causes.]

7. Billy Longley: The Texan

Murderer, gunman, assailant, receiver and thief. He is one of Melbourne's most dangerous and vicious gunmen and has been charged with murder on several occasions only to be acquitted.

[Convicted of the 1973 murder of Painters and Dockers secretary Pat Shannon. Much later, The Texan's revelations on waterfront corruption resulted in the Costigan Royal Commission. In his later years, he teamed up with former Victorian detective Brian Murphy in a mediation business with the motto: 'Everything can be negotiated'.]

8. Stanley Smith: Stan the Man, Stately Stan and Stoner

Assailant, gunman, shoplifter, sexual offender and drug pusher: Became actively involved in a shop-stealing organisation committing numerous thefts. The offender has the reputation of being one of Sydney's most dangerous gunmen.

[Made the mistake of trying to expand into Melbourne, allegedly as a rock concert promoter. In 1973, detectives grabbed him at Melbourne Airport and found a small bag of hashish in his pocket. He claimed it was planted but was subsequently convicted and jailed. Many years later I asked the detective involved if the drugs were planted. He just smiled and said: 'Any port in a storm', which was ironic as we were drinking port at the time.]

9. Ronald Albert Feeney
Armed assailant, false pretender, forger, utterer, house-, office-, shop- and storeroom breaker, car and motorcycle thief, stripper and sexual offender. A violent and dangerous offender.

[Feeney ended up the part-owner of the notorious Mickey's Disco in St Kilda, where he employed the unhinged hitman Christopher Dale Flannery. How someone with Feeney's underworld reputation and criminal record was allowed to have a stake in a licensed premises remains a mystery.

Legend has it that when police learnt he had accepted a contract killing they decided the only way to stop him was to plant a gun on him. He was later jailed for being a felon in possession and the murder plot was thwarted.]

10. Michael John Sayers: Melbourne Mick
Thief, gunman, safeblower, housebreaker: When this offender is released he will continue to commit violent crimes – he is a man to be treated with caution.

[One of those Melbourne crooks who moved to Sydney for easier pickings. He became a contract killer with two confirmed hits and was involved in the Fine Cotton ring-in affair. Ultimately the interstate move proved a poor career choice; Melbourne Mick was shot dead outside his home in February 1985.]

11. John Stewart Regan: The Magician
Assailant, gunman, sexual offender, forger and false pretender: A stand-over man among Sydney criminals and prostitutes. Known to use knuckle dusters and iron bars to commit assaults.

[Dubbed The Magician for making rivals disappear. On 22 September 1974, he left home without his bulletproof vest and was shot dead by George Freeman and two gunmen.]

12. George David Freeman
Shop stealer, clubhouse-, hotel-, safe- and shop breaker, gunman and thief. A plausible offender, travels extensively and can invariably be found in the company of others of the criminal element.

[A murderer, race-fixer, illegal casino owner with links to US organised crime. Prodigious corrupter of police, lawyers and the judiciary. Survived being shot in the head only to die from an asthma attack in 1990.]

PART 2
THE GOOD GUYS

The reason I have survived so long in this business is because for every act of evil, there is an act of decency. Over the years, I have met cops, judges and lawyers who have devoted their lives to justice and the underdog.

There is, for instance, the judge whose grandfather was a Chinese opium dealer, the Greek lad who grew up to be one of Australia's first undercover police officers, and the cop who, as a junior officer, was plucked from obscurity to head a taskforce that became known as 'The Incorruptibles', and who later became Chief Commissioner.

Sometimes it takes years before the good guys feel comfortable telling their stories.

The headlines usually go to the bad guys. This is an attempt to balance the books.

THE SECRET SOCIETY OF MEN IN BLACK

It was at the Victorian Special Operations Group 30th anniversary dinner that I saw first-hand how the 'Soggies' demand excellence and find it difficult to compromise on even the smallest detail.

The hired comedian was performing a 40-minute monologue, which began slowly and tailed off quickly.

Anyone who tells jokes for a living knows that some days you just die on stage, although it is probably advisable not to do it in front of an audience trained to kill.

I was sitting at the organisers' table that night and saw one of their mobile phones light up with a text. 'Get him off or we'll shoot him.' It came from the snipers' table. These are people who can hit you between the eyes from a distance of more than a kilometre. It's best to keep them on side.

We are told it is no longer a matter of if, but rather when, we are confronted by a major terror attack, which means we have never needed the SOG more. The squad has been expanded and re-armed in preparation of what is likely to come.

We had a taste of it when a deluded criminal with a history of ice abuse held a woman hostage and killed a man in Brighton to lure police to a fatal confrontation – all in the name of Islamic State.

If he had a plan, it was a pretty bad one. He ran at a contingent of SOG police, injuring three with blasts from his sawn-off shotgun. They returned fire, hitting him 37 times.

The Soggies are the police other cops call when they are in trouble. Even their selection process is brutal, with some of the fittest and strongest washing out as instructors deliberately try to break them.

There is a mystique about the men in black – they work in secret, often raid in the dark, give evidence without revealing their names and wear masks to protect their identities.

Which makes the book *Sons of God* by Heath O'Loughlin all the more remarkable. O'Loughlin reconstructs some of the SOG's biggest operations through the personal recollections of the members involved. It is riveting reading.

In fairness, O'Loughlin may well have been born to write this story. His father, Doug, and uncles Neil and Robert were all officers in charge of the squad.

At one point there were 13 O'Loughlins in the Victoria Police and while Heath didn't join the family business, as a schoolkid he was able to do his work experience with the SOG.

The upside was that while his mates were pushing pens around an office, he was acting as a hostage or a gunman in scenario training, or blasting away with a high-powered sniper rifle at the range. (They weren't too big on OH&S back in those days.)

The downside was that his father marked his work experience performance as satisfactory, saying you had to be exceptional to get top marks. It seemed to be an O'Loughlin trait, as for years Neil refused to make Soggies eligible for Valour Awards, arguing that what was considered exceptional elsewhere was expected at the SOG.

In the book, O'Loughlin interviews SOG members (using their

operative names) who opened up on what has nearly become a police secret society.

For example, veteran instructor Lima says: 'Am I brutal? I'm not sure. Am I hard? Definitely. We have to expose candidates to levels of discomfort and pain they never thought they were capable of enduring.

'I don't care if a man cries for three hours, so long as he keeps going. I remember holding a bloke's legs while he was doing sit-ups one year – he must have done a thousand sit-ups that day. I was inches away from his face and he had started to cry but kept going. He'd do a sit-up, and when he reached the top he'd say to me: "You're a c---." He'd do another one and repeat it: "You're a ----." He earned a lot of respect that day.' (And a sore tummy.)

One Soggie told me general duties police were in more danger because they were in an uncontrolled environment, where most SOG operations were planned, practised and precise.

The SOG complete more than 400 operations a year, with more than 100 considered high-risk and life-threatening. These jobs include sieges, forced entries, cordon-and-contain operations, mobile intercepts and arresting violent local criminals and terror suspects.

During Melbourne's underworld war, some of the major players were relieved to find that the armed masked men ordering them to surrender were the SOG and not gangland rivals. At least then they knew they weren't going to be shot.

The Soggies' philosophy has always been to overprepare when they can to avoid violent confrontations.

While they train for hundreds of violent scenarios, there are jobs that evolve so quickly, life-and-death decisions have to be made in the field – such as in April 1996, when a deeply disturbed young man named Martin Bryant killed 35 people and wounded a further 23 at Tasmania's Port Arthur in what is Australia's worst massacre.

Bryant has never explained what motivated him and in all probability wouldn't know. Murder is murder, whether it is wrapped in a warped political dogma, an irrational grudge or a pathetic grasp for infamy. Now [2017], for the first time, Heath O'Loughlin takes us inside Port Arthur through the eyes of the SOG sent to reinforce the local police.

And he reveals that despite Bryant having killed more than 30 people and continuing to fire at police, a senior local policeman refused to authorise the snipers to take the kill shot.

Tasmania had a small, part-time and well-trained SOG that simply wasn't big enough to deal with the massacre.

Sierra (a world-class sniper) was at home with his wife and child when the news broke.

'I remember saying to my wife: "I'll be going to that." Just minutes later the call came through, and I was summoned to the Essendon Airport for immediate deployment to Hobart.'

The death toll was terrible, but according to Tasmanian SOG member Mojo, it could have been worse. Bryant had planned to board a ferry with 80 tourists for a trip to the Isle of the Dead but he parked his car illegally and the boat operator wouldn't let him aboard until he moved it. By the time he reparked and returned, the ferry had sailed.

'It could have easily been a double headcount had he been able to get aboard that boat,' says Mojo.

Instead of being sent to Port Arthur, when the SOG touched down in Hobart they were diverted to a nearby disused police station to be sworn in as local constables.

According to Sierra: 'We were wasting time on a silly formality when we could have been saving lives. It was absolutely ridiculous. Making matters worse, they couldn't find a Bible for us to swear on, and precious time was just ticking away.'

Once at the scene, Sierra and a local sniper positioned themselves in a forest about 200 metres from the gunman, who was set up in a guesthouse.

'When we arrived, we had to seek permission to engage Bryant if anyone spotted him. However, our request for a green-light was surprisingly denied. In my opinion, putting a single round in his head was the only and best way to end it.

'What came next was equally staggering, though. If we saw him, we were told we could shoot at his legs. I had to explain that that's not how things are done. Only a fatal shot to the head would negate him as a threat. If we shot Bryant in the leg or another limb, he would still be able to shoot and kill a hostage or police officer.'

But the world has changed since then and the threat of terror means police will be quicker to use deadly force. Then Chief Commissioner Graham Ashton sought clarification on the law from the government, which really meant SOG snipers would be given the green-light to shoot to kill the moment a terror suspect takes hostages.

At one point, Sierra caught sight of Bryant standing behind a screen at the guesthouse.

'I flicked the safety off and placed my finger on the trigger. I was ready in case he came out with a weapon and started firing, because that would be enough for me to justify taking him out. But Bryant stayed behind the thin veil of protection the flyscreen gave him and never came out. I decided not to take the shot and flicked the safety back on because under those circumstances, I would not have been justified.

'We don't get paid to take lives in the SOG; we get paid to save them and put criminals like Bryant before the courts.'

JUDGE HAS SEEN THE BEST AND WORST

It was entirely appropriate that Justice Coghlan's last case involved sentencing a serious organised crime figure for a brazen gangland murder. Coghlan has spent more than 50 years investigating, prosecuting and judging serious crooks on serious crimes, and he didn't miss on his last day on the bench, sentencing George Marrogi to a minimum of 27 years for the 2016 murder of Kadir Ors outside the Campbellfield Plaza.

Marrogi is violent and ruthless but not necessarily a forward thinker. He fired 13 shots at Ors, hitting him seven times. Then he had to fire more at two of Ors's friends who drove after him. Even so, it took four trials to convict him.

For Marrogi, it was a body blow. For Coghlan, it was another day in the office.

Unlike many who dive deep into the murky world of gangsterism, Coghlan appears to have emerged unscathed. 'I'm lucky because I don't seem to worry [about traumatic cases]. I'm able to shut the door of the chambers and not take it home.'

As we sit at a coffee shop opposite the Supreme Court, the 78-year-old peppers his recollections with anecdotes, insider nicknames and a veteran's observations. Clearly, he is a man who has loved his job.

He misses the days when serious work was punctuated with fun – when he worked as part of a team of prosecutors or the legal adviser for police taskforces on complex cases. Cracking jokes on the bench can backfire if the Court of Appeal lacks a sense of humour.

He lives a relatively anonymous life but on his visits to his local market, he often receives unsolicited advice on the justice system. Dealing with the public remains the great leveller.

There is one case that sticks. He was the murder trial judge for Arthur Freeman, who in 2009 threw his four-year-old daughter off the West Gate Bridge. 'I live near the Freeman children's school and I think of it every time I go over the West Gate Bridge.'

As a Supreme Court judge for 15 years and the Director of Public Prosecutions for seven before that, he has dealt with the dangerous, the deranged and the downright dastardly. He is both bemused and amused by how crooks who would have been better off keeping a low profile actively sought the headlines.

'There is always underworld violence but in the Purana [Taskforce] days [of the Melbourne gangland war], there was a certain amount of madness. They were always going to get caught. Carl [Williams] called himself "The Premier" because he thought he ran Victoria.'

And then there was prodigious drug dealer Tony Mokbel. In a secret meeting with police which both sides promised not to record (both sides lied), Mokbel tried to broker a deal. Too many people were getting killed and there were far too many murder investigations for his liking and he just wanted everyone to calm down and get back to their core businesses.

'He said he would get people to 'fess up to drug dealing and we could call it quits. He said, "I'll get Con [Heliotis, QC, his barrister] to talk to Paul [Coghlan] to work out the details,"' Coghlan recalls.

There were to be deals, but they would not be to Mokbel's liking.

In Victoria, we have had many underworld wars and rarely have there been successful prosecutions because of a 'code of silence'. For the first time, Coghlan facilitated deals where killers were offered discounted sentences to give evidence against the syndicate bosses. 'We made offers too good to refuse. It was better to be in the brief [as a witness] than on it [as the accused].'

Beneficiaries included one of Williams's paid killers, who was taken secretly to Ballarat to plead guilty to reduced murder charges in exchange for becoming a prosecution witness.

Of all the gangland murders, the one that puzzles Coghlan most is that of Graham Kinniburgh, gunned down outside his Kew home in 2005. Possibly Australia's best safebreaker, he lived modestly (except for regular visits to the Flower Drum, where his tab died with him. He once claimed to have spent '50 grand on fried rice').

'He was trying to be the peacemaker,' says the judge. 'He was never going to be a give-up [police informer].'

Coghlan is living proof that those who claim judges are not from the real world need a reality check. Many believe the Supreme Court bench is inhabited by crusty men who ate crustless sandwiches at elite private schools before progressing to rowing on the Yarra, studying at Melbourne University and dining at the Melbourne Club, invariably taking on dozens of oysters and gallons of white burgundy.

Coghlan shows this is just a cliché. The grandson of a Chinese merchant, innkeeper and opium dealer, Chien Ah Foo, far from being regulars at the Flower Drum, his family were given an extra rice coupon during rationing because of their heritage.

Coghlan, the youngest of four, went to the local Catholic school and enrolled in medicine at university before jumping across to the law. In 1969, he began practising law.

The process in those days was a touch more robust. There was no DNA, phone taps, CCTV or taped interviews. It was the day of the typed record of interview, where the accused would often claim confessions were fabricated.

In one case, Coghlan recalls, when a detective was asked why it took two hours to take a three-page statement, he responded: 'I'm a slow typer.'

Today's trials are more complex, more demanding and longer, with the delays stretching for years, leading Coghlan to call for reforms, starting at the magistrates courts. Each year, he says, about 74,000 arrest warrants are issued at the magistrates courts, adding to the backlog and forcing police to rearrest offenders.

In many cases, the warrants are issued when an accused fails to attend a hearing on minor charges. Coghlan wants the matter finalised with a guilty verdict, leaving the accused the right to appeal if there is a reason they didn't attend the hearing: 'Give them a court date that says the matter will be dealt with in their absence and stop clogging the system with rubbish.'

He wants judges involved in the plea-bargaining process, where the accused is informed what sentence to expect if they plead guilty or decide to go to trial. 'They should put a number [of years] to it.' As of 2022 this process, known as 'sentence indication', is now in effect; the retrial of Jason Roberts is the first application of this court proceeding.

As it stands, the offender can wait to test the case at a committal hearing, then get a sentence discount by pleading guilty later. 'With trials taking four years to be heard, why would you plead guilty early when anything could happen?'

The earlier the plea, he says, the greater the discount should be, because it spares victims and witnesses the trauma of giving evidence in trials, although he is quick to add that 'There are some crimes that are so horrific there should be no discount.'

Coghlan knows that while the accused has rights, victims need protection. There can be no greater example than the murder of Mersina Halvagis, killed in 1997 tending her grandmother's grave at the Fawkner Cemetery.

The star suspect was serial killer Peter Dupas but for years there was insufficient evidence to charge him. When the breakthrough came, Dupas had already been sentenced to life with no minimum over two murders.

Even though Dupas would not serve one extra day's jail as a result, Coghlan, as DPP, authorised the prosecution so the Halvagis family would receive justice. 'There was never any doubt we would run the case,' he says.

Despite the complexity of trials, he remains a staunch supporter of the jury system, where citizens plucked from the street spend months digesting the minute details of crimes committed years earlier. 'Juries are fantastic. It is the best system possible.'

In one of the Marrogi trials, he discharged the jury after one member reported seeing a man she earlier spotted loitering in her apartment building turn up at court to chat with the accused.

In one case, he was surprised when a mafia boss he prosecuted was acquitted when the evidence seemed strong. 'I was told the jury was scared.

'There was one mafia figure who had a remarkable run with juries,' he says, without further comment.

Coghlan shuts the door on his chambers with a lifetime of memories and no regrets. 'I've had a fantastic life in the law.'

But he isn't ready for full-time retirement. The man who prosecuted crooks has just been appointed special adviser to former Supreme Court and Federal Court judge Mark Weinberg's probe into alleged war crimes in Afghanistan.

CITY IN BLUE ILLUMINATES OUR BIND TO POLICE

The police force is like a giant family that can squabble about the most insignificant issues. The troops often say the bosses have no idea, and the bosses sometimes say the newbies lack a work ethic. Old detectives say younger ones are soft, and the newer ones say the veterans are dinosaurs. Both the top and the bottom label middle management as risk-averse.

Professional standards investigators are headhunters, road police are humourless ticket machines, unsworn members are pen-pushers and crime squads hog the headlines and take all the glory.

Then there is a crisis and all that is forgotten. Then this giant blue family comes together as it has over the death of four police on Wednesday on the Eastern Freeway. Rank, age and experience doesn't count – grief is the one great leveller.

The recruits in the academy have lost one of their own – Probationary Constable Glen Humphris graduated a few weeks ago and was on extended training placement with road policing.

Take a moment to reflect on the profile of the four victims: Glen, Josh Prestney, Lynette Taylor and Kevin King. They were all so different. Two were parents, one was preparing for retirement, two had just started their professional lives. It reminds us they are three-dimensional people behind a two-dimensional badge.

During the lockdown the academy has stopped parades. On Thursday recruits and staff massed on the parade ground for a minute's silence. Sometimes it is the little things. On the day they removed the bodies from the freeway, two fresh squads graduated – just as Glen had done the previous month and Josh just before Christmas. More than 50 new police determined to make a difference – just like Josh, Glen, Lynette and Kevin.

On Thursday station sergeants and welfare officers contacted all the victims' immediate work colleagues, offering guidance and help. Police Legacy has begun a lifelong commitment to the bereaved families.

For Graham Ashton it is the day every chief commissioner dreads – death on duty. Publicly he must be brave – putting on a stolid face and not giving in to anger and sorrow. Privately he must show compassion to the workmates of the fallen, the police force as a whole and, most importantly, the relatives of the four members who lost their lives.

He will be drained as never before. One of his predecessors once told me he didn't understand how important the role as standard-bearer was until he took the top job. During the average day you are the chief executive. During the worst ones you are a field marshal.

Police across the state will be in shock and will be reminded of the inherent dangers of their job but history shows there will be an unexpected reaction. Morale will go up. Officers will find comfort with each other and a boost from the public sorrow.

Police have spent weeks now trying to enforce coronavirus lockdowns. Before that they were being battered by the Nicola Gobbo royal commission. They spend much of their working lives dealing with the angry, the unhappy, the unhinged and the violent. Often, they are beaten down by an endless river of misery. They spend 95 per cent of their working lives dealing with 5 per cent of the public.

What can get lost along the way is they spend 95 per cent of the time protecting us from that 5 per cent.

Then there is an event such as the Eastern Freeway. The driver of the speeding Porsche, mortgage broker Richard Pusey, left the scene where three police were dead and another was dying after they were struck by a truck. Many more cars stopped as ordinary people ran to the scene to try to help.

The first responders and investigators from the major collision and homicide squads were methodically thorough. They knew the only way to truly honour their dead was to remove their emotions and remain coolly professional. The investigation needed to be perfect.

In Bourke Street in January 2017 when James Gargasoulas drove into the mall, killing six people, pedestrians fled from the speeding car only to flood back to help the wounded and the dying. The motorists on the Eastern Freeway behaved exactly the same. It is part of the invisible contract. Our police are not and never have been an oppressive force – they are a community presence. The homicide solution rate here smashes just about any regime in the world, not because our investigators are necessarily more efficient but because witnesses cooperate where in many other places they just don't want to become involved.

Despite all the conflict there is a trust. We believe most police officers will do the honourable thing most of the time. And most of the public will support them most of the time. This invisible contract is only illuminated in the darkness.

Melbourne glowed blue in tribute on Thursday evening. It was just a gesture but an important one. A reminder that we live in a civil and peaceful society is that the death of police – any police – still shocks us. When the fatalities are so random, it reminds us of the dangers.

In 1986 Constable Angela Taylor was heading off to get lunch when she was caught in the Russell Street bombing. Two years later Constables Steven Tynan and Damian Eyre were shot dead in an ambush in Walsh Street. Ten years later Sergeant Gary Silk and Senior

Constable Rod Miller were shot dead when they pulled over a car while on stakeout duty.

We report heavily on organised crime and the activities of gangsters but it is the general police that are at the most risk. Trevor Given was not long out of the academy in November 1989 when he was assigned to escort a donor heart from Essendon Airport to The Alfred hospital. He crashed and died during the dash. The heart was rescued, the operation was a success and the 53-year-old patient lived another 20 years.

Kenneth McNeil graduated dux of his course when he walked out of the academy on 28 January 1974. Four months later he suffered a severe brain injury when he was struck by a tram while on traffic duty. It left him disabled for life and more than 25 years later he died from his injuries.

A Special Operations Group officer who had been involved in more than his fair share of raids always said general policing was the most dangerous job in the force. 'We were usually able to plan our operations and usually had the odds well on our side. On the road in uniform the most basic call can turn on you.' He said the closest he came to death was as a young constable when a seemingly harmless offender pulled a knife on him during the day at a suburban railway station.

The hardest battle for police is the day-after-day grind and the feeling that whatever they do it doesn't really matter. The public reaction this week shows that it does.

UNDERCOVER COP IN NICK OF TIME

In the middle of the Melbourne Cup Carnival, while we wager more than $650 million, it is a fair bet not many will reflect on how the Sport of Kings turned from an expensive local hobby into a huge international industry.

There are only a few men left who know the real story. One is former chief commissioner Mick Miller and another is Victoria's first undercover cop, Nick Cecil. They were part of a small squad known as the Special Duties Gaming Branch – Mick was the boss – which was set loose in 1955 on the huge illegal off-course gambling industry at a time when police around the state were bribed to look the other way.

After hundreds of arrests, it became clear the desire to place bets by off-course punters was insatiable and, after a royal commission, the government established the Victorian TAB.

While the squad had success at smashing their way into the fortified headquarters of the SPs, they were struggling to infiltrate the big ethnic clubs that ran huge gambling dens. Miller raised the problem while lecturing new police at the St Kilda Road Depot. Following the talk, the brash and bright Cecil stepped forward to say: 'I can get in.'

It was not an idle boast. Back then, Victoria Police was filled with taller-than-average men of Australian or British descent, which made Nick an oddity because he was of Greek heritage. His father, Harry, left Greece by sailing ship for Canada but returned to fight for his country in World War I, leaving him with a scar on his forehead from a Turkish bayonet. He eventually settled in Yarraville to run a thriving fish shop.

Cecil was seconded to Miller's squad and sent to the baccarat games, posing as a punter and mingling with notorious gangsters such as Normie Bradshaw.

Mick's team was soon dubbed 'The Incorruptibles' and my father, Fred Silvester, was one of them. At a time when his wage was £20 a week, Fred was offered £10,000 a year to protect the top 10 SPs in Victoria (which equates in today's money to about $850,000). They were all driven out of business, although years later another one set up shop interstate and was dubbed 'Tweety Pie', because he was the one 'Sylvester the Cat' couldn't catch.

The Special Duties team was filled with young idealists not constrained by the failures of the past. Faced with a problem, invariably one would find an imaginative solution. When they wanted to trace a network of bookies who received their daily odds by telephone from a Flinders Lane pricing agency, Nick took the counting device from a seized pinball machine and connected it to the solenoid in a telephone, so when it was clipped to a phone wire it recorded the numbers as dialled.

Nick and Fred clambered onto the roof and drilled a hole in a sink exhaust pipe to tap the phone line. 'Fred slipped and fell flat on his back onto a narrow ledge. If he had gone a little further (and missed the ledge), he would have been dead,' Nick says.

That Saturday the two sat on the roof, collated the numbers as they rang, put them in a capsule and threw them down into the lane to waiting police. A security officer at the postmaster-general's then took the numbers and returned with the matching addresses. 'We were able to knock off at least 30 SPs because of that,' Nick says.

When they couldn't get into a fortified SP headquarters in Russell Street, they arrested a barber who worked on the ground floor: 'We said we wanted to question him over stolen razor blades.'

While he was being interviewed, they secretly took his keys to have a second set cut. 'Early the next Saturday Fred just unlocked the door, went upstairs and hid in the ceiling, drilling tiny peepholes so he could see what was going on,' Nick recalls.

When The Incorruptibles wanted to move on country SPs, they knew the bush telegraph would warn their targets long before they gathered any evidence. This was where Nick's other great skill became valuable. An accomplished singer and guitarist (from the band The Harmony Buckaroos), he travelled to Castlemaine as a troubadour.

At a pre-arranged time, Nick placed two £20 bets using marked notes. He won, but before he could collect his 200 quid, his colleagues launched the raids.

One of the squad, a gun footballer, was sent to Mildura, where he starred for a month while secretly identifying local bookies. In one weekend the town lost its best footballer and most of their SPs.

Another time two worked as trench diggers in Sale. According to Nick, one worked so hard he became foreman, while the other was a little slacker. The day before the raids, the foreman sacked his squadmate. Clearly he was a better detective than ditch digger.

In Shepparton, when Nick couldn't get access to a hidden gambling den inside a restaurant – the entrance was a hidden door inside a wardrobe – they sent another detective dressed as a visiting sailor looking to punt his pay. He got inside easily and the squad had another pinch.

In Melbourne they dressed as painters and started working inside an SP bookies' building, then hid in the roof cavity to gather evidence. They also posed as abattoir workers, lugging large open tins of pigs' remains through laneways. In another operation, one stood in plain sight on a street corner, watching a gambling den. His cover was to hold a bunch of flowers and repeatedly check his watch for more than an hour before wandering off, apparently having been stood up on a date (this was in the days before Tinder).

Nick was seconded to the Homicide Squad to work on ethnic murders, investigate arson and build up an impressive network of informers. One was a Greek man who wouldn't talk to other police. When asked why, he said: 'Nick, you are Greek. I want to see you kick on.'

While he wasn't racially vilified in the police force, the sporting field was different. He played Australian Rules with an all-Greek side. 'They called us dagos, I hated that. It took us five years to win the premiership. We won the footy, we won the fights and we got all the girls.'

Cecil earned a reputation as a free-thinking innovator and was placed in charge of the Crime Intelligence Bureau, a secret unit that gathered information on Victoria's most dangerous gangsters.

In 1969 they were assigned to find Great Train Robber Ronald Biggs. The plan was simple: follow his wife, Charmian, then living in Blackburn. 'She was a friendly, intelligent woman. I liked her.'

It was pointless to skulk around because she knew police were on her tail, so they used 'open surveillance', hoping Biggs would eventually want to see his wife and three children.

'They were fantastic kids, we'd play cricket with them in the street. I had them home to play with my kids,' says Nick. 'The youngest was a natural nit-keeper (lookout). He'd bounce about in his car seat as a warning when he saw us.'

No one is sure how Charmian kept slipping the net to meet up with her husband, but one day she said: 'Nick, believe me, he's gone. He's left Australia.' After hiding for months, Biggs had sailed to Panama using an altered passport and moved to Brazil. They divorced in 1976.

Cecil's team was also assigned to chase the Bedroom Bandits, a gang who robbed rich families, usually around Brighton. When the robbers' car wouldn't start due to a flat battery, the undercover police came to their aid. 'We got out and gave them a push.'

They were later arrested, and no doubt very surprised to learn in court that the good Samaritans who gave them a jump-start were actually undercover cops.

THROWN INTO THE DEEP END OF UNDERCOVER POLICING

It took two days on a train for 16-year-old Keith Banks to travel 1300 kilometres from Townsville to Brisbane's Police Academy in Oxley.

Fit, idealistic and eager to learn, he sucked in as much knowledge as he could – he learned how to march and leave his room spotless – before graduating into a police force rotting from the top.

By the time he was 21, the clean-living country kid was a dope-smoking, binge-drinking undercover agent regularly risking his life to infiltrate drug syndicates, all the time knowing his targets could be tipped off by corrupt cops.

There was a group of them – Keith, Harry, Spider, Giblet, Zulu and Larry, all in their early 20s, all super keen and all hopelessly ill-equipped to be Queensland undercover operatives.

They were selected because they were young and didn't look like cops, but it would come at a terrible cost.

Harry joined as a non-drinking devout Muslim. He left five years later as a heroin addict who would commit armed robberies in two states.

'In Cairns, Harry was forced to use heroin to maintain his cover,' says Banks. He returned to uniform, managing to hide his addiction for years.

Eventually he was pensioned off as medically unfit without an apology or rehabilitation.

'He did three years' jail in Adelaide and seven in Brisbane. He nearly died of a smack overdose inside. It was coppers who gave him smack when he was undercover. It was callous and cold-blooded because they could use him to get inside places they couldn't,' Banks says.

The police who exploited Harry were the same ones who one night in the Brisbane police club asked Banks and a mate to sell seized heroin.

'We'll give you some powder, you offload it when you are on a job and we'll split the profits,' they said.

Little wonder: the commissioner of the day was Terry Lewis, who would be jailed for bribery and oversaw a police force that was politically compliant and infested with corruption.

One day Banks walked into the drug squad to find detectives bagging seized drugs to resell. They just looked up and kept working.

The UCs [undercovers] had keys to the exhibit room and could take as much dope as needed, officially to use in undercover stings but unofficially to use whenever they liked.

They had a standing $20 bet on who could engage the highest-ranking officer in a chat at the Police Club while high.

Banks has told his story in a raw and honest autobiography, *Drugs, Guns & Lies*. It is the best true crime book published in Australia in the last decade.

It tells how in the 1980s UCs fended for themselves and lived on their wits. Banks took to wearing moccasins because they were comfortable and wide enough to hide his .25 Browning pistol: 'There's no training course, you have to figure it out.'

He says the bosses saw them as expendable, declaring there was 'complete indifference from the men who were supposed to be looking out for us'. The undercover operatives became real-life actors, taking on different characters for infiltration.

'I was a nice, well-mannered guy from the bush, but I learned to play the heavy or the wimp depending on the circumstances. That was the fun part.

'It was NIDA [National Institute of Dramatic Art] on steroids.

'You could get on the gas, smoke weed and there was no supervision. You had guns and a shitload of cash. What's not to like?' (These days UCs are drug tested and better supervised.)

Think of how often you have a chance meeting with someone you know. Now imagine you are undercover, leading a double life. Every one of the UCs has a story of that chance meeting and how they had to think on their feet to survive.

One Victorian UC infiltrating the Mafia saw a policewoman from his academy squad walking towards him at a nightclub. Much to her surprise he kissed her passionately and led her to the dance floor, nuzzling her neck so that he could whisper he was undercover. Another, who was inside a bikie gang, hid behind his Harley-Davidson when a neighbour pulled up next to him at a service station.

Banks says a mate was in a car with a drug dealer when a cop drove past and waved. '[The dealer] backhanded the bloke and said "you must be a dog! That cop waved at you!"'

In one deal, Banks didn't know the friendly dealer he was targeting was an escapee and double murderer. While Banks was setting him up, the dealer was planning to kill him for the money.

'I wanted to arrest him, and he wanted to kill me. He was quite an affable guy when he wasn't planning homicides.'

That is why undercover work is so dangerous. 'Being undercover is like being an informer, you get close to people to betray them. I met some bloody good blokes who happened to be drug dealers.'

The UC was caught in the middle. Many traditional cops resented their wild lifestyles and the crooks felt they were sold out by so-called friends. As Banks wrote: 'You're not yourself and you are not the person you pretend to be. You're nobody.' They also broke the same laws they were enforcing: 'We smoked as much as the dealers we arrested.'

Many did not recover from their time in the shadows. Some left the job and cut all ties with police, some continued to use drugs while others would spend the rest of their lives looking over their shoulders.

Banks wasn't addicted to drugs – he took speed once on a job and spun out so badly he swore off powders – but perhaps he was addicted to adrenalin.

When he returned to orthodox policing he joined the tactical response group and in 1987 was on the raiding party sent to arrest Paul Mullin, a violent armed robber who had been on the run for nine years.

Mullin, armed with a high-powered .223 rifle, fired through the door, fatally wounding Senior Constable Peter Kidd and injuring Senior Constable Stephen Grant. Banks and others returned fire, killing Mullin: 'We sent him on his way.'

In the days before professional counselling, Banks suffered 'survivor's guilt', replaying in his mind the raid and nursing his dying mate in his arms.

Friends of Mullin's took a contract out on Banks and other members of the tactical response group and the officers were told to carry their guns at all times.

'I was pissed every night. Two months later I put a gun in my mouth at home. I cocked it thinking I wanted to feel what Peter did. What stopped me was I didn't want my girlfriend to find the blood splatter and have to clean it up.' When he came to his senses, he dismantled the gun and placed it in different parts of his home. While no longer suicidal he was, he admits, homicidal. He was angry, anxious, suffered nightmares and kept thinking about his fallen mate. Years later he would be diagnosed with post-traumatic stress disorder.

Instead of shrinking from danger, he hunted it. 'I wanted to knock someone. I volunteered for the most dangerous jobs in the hope there would be a fatal confrontation.'

Eleven months later he was on a raid on the Gold Coast where the suspect was shot and badly wounded. Two years after he had lost his mate, Banks knew he shouldn't be in the tactical response group. 'I told the boss "I've gotta go".'

But Banks refused to find a safe spot to work. Six years after he shot Mullin as a detective sergeant, he confronted an armed man and the result was entirely different.

The offender walked into Brisbane's MLC building armed with a rifle, hand grenade, 16 sticks of gelignite and three detonators. After the gunman fired shots, Banks was one of the first on the scene. He and another police officer spent 90 minutes persuading the gunman to surrender even after he threatened to detonate his bomb and kill them all.

Banks is one of the few police in Australia to win two Valour Awards, for the Mullin raid and the MLC building siege.

A few years later he was drinking in the Melbourne Police Club when he was introduced to Mark Wylie, who in 1985 was shot arresting a suspect for the Russell Street bombing.

'Big Jimmy Venn [ex-Special Operations Group and Valour Award winner] introduced us. He said: "You've got something in common. You've shot someone and he's been shot."'

Wylie, who had resigned from policing, later head-hunted Banks to work with him at Myer. It is 25 years since Keith Banks retired from policing, but it is still in his blood. He manages his PTSD, saying you can control it but it always remains in the shadows.

Wylie battled those demons for years. In 2014 he took his own life.

Banks says one of the reasons he wrote the book is to highlight PTSD and the toll policing takes on career cops.

'Almost everyone I worked with ended up wracked by trauma, substance dependency and mental instability . . . It is an epidemic.'

HURRICANE HOWARD, THE JUDGE WHO COMMITTED THREE DEADLY SINS

When Howard Nathan was appointed to Victoria's Supreme Court bench, he was immediately blacklisted by some brother judges for committing three unforgivable sins: 'I was Jewish, gay and left-wing.'

He still doesn't know which upset them the most. It was a time when judges were male and usually crusty, privileged and ferocious supporters of the many legal traditions that even then belonged to another world.

And they all presented as enthusiastically heterosexual. The fact that Nathan was comfortable with his sexuality drove them nuts. One refused to speak to him under any circumstances while others cut him dead, professionally and socially.

'They were not all bad, but the majority were miserably minded, misogynistic and simply unpleasant socially. They were the ones who were unbalanced,' he says. 'When I arrived, it was: "How are we going to deal with this?" Some were puerile and quite infantile.'

It was only when a lawyer threatened to name judges living double lives that Nathan discovered why some of his colleagues were so openly homophobic. 'When this threat was made, I went to one of the senior judges and said we have something to deal with, and there was this ashen-faced senior judge almost perched on the windowsill, ready to jump. I had no idea then that he was a closet gay man. I went to another judge who said he was in the same position.'

He speaks with sadness of a time when so many gay men felt the need to pretend to be something else. 'They lived fake and phoney lives. From the minute they got out of bed, they lived a deceit for years. Often the wives were suspicious but non-confrontational.'

(They include, he says, prominent politicians, senior clerics, high-ranking police and a sprinkling of judges.)

Working on a government law committee, the police representative began to stutter when he saw Howard, realising they had met before in different circumstances. Nathan had to assure him private matters would remain exactly that.

Nathan is the perfect example of someone who wrings the most out of life. Truck driver, teacher, barrister, senior counsel who narrowly avoided being shot in court, government adviser, South Melbourne mayor, Supreme Court judge in Victoria and the West Indies, reformist, art patron, professor, sheep farmer and the baker of what he says are 'dentally challenging' muesli cookies.

He lives happily in a beautiful cottage on the outskirts of Bendigo with his long-time partner. The generous art patron's sheep farm has a three-metre statue of a naked Ned Kelly and his home is filled with art works. Having worked the farm for years, Nathan says he would be happy never to see a sheep again. 'I have had my hand where no Jewish boys should.'

The miracle is not that Nathan has made a mark on so many canvases but that he made a mark at all. His family eventually settled in a Gippsland dairy farm town. In World War I, his father, Bob, drove a mule train that took ammunition to the front line and then collected the bodies.

In World War II, by then a doctor, Bob volunteered a second time. At the age of four, Howard Nathan was sent to an Anglican boarding school in St Kilda: 'It was really a child farm.'

His mother was an infrequent visitor and when his father returned from the war, Nathan was thrust into a world of violence and hate.

'He bought a medical practice in a declining country town. He was cruel, he was vicious – he was self-absorbed and a drunk. He broke a broom handle over my backside once and took to me with a knife. That ultimately led me to leave home.'

Nathan now knows the wars turned his father into a tyrant: 'I didn't know how damaged he was until around the time of his death.'

Instead of descending into self-pity, Nathan became driven, winning scholarships to private schools and universities, 'seeking the praise from a father when it was never going to be forthcoming'.

He loved his time as a teacher at Collingwood Tech, remembering when a student fired a shot in another class from a gun made in the metal shop.

There is a case from 1980 that haunts him. His client, Nazire Dragovic, was the victim of a domineering brother-in-law, Sulejman Kraja, who beat her with the rubber hoses from a washing machine and controlled her money.

Nathan won the case, requiring Kraja to return $13,500 and pay $2000 in restitution for the assault. 'We won the case hands down. During the trial he had threatened the interpreter and I raised it with the judge.'

After the trial, Kraja's barrister, Peter Vickery, warned him: 'Howard, I've got to tell you, my client threatened to shoot you all.'

Nathan says: 'Smartarse me, instead of taking it seriously I said: "They all say that."'

Kraja, armed with a pistol, was waiting. 'We came down the stairs – a hapless witness, a bodyguard, my instructing solicitor and my client. Kraja came out of a side corridor and I heard the shots. He came up behind the interpreter and blew the top of his head off, he then moved to the bodyguard, put him in a headlock and blew off the side of his head.

'He moved to the witness, an old man who was supporting my client. He looked up and blew his entire head off from his mouth upwards. He then shot my client, shot her jaw off and she staggered away, and my instructing solicitor, a woman of immense courage, poise and sense. She fell down and he shot at her, grazing her arm and exploding on the wall next to her eye. Three dead, two wounded and he then came looking for me with one shot left in the pistol.

'A policeman, not knowing what had happened – another brave copper who went unrecognised – tackled him with a rugby tackle and brought him to the ground.'

Kraja murdered Jon Myeda, who was acting as a bodyguard, witness Mehemet Zeneli and interpreter Luke Cuni, a relative of Mother Teresa. He wounded Dragovic and instructing solicitor Mary Anne Serafini.

'I was pretty good at the time but 10, 20 and 30 years on, I am riven with guilt for not taking up the offer of Vickery.'

We talk of the law, his interest in art and being a fly-in fly-out judge in the West Indies, where he was known as Hurricane Howard. Then comes a bombshell: as a teenager, the judge was the victim of a crime.

When Nathan was 13 or 14, he was walking through an Elwood car park often used by learner drivers when a middle-aged paedophile opened the door of his black car and said: 'Sonny, do you want to hop in to learn to drive?'

There were repeated encounters between the pair over nearly two years, with the offender taking the teenager to his home. 'There were multiple toothbrushes in the bathroom, so I knew he was married.'

Then he disappeared. 'I realise now I had become too old for him.'

Decades later and now a judge, Nathan was invited to address the Detective Training School. At the conclusion, an officer addressed the group, saying it was good to see so many female students and pointing to the portraits on the wall that were exclusively male.

'Well, I nearly fell off the platform because there he was [on the wall], Sergeant Jim Barritt, no doubt at all.'

That officer on the wall, we now know, was part of a conspiracy to protect a paedophile priest in Mildura, uncovered by detective Denis Ryan.

When Ryan was transferred to Mildura in 1971, the vice-principal of the local St Joseph's College told him Monsignor John Day had molested a 12-year-old female student. He also told him Day was being protected by local detective Sergeant Jim Barritt.

Ryan launched his own inquiry and soon had more than a dozen statements from boys and girls that Day had assaulted them. Because Ryan would not stop, he was forcibly transferred back to headquarters. His son suffered asthma so he could not return to Melbourne and was forced to resign. Many years later, Ryan received an apology and compensation for the cover-up. He was never charged and died a free man.

Nathan says the man in the black car had worked in Mildura, risen to senior ranks and was involved in the transfer of Ryan. 'Dinny Ryan was the victim of a connivance to thwart criminal justice on an almost unimaginable scale.'

Nathan condemns the lawyers and judges who cling to the traditions and archaic customs of the courts at the expense of justice. He praises the new Bendigo Court for embracing a more equal system that doesn't hide behind a coat of arms. 'I'm not sure that lions and unicorns ever roamed around Victoria.'

He believes much of the modernisation is down to the work of Marilyn Warren, Chief Justice of the Supreme Court of Victoria from 2003 to 2017. 'When she was appointed chief justice, she steered that ship through the shoals of discontent, improving the quality of work and the environment. She was marvellous.'

FROM A YOUNG CROWE TO MURDER

The young skinhead tried to explain to the stern sergeant at the South Melbourne station that looks can be deceiving. He and a few of his gang were hauled in for kicking over rubbish bins, hooning around and apparently looking for trouble. By way of explanation, the young man said they were not bash artists but dramatic artists – actors playing neo-Nazi skinheads in a cutting-edge movie.

The budding actor would later recall the sergeant seemed unimpressed, responding: 'Is that right? Well, I hope you're a method actor, son, because you're really going to enjoy this. Put him in the fucking cell.'

'At the time, I was really kind of angry,' the actor recalls. 'But over time, you cannot help but laugh at that. That's funny as hell.'

Nearly 30 years later, the sergeant denies using such rude language but acknowledges the young man was given four hours in the cells to reflect on both his acting methods and street behaviour. 'Actually, he didn't seem a bad bloke.'

It turned out the prisoner was telling the truth. He was in the movie *Romper Stomper*.

The sergeant, Mick Hughes, would become the 29th head of the Homicide Squad. The actor, Russell Crowe, graduated to Hollywood.

After 43 years, Hughes retired from what he says is 'the best job in the world'. But it has come at a cost.

Hughes followed the family tradition, joining the army and after 10 years – seven of them as a military policeman – joining the Victoria Police.

A missing person's case that turned into a murder gave him a taste for homicide investigations. Insurance broker Jimmy Pinakos went missing in April 1989 and Hughes was convinced he had been murdered. Associate Ron Lucas was also missing, either because he was on the run or had also been killed.

Three months later Pinakos's dismembered body was found packaged in two shallow graves at Rye. He had been shot in the heart with a crossbow. Lucas was arrested in Adelaide wearing some of Pinakos's jewellery. He was convicted of the murder.

Hughes joined the Homicide Squad in 1992, working under legendary Senior Sergeant Rod Wilson. 'Rod was a great boss who taught me what I call humane leadership. He had great interpersonal skills.'

He quickly learnt that murderers can't be typecast. 'So many killers are not the face of evil that you expect. They can be quite unremarkable.'

One of his first jobs was a double murder in Kinglake. Career criminal John Lindrea was invited to a housewarming party for Kayleen McDonald, a widowed mother of three. When he was asked to leave, he went to a car, returned with a gun and opened fire, killing McDonald, guest Andrew Johns and wounding a third man.

We see stern-faced Homicide Squad detectives on the TV news walking into crime scenes – impressive, impassive and ice cool. Often it is a professional mask. There are some memories that never dim.

For Hughes an early morning call on an unseasonably cold December morning still affects him. As he recalls that time, his voice wavers and his eyes glisten. He had been called to the suspected hit-run death of eight-year-old Kylie Gill. Hughes quickly realised it was murder. 'It was a bitterly cold night and she was wearing no slippers and only pink flannelette pyjamas. Her mother [Mary, who was confined to a wheelchair] told us Kylie was afraid of the dark. We knew she hadn't wandered or run away.'

As a father of young kids, it hit him hard. 'She was a beautiful little girl.'

In those days you didn't show your emotions, just kept your game face on and solved the crime. They caught the killer, who was sentenced to 25 years with a minimum of 15.

Nearly 30 years after he arrived at the Springvale crime scene, Hughes now knows he never really left. It is called Compound PTSD, brought on not by one traumatising episode but dozens or perhaps hundreds. 'It was explained to me as each incident is a book that you carefully put on the shelf until there are so many that the bookcase collapses,' he says.

That would come, but back then there were killers to catch – none worse than Frankston serial killer Paul Charles Denyer who, in the winter of 1993, killed three women and stalked many more.

After the second fatal attack the head of homicide, Detective Chief Inspector Peter Halloran, knew they were hunting a serial killer who would continue to murder until caught. He assigned crew seven under Rod Wilson as the lead investigation team.

Denyer always struck when it rained, hoping it would wash away forensic clues. And it was a wet winter.

Homicide detectives are trained to be meticulous and travel slowly, with a successful prosecution at the Supreme Court the ultimate goal. This time it was different. The need to identify and arrest was urgent because every time it rained, there was a chance someone would die.

'We knew if we didn't get him, he would strike again,' says Hughes.

Elizabeth Stevens, 18, a student, was stalked and killed on 11 June. Debra Fream, 22, a young mother, was abducted and murdered on 8 July.

On Friday 30 July, the 10 key investigators met to review Operation Reassurance, a massive doorknock planned for the next day. As they talked tactics it began to rain – heavily.

Around the time police were meeting, 21-year-old Denyer drove a short distance from his Frankston home to Skye Road and cut three holes in a cyclone fence next to a bike track near John Paul College, a local secondary school. His aim was to ambush his victim and drag her into thick scrub, away from potential witnesses.

As he sat in his car Natalie Russell, 17, a John Paul student, walked past heading down the bike track as a shortcut home. Denyer followed and stabbed her to death.

An alert postie saw a man in a car who seemed to slump down to avoid being seen and reported her suspicions. Two police units were dispatched and logged Denyer's now empty car.

When Russell's body was discovered, police computer checks showed Denyer's car at the scene of the murder. Further checks revealed Denyer had lived in Long Street, the street where Elizabeth Stevens was grabbed.

Using Operation Reassurance as a cover, police went to Denyer's home. He was out and they left a card asking to make contact. He did.

Denyer was enthusiastically co-operative and he remembered his exact movements at the time of the murders. 'His answers were just too neat,' says Hughes.

Wilson asked Hughes: 'What do you think?'

'He's our man,' came the reply.

During the interview Wilson adopted a courteous, almost friendly approach. Meanwhile the pathologist found a piece of skin in his last victim's throat that came from Denyer's hand.

When Wilson raised the evidence Denyer tried to explain but eventually confessed.

Hughes moved out of the squad, returning twice – once to run a crew and then, in 2014, as head of the squad. 'It was a fantastic job. It was like being the coach of the best team in the AFL.'

Always concerned about the welfare of his team, he ignored his own gathering clouds. He was tired and had broken sleep but put it down to the pressures of the job. When a receptionist asked: 'Boss, are you OK?' he brushed off her concerns.

'She knew something was wrong. I didn't.'

Hughes was considering retiring at the end of his stint at homicide. Instead in 2017 he was called in and told he had no choice – he was to be transferred.

Feeling abandoned and betrayed, he took six months off for an overseas trip, spending most of it feeling dispirited and ill. He wanted to return to work only to be told: 'Mick, you are too angry to come back, you need assistance.'

'I thought they were trying to get rid of me.'

He was angry, depressed, couldn't sleep and suffered flashbacks. He sought help and was diagnosed with PTSD. 'That was the first step in recovery. Then you can do something about it.'

His counsellor asked him to rate his tolerance. He gave himself a rating of five out of 10. He asked his wife, Sue, to rate him: 'She said I [didn't score] one.'

It was a long way back but Hughes is in a good space. He has lost 20 kilos and walks eight kilometres a day. 'I'm fitter physically and emotionally than I have been for 10 years.'

There is an expression in policing he hates: 'There is nothing more ex than an ex.' He says it is vital for former police to be valued for their contributions and to remain connected. He urges his colleagues to reach out to old mates who may be struggling: 'It can make all the difference.'

JUDGING THE JUDGE: VINCENT'S WORK WAS A MASTERPIECE

We tend to think of judges as a privileged bunch, born with silver spoons in their mouths, educated in wealthy schools and at risk only from a mishandled cheese knife at the Melbourne Club.

Frank Vincent, AO, KC is entirely different.

He was born in 1937 to Frank snr, a wharfie and Waterside Workers' Federation union official, and Tess, a factory worker. Eventually, they moved to Launceston in Tasmania but after Frank won a Commonwealth scholarship to Melbourne University, they returned, living in Camp Pell, the former World War II army camp in Royal Park, then a migrant hostel and cheap temporary housing.

He joined the Victorian Bar and with his grasp of the law and his work ethic he could have made a fortune in commercial litigation. 'I soon became dissatisfied by my involvement in an absurd system that benefited principally those involved in its operation.'

Instead, he became a crime specialist: 'I was attracted to the work and had no interest in the much less demanding and considerably more lucrative role of arguing about other people's money.' Soon, he was taking on murder cases, eventually becoming the go-to guy for homicide defences, doing nearly 200.

They came at a cost. Each is like a heavyweight fight in an emotion-filled court where someone has lost their life and the accused faces losing decades of theirs.

Vincent was always honest, perhaps too honest. 'When one of my Victorian clients asked for my view of the prospects of a successful defence, I informed him that they were poor. He thanked me profusely and immediately absconded. He was caught two years later.'

At the eventual trial the defence was going well; that is until the client, who was on bail, panicked, jumped in a cab outside court and disappeared. The judge, no doubt sensing the jury was set to acquit, didn't issue an arrest warrant but gave Vincent a chance to find the accused.

'About two hours later the client rang, apologising and obviously drunk. He assured me that he would be there when it resumed. Over the weekend, I was running in a marathon when I saw him at the edge of the road cheering me on.

'As promised, he came to my room on the next morning. This time, I walked across with him. Nothing was said to the jury and the trial continued, resulting in his expected release.'

It wasn't all high-profile murder cases. Vincent had a second career, defending the underprivileged First Nations people in the Northern Territory. In one case he knew the prosecution was doctored, learning the so-called confessions were forcibly obtained. 'The police would indicate the place where the confession was to be signed, or an adopting mark made, by tapping it with the barrel of a revolver.'

Murder motives, he says, are rarely as glamorous as those portrayed in gritty movies. 'I have been involved in cases where the death of a person has been precipitated by the most trivial of matters, such as the purchase of a Christmas tree.' (Whether it should be real or plastic.)

'In one extraordinary case, the perpetrator stabbed his fiancée to death in a dispute over the design of their wedding invitations.'

For 16 years, he was on the Adult Parole Board, 13 of them as chairman. He conducted about 10,000 interviews with inmates wanting release. Some cases stuck, such as the 14-year-old who turned to crime to care for his 10-year-old sister when they were orphaned. Living as runaways 'the young man made sure his sister continued at school, and he earned money whenever and however he could. He was proud that he had always looked after her until she reached adulthood and that she was now married and had a good job.'

One prisoner showed all the signs of reforming until his mother's partner murdered her by dousing her in petrol. 'He wanted to stay in prison so that he could eventually be near the man and kill him.'

Some were so institutionalised, they were terrified of leaving. While travelling to see his daughter, who he had not seen since she was 16, one parolee started to think about what he could say about those lost years. He got off the bus and bought a knife. 'He held up a chemist's shop on the other side of the road and then waited at the bus stop for the police to arrest him so he could return to prison.'

One long-term prisoner was granted compassionate leave after his infant son was bitten in his cot by a rat. 'The prisoner was accompanied by a prison officer who worked with him over a weekend, blocking rat holes and setting baits.' When this prisoner returned, he wrote draft after draft of what he wanted to say to the parole board. 'I had never encountered anyone who was as obviously terrified as he was when he entered the room clutching his piece of paper. We made the order for his release and he left. A short time later, we became aware of a sound outside. He was curled up underneath the window sobbing uncontrollably into the grass. He was so ashamed of the position in which he had placed his wife and children that the pattern of his life was broken, and he was never again seen in the system.'

Appointed to the Supreme Court in 1985, Vincent heard some of Australia's biggest crime cases: the Russell Street bombing trial, the murder of two police in Walsh Street, South Yarra and Paul Charles Denyer, the Frankston serial killer.

As a judge he was unable to show emotion in front of juries but, as he says, no one gets out of murder cases unscathed. Even now he avoids movies that show personal distress, having seen too much in real life.

Despite a career in criminal defence, he enjoyed some of the civil work. 'Watching the antics of fiercely competing relatives in wills cases was often quite entertaining and informative. In one of these cases, an elderly and frail-looking female friend of the deceased was called as a witness. She was clearly appalled that the capacity of her long-time companion in an aged care home to decide who she wanted to leave her money to was being challenged by greedy relatives.

'When she entered the witness box and was handed the Bible to be sworn, she said, "You want me to take an oath to tell the truth" – her gaze and sweeping arm encompassing everyone in the room with obvious disgust as she continued with real venom – "just like all these people here."

'When counsel for the claimants asked her for her occupation, she responded that she was a pensioner and what would he expect at her age. He looked at me to intervene but I said nothing, sharing her general view of the unedifying performances of the people involved. She was a smart and dangerous witness who was quickly excused from the court. Although she gave little evidence, she was a powerful advocate for her old friend.'

Retiring from the bench in 2009, Vincent conducted a number of inquiries, including as senior adviser for Victoria's parliamentary investigation into sexual and physical abuse of children in non-government care.

'The institutional hypocrisy evident within the leadership of major religious organisations and their determination to protect their status and reputations in total disregard of the terrible damage to the many victims over decades was sickening,' he writes.

'The Catholic church hierarchy, in particular, expressed feigned surprise at the disclosure of the endemic nature of a problem which they had been well aware of for decades and, once confronted with it, their primary objective was to limit the consequent damage to their reputation and finances.'

At a time when the ethics of more than one lawyer is being called into question, Vincent shows why we need the good ones.

HASTY END TO TWINS' CRIME SPREE

It took Rick Hasty 20 years, two marriages and a couple of thousand beers to come to terms with the day he should have died. A sixth sense got him into that mess; quick reflexes and a dose of luck got him out.

The story of country copper Hasty, his mate down the road, Senior Constable Ray Koch, and the twins Peter and Doug Morgan is the least-known legendary crime story in Australian history. It is a (relatively) modern-day bushranger tale that could have ended with the murder of two police.

If you believe in breeding, then Peter Kay Morgan and Doug Kay Morgan share more than a name with their father. On 15 December 1949, Kay Morgan tried to rob the Eltham State Bank, firing three shots at a bank officer who promptly grabbed the branch handgun to fire 15 shots at the bandit, who wisely withdrew without any cash.

Morgan escaped, only to crash his getaway car into a ditch. He was arrested a month later, finally serving nearly three years' jail for the failed armed robbery.

Dad set the boys on the road to crime when they were still in primary school – they were only 10 when they acted as lookouts while he committed burglaries.

As young adults they started on the straight path as moderately successful building contractors, but when the industry suffered a dip in 1977, they returned to the family business, committing 24 raids on country and outer-suburban TABs and banks in the next 23 months.

New at the game, the rookies invented an ingenious crime tactic, using their identical looks to baffle detectives. The twins used double hits – one raiding a country TAB with the second hitting another branch in a nearby town about 20 minutes later wearing identical clothes to add to the confusion. As police believed one suspect was responsible, they would move their roadblocks to the second site while the brothers hid in the bush, using pushbikes, motorbikes or hiking up to 50 kilometres through the scrub to freedom.

When Peter robbed the TAB in bayside Edithvale, he paddled four kilometres in a canoe across Port Phillip Bay and into the mouth of the Patterson River. Doug once had to cross a flooded river near Heyfield in Gippsland after a robbery. 'I lost my grip and was swept into the middle of the river. I nearly drowned,' he later told police.

The brothers paused their robberies in daylight saving months, leading police to the logical conclusion the 'bandit' preferred to strike near closing time, using darkness to cover his escape.

But the truth was the latter-day bushrangers had another reason for not striking in summer: Peter Morgan was afraid of snakes. It was in the middle of the crime spree that *The Sun*'s chief police reporter, Geoff Wilkinson, dubbed the unknown robber the After Dark Bandit.

It was always Wilkie's story, and he was the first reporter to learn they were twins. For Wilkinson it has been 40 years but he has finally finished the book on the crime twins he has threatened to write since 1979. Written with colleague Ross Brundrett, *Double Trouble* is the riveting account of the Morgans, their robberies and the aftermath.

(Wilkie has always been deliberate to a fault, often moving at a speed that makes a dugong look like a dolphin. I lost five years of my life waiting for him to choose between the strawberry gateau and the cherries jubilee at late-night restaurants where even the dim sims have tattoos.)

On 27 April 1979, Peter Morgan was set to rob the Heathcote CBC bank, which he had raided twice previously. This time he was confronted by the local policeman, Senior Constable Ray Koch.

Morgan shot Koch twice, then forced him into the bank and took $11,000. Wilkie was recovering from meningitis so I was sent to do the job. We followed the Homicide Squad up the highway because Koch was not expected to live.

Hasty was on duty at Bendigo that day and wanted to join the manhunt but was told he would be needed the next day.

Hasty was an old-fashioned country cop who relied as much on experience and common sense as the rule book. More than 10 years as a knockabout working on the land taught him people skills, and when a 1971 drought dried the land and his income, he sought the security of a police wage.

There was a skeleton crew of five police on duty in Bendigo when Hasty was returning from visiting Jean Koch, Ray's wife. Stationary at the lights in the divisional van near the RSL, he saw a man walking towards him with a red Zapata moustache, blue jeans and a jumper, carrying a blue suitcase.

'I don't know why but I just knew he was the bloke who shot Kochie. And I also knew that he knew that I knew.'

The man kept walking while Hasty watched him in the rear-view mirror, disappearing down Victoria Lane in the shopping strip. His destination and ticket to freedom was the railway station, 10 minutes and one kilometre away.

Hasty, who was unarmed, made a U-turn and wandered after the suspect.

'He was walking back towards me and I thought: "That's the bastard who shot Ray." I stopped him and asked his name, he said: "Peter Morgan, why?" I said: "Because I run this fucking town and I want to know who's in it."'

Hasty asked what was in the suitcase and Morgan replied: 'Bits and pieces.' Hasty scanned the man in the lane and, seeing no bulges suggesting a hidden firearm, opened the case.

Inside was a can of Coke, a newspaper and a blue haversack. Hasty opened the sack to find it contained a shotgun, a monkey mask and the cash from the Heathcote robbery.

Morgan, knowing the jig was up, grabbed the pistol concealed in his back pocket and, using his left hand, stuck it in Hasty's midriff. 'What flashed through my mind was "toy or death". I grabbed his wrist but he was too strong, so I flicked his elbow up and the gun went over his shoulder and dropped on the ground.

'He was left-handed, the safety catch was for a right hand and he couldn't reach it with his left thumb. When he shot Ray, he had to switch it to his right hand,' Hasty recalls. 'He couldn't get the safety off to blow me in half.'

When Hasty grabbed the gunman by the throat and pushed him against the wall, Morgan managed to say: 'You've got me, you'll make a hero.'

'I couldn't believe his ego,' Hasty says.

The policeman then issued an unambiguous instruction: 'Move and I'll kill you as you stand there.'

When back-up arrived, one of the police was shaking so much he dropped his gun. 'I said: "For Christ's sake, pick it up."'

Taken to the station, Morgan – who less than 24 hours earlier had shot a policeman twice in the back and left him for dead – calmly asked for a white coffee with 1½ sugars.

In those days there were no counsellors for police and as Hasty started to realise how close he had come to a bullet, he 'necked six stubbies'. Then someone asked his blood type, which was O positive.

'I was told to get down to the hospital and donate blood, because Ray needed it.'

Doctors gave Koch 15 litres of blood as they removed his spleen and repaired 17 punctures in his stomach and intestines. But they were only able to recover one bullet, despite finding two entry holes. Ten days later they discovered the second bullet was lodged in his heart, having moved there through a blood vessel. The tough old country cop survived the second round of surgery and lived another 16 years.

Once Peter Morgan was interviewed it didn't take too long to discover twin brother, Doug, was also involved. While most identical twins remain close during their lives, the Morgans were exceptions – they can't stand each other.

There was no psychological assistance for Hasty after his near-death experience and he admits he ran off the rails for a while, often drinking to forget: 'For 20 years I wouldn't speak about it.'

When it came to compensation, Ray Koch received $5000 and Hasty $4000. 'I said to Kochie, "I'm glad we didn't get $10,000 because we would have had to get cut in half to earn it."'

Hasty now lives in a peaceful part of Victoria, on a dead-end dirt track near a creek. Next to the house is his garden, where he grows flowers and watermelons. 'I gave one to a mate, he said it was the best he had ever eaten.'

Hasty is one of only six Victoria Police to have been awarded the Queen's Gallantry Medal. A couple of years ago, when he was caught driving well over the speed limit, he wrote a note asking for a warning, signing it 'W.R. Hasty QGM'.

'They let me off but said, "Don't try this again for three years."'

'RAGTAG' TEAM'S COURAGE UNDER FIRE

If courage is the capacity to perform under fire, then the investigators chasing two dangerous escapees had it in spades.

One of the escapees, bunkered down in a bush foxhole, had killed before, had a pathological hatred of cops and was armed with an automatic rifle and hundreds of rounds of ammunition. To make matters worse, the Special Operations Group had engaged the man in a gun battle, leaving the detectives in thick bush at risk from friendly fire.

When the battle was over, two people were in custody, one was dead and five police and a police dog were recognised for their bravery.

But the detectives who actually made the arrests were ignored. Now, nearly 30 years later, there is a push to have the omission rectified. The police Honours and Awards Committee has been asked to review the case.

The story began on 7 March 1993, with a Hollywood-style escape from the Melbourne Remand Centre (now the Melbourne Assessment Prison) on Spencer Street by armed robbers Peter Gibb and Archie Butterly, who used smuggled explosives to blow out a window, and prison sheets to clamber to the ground.

In the waiting getaway car was a handgun that Butterly would use on anyone who got in his way.

A prison officer gave chase in a taxi and Gibb crashed the getaway car at the entrance to the West Gate Freeway. When an unsuspecting motorcyclist stopped to help, the escapees stole the bike before crashing again.

When police arrived, Senior Constable Warren Treloar drew his baton and approached the two men. He was shot twice by Butterly.

Treloar's partner, Senior Constable Jan Schoenpflug, drew his gun and exchanged shots with Butterly until he was forced to back off when the gunman threatened to kill the injured Treloar.

The escapees hijacked the police van and drove to a Seaford warehouse, where they swapped cars. Gibb had a damaged left arm while Butterly had suffered serious internal injuries.

The escape and the hunt would normally have been assigned to the Major Crime Squad – except that 'the Majors' had been disbanded after a series of scandals.

Instead, a 'ragtag' group was brought together. The first two men picked were Graeme 'Spook' Arthur and Cameron Duncan, who had previously arrested Butterly over an aggravated burglary. They were backed by a small team which included Gary Silk from the prison squad. (In 1998, Silk and Senior Constable Rod Miller were murdered in Moorabbin.)

For Duncan, the stakes were high. Butterly had threatened to kill him and his family. Duncan's children were relocated after the escape. 'In my career, he was the most dangerous crook I had to deal with. He was an absolute nutcase,' Duncan recalls.

Butterly accidentally (he claimed) shot and killed a man during a Melbourne armed robbery and was sentenced to 10 years for manslaughter. During the armed robbery of a Perth department store, Butterly shot and wounded a security guard. He was arrested in Sydney a week later. As a crook, he was a failure, spending more than 35 years in jail or on the run.

He had arrived in Australia from Scotland as a 10-year-old, was in trouble with the law four years later and in an adult prison by the age of 18.

Gibb was facing armed robbery charges when he escaped. It was a dim-witted plan because he was later acquitted of the stick-up, meaning he could have walked out the front door rather than slithering out a window.

Prison officer Heather Parker was missing and believed to be with the escapees. First police had to establish whether she was a hostage. When the team checked her home, they found love letters from Gibb that showed Parker had assisted in the escape. In a selfless act, the injured Treloar spoke to Parker's two children, assuring them their mother was not a bad person but had done a bad thing.

The two injured escapees sought treatment at the Gippsland Latrobe Valley Hospital, then travelled to Woods Point, taking a room at the 125-year-old Gaffney's Creek Hotel. Gibb and Parker dined at the bistro before taking a meal to the wounded Butterly. He had lost so much blood that they set fire to the hotel to try to hide the evidence.

When members of the public found the getaway car partially hidden with bracken at Picnic Point on the Goulburn River six days after the escape, Arthur, Duncan and Silk – armed with shotguns – joined the search in thick bush.

Police had planned to sit off the car and grab the crooks when they returned but when media helicopters flew overhead, the escapees knew they were being hunted. Butterly – incapacitated from his injuries and armed with a Colt automatic rifle (the shortened version of the M16), bags of ammunition, a pump-action shotgun and a .38 Smith and Wesson stolen from Treloar – decided to shoot it out.

When the police reached a range of about 20 metres, Butterly opened up. Duncan, Arthur and Silk took cover behind trees. 'There must have been more than 100 shots fired,' Duncan says. He didn't need to guess how close the shots were because he was hit by leaves dislodged from bullets flying just above his head.

Meanwhile, the Special Operations Group returned fire, shooting 55 rounds in the direction of the foxhole.

SOG operative Damien Hehir, despite being shot in the back of the right leg, remained in position. His partner, David Empey, dove into the river and reloaded underwater before continuing to exchange fire with Butterly.

Gibb and Parker tried to slip away along the river. Although there was still gunfire, Duncan and Arthur broke cover and, pointing their shotguns at the couple, told them not to move.

Duncan says Parker jumped into Gibb's arms in an apparent effort to shield him from being shot. Arthur grabbed Gibb, Duncan grabbed Parker and they dove to the ground as the shooting by the SOG continued.

'She was actually laughing,' says Duncan.

Then it was quiet. Police dog Shamus was sent in and returned with blood on his snout. Butterly was dead with a bullet wound behind his right ear.

The shot had been fired from the stolen police revolver.

One theory was that he agreed to provide cover while the others escaped and then, when they were gone, shot himself. (He had shot himself before. Years earlier, Butterly was chased up a tree by a police dog, fell out and accidentally shot himself in the head.)

Gibb and Parker were wary of the erratic Butterly. Certainly, Gibb felt that when Butterly shot Treloar after the escape, he had signed both their death warrants. According to police, Gibb said in his record of interview he believed it was 'an unwritten rule that if an officer gets shot, that's it'.

Why then would Butterly, who hated police, end the gunfight by taking his own life when he had plenty of firepower? And why shoot yourself behind the right ear? (He didn't die instantly, surviving the shot for at least 30 minutes.)

As Coroner Graeme Johnstone found: 'There are a number of factors that create a difficulty in finally concluding the circumstances surrounding the shooting . . .

'Even though Butterly was erratic and injured, it is difficult to reconcile the fact that in a shootout with police, he did not continue to fire until his supply of .223 ammunition was exhausted.

'When it is realised not only did he have a number of full magazines in the kitbag, but also the rifle was found with one round in the chamber and six in the magazine, it becomes even more puzzling.'

The other theory is that his mates did it because he wouldn't let them try to escape.

Later gunshot residue tests found .38 traces on one of Parker's hands, but there was insufficient evidence to establish what had happened.

Then Director of Public Prosecutions Bernard Bongiorno found 'there is ample evidence that one or other of them killed Butterly' but it was impossible to say which one or disprove the possibility that Butterly had asked to be shot.

Arthur and Duncan had been under fire for at least 15 minutes and had to think they could have been shot when they broke cover to make the arrests. But for some reason, their bravery has not been acknowledged.

Recently, a retired detective took it up with Chief Commissioner Shane Patton, asking for a review. 'I am shocked that all these years later, the true nature of the circumstances has not been recognised and noted accordingly,' the detective wrote.

Is it really too late to review this case? After all, heroism doesn't go out of fashion.

[After this story was published the case was reviewed, and in July 2023 Arthur and Duncan were honoured with Command Commendation certificates presented at police headquarters.]

'SOMETHING HAD TO BE DONE, DON'T YOU THINK?'

It was four days before Christmas in 2017 and Melbourne was packed with last-minute shoppers, tourists and office workers when more than 70 pedestrians stepped onto Flinders Street at the start of peak hour.

Sitting behind the front row of cars was Saeed Noori, idling quietly in his mother's Suzuki Vitara SUV, 36.5 metres from the Elizabeth Street intersection. Noori, then 35, waited seven seconds after the pedestrian signs turned green to make sure one of Melbourne's busiest crossings had reached maximum capacity, then pulled out onto the tram lane and flattened the accelerator.

The car responded immediately and had reached 50 km/h when it hit the first walker. He would strike 16 more, missing others by centimetres.

Antonios Crocaris, 83, was 18 when he migrated from Greece to Australia in 1952, married 10 years later and raised three children. In retirement he tended his garden, growing fruit and vegetables, and loved to fuss over his three grandchildren. He was hit by the car at around 4.40 pm and died eight days later.

At first report there were fears of multiple fatalities and there was a sense of relief that 'only' one person died. But many received life-altering injuries, while others will carry mental scars forever.

Kees Green, then 43, saw the SUV heading towards him and pushed two women clear before he was struck. He suffered several spinal fractures plus cuts and deep bruises to his head, shoulder, chest and knee.

A tourist carrying his grandson was hit and critically injured with head wounds. The little boy suffered a fractured skull. A 24-year-old Chinese student received multiple skull fractures and breaks to facial bones, spine and ribs. A service delivery driver suffered broken legs and injuries that required orthopaedic surgery. An administrative assistant, 35, sustained brain bleeding, fractured wrists, a broken arm and three breaks to the legs.

What motivated Noori has never been established but he had a hatred for ASIO, feeling the spy agency unfairly targeted Muslims, and he was fascinated with international terrorist attacks. One of his home computers contained encrypted entries on vehicle attacks in London, Charlottesville and Barcelona. Clearly, this was a copycat ambush.

How long he had been planning the 21 December 2017 attack will never be known. In the months that followed, homicide investigators were able to piece together his movements without proving a motive.

He was one of 10 children and aged 12 when the family fled Afghanistan to escape the Taliban. He arrived in Australia as a refugee in 2004, becoming a citizen two years later. Initially considered a hard worker and family man, he became a heavy gambler and drug user. An addiction to ice, a history of mental illness and a fascination with terrorism were in the mix but in the end, it is about what he did, not why he did it.

The previous night he spent gambling at Crown Casino and that morning went to the bank and withdrew $7000, depositing $3000 in his mother's account. Around 1 pm he left the family's public housing unit in West Heidelberg, saying he was heading to town to shop for a family New Year's Eve party. Instead he caught a bus down Bell Street to the Preston Avis car rental branch where he tried to hire an SUV but, as none were available, he headed to the nearby Europcar office to hire a van similar to those used in overseas attacks. He was knocked back because he didn't have a sufficient limit on his credit card.

Noori then caught a bus to his mother's Oak Park house and borrowed her Suzuki, saying he had a doctor's appointment. He then drove to the city, a 15-kilometre trip.

In sentencing him to life with a minimum of 30 years, Supreme Court Justice Elizabeth Hollingworth said: 'In the midst of the chaos and mayhem at the intersection, many ordinary people did extraordinarily brave and compassionate things that day. Some people risked their own lives pushing others out of your path.

'An off-duty policeman quickly went and restrained you on his own, without concern for his personal safety.

'One of the people whom you hit wrote to the Crocaris family, to let them know that strangers had comforted Mr Crocaris and held his hand as he lay there, critically injured. She concluded her letter by saying: "Please remember, as we are struggling to, that most people are kind and decent to each other. I saw one man do something hateful, but I saw many more people do something loving that day".'

The hero policeman was Sergeant Francis Adams. He has not spoken publicly about what happened that day until now.

Adams is a 30-year veteran with a history of sharp-end policing who has moved into training and strategy (he has a Masters in Education). He was one of the first police on the scene at Moorabbin in August 1998 when Sergeant Gary Silk and Senior Constable Rod Miller were ambushed and murdered.

On 21 December 2017, Adams looked at the clock at the Victoria Police Centre and realised he was running late as the pre-Christmas road safety meeting had run over time. He was due at the corner of Flinders and Elizabeth streets to meet his sister. Typically, he would later say, he had not bought a single Christmas present and planned to blitz the shops.

Outside the building he jumped on a tram to travel just over a kilometre to claw back a few minutes.

Two minutes earlier or two minutes later, Adams would not have been the man on the spot. But he was, and even though he was off duty, he knew he had to act. No one could blame him if he had stood still, taken cover, walked away or shepherded his sister to safety.

No one, that is, except Adams.

While he stood there he heard the car accelerate, flicked his eyes to note the pedestrian light was green and immediately concluded this was no accident but, in all probability, a terrorist attack.

Like most police he had wondered what he would have done if he had been in Bourke Street 11 months earlier, when James Gargasoulas mowed down pedestrians, killing six and injuring 27 more.

But Adams always thought if he was in those circumstances, he would be fully equipped and on duty, not unarmed, unprotected, unprepared and on his own. 'I believed he was an active armed offender who had launched a vehicle-borne attack and I thought it was a coordinated attack. I thought: "The job's on here", and I just ran at him.

'Something had to be done, don't you think?'

Adams is a big man with a quiet, thoughtful manner, laconic sense of humour and a reasoned approach to life. When asked why he became a police officer, he smiles slightly, looks away and says: 'World peace.'

In reality he saw powerless people being stepped on and powerful people who didn't care. It is clear Adams, 48, has a healthy distaste for bullies: 'There are those who try and walk through life as if they are untouchable.'

Within moments Noori's Suzuki was stationary, smashed against the tram barrier. Middle Eastern music was blaring from the radio and Noori was ranting. More than a dozen people lay injured and the off-duty policeman believed many were dead or dying. There was a smell of petrol in the air.

Adams knew that in similar attacks a terrorist had usually left his vehicle and tried to kill as many people as possible before being shot by police. 'I thought if he had a knife or a gun I would try and take it from him. I also thought he might try and detonate something.'

Noori was still sitting in the driver's seat with his seatbelt attached when Adams launched, unlocking the belt and dragging the attacker from the car.

'I tried to keep control of his arms so he couldn't detonate a bomb. I remember taking a big breath and thinking: "If he detonates, I'm screwed."

'I accepted that if this thing goes bang with me on top of him, I will get it.'

Noori, a big man himself, tried to struggle and Adams, an expert in Operational Safety Tactics Training, applied a chokehold that he would not release until there was no threat. 'I was prepared to deal with the consequences later.'

Filled with adrenalin, a desire to protect the wounded and those who ran to help the injured, Adams was unaware that he was seriously hurt. The little finger on his right hand was badly damaged and his left shoulder smashed (it needed a full reconstruction and requires further surgery).

Sixteen months after he ran towards a man honestly believing he was likely to die at the hands of a suicide bomber, he knows that – like the wounded and traumatised victims of the attack – there is work to do before he recovers.

'I am mentally and physically repairing. This isn't my first rodeo.'

PUTTING FACES TO THE CRIMES

When we look at a painting we all interpret what we see. And if we are unfortunate enough to be caught in a crime our memories capture unique (and not necessarily accurate) impressions.

For 23 years Adrian 'Patto' Paterson was the head of the Criminal Identification Squad, working patiently to sift through people's memories in the hope of creating images accurate enough to identify offenders.

Today the go-to is CCTV, dashcams and people who pull out their phones quicker than Wild Bill Hickok could produce his ivory-handled Colt revolver.

For Paterson and his colleagues, it was a matter of interviewing and coaxing out memories from 'eye' witnesses who had only seconds to remember details of offenders in moments of incredible stress.

We have all tried to put a name to a face. This lot used art and science to put a face to a crime. They must have done something right, for in those 23 years CIS identified 4709 offenders – a success rate of better than one every 48 hours.

Patto was in policing for a staggering 54 years, including eight years as a part-time law instructor, retiring in 2018 at the age of 74.

In that time, he saw identification move from sketches and Photofit boards to sophisticated facial recognition technology.

Some witnesses, he says, see nothing but an event. 'Someone is caught in an armed robbery, and you ask them to describe the offender, and they will say: "All I saw was a bloody big knife."'

People need a point of reference, he says. The hairdresser seeing a robber running through a shopping centre identifies his hair colour and cut, a woman who sees a bandit says he looks like the star from the movie she watched the night before. The boy nearly abducted from a park gives a detailed description of the offender's dog. Locals quickly identify the man who regularly walked his pet in the area.

Sometimes a crook can just pick the wrong house, such as the time William Ellis Green disturbed an intruder in his home. Green was better known by his initials WEG, the legendary cartoonist for the *Herald*. When police asked for a description, WEG let his black marker pen do the talking, banging out a quick caricature. It proved to be an accurate (if exaggerated) representation of a burglar caught in the area later that day.

A CIS investigator created an image of a sex offender after interviewing a victim. On the way back to the office he saw the offender drive by on a bike and immediately made the arrest.

One of the best witnesses Paterson interviewed was a 10-year-old country boy caught in a car in South Yarra back in 1986 when it ran out of petrol.

'The husband left his wife and child in the car while he walked off to try and find a service station. Shortly thereafter, two vehicles (one previously stolen) pulled up behind their car. Two offenders got out of these cars and primed an explosive device designed to blow up the Turkish Embassy [Consulate].

'The young boy, kneeling on the back seat of the family car, looked out from the back window at the activities of the two men, concentrating on one in particular. As a result of the subsequent explosion, the family came forward. I had the benefit of interviewing the young boy at two o'clock in the morning.

'The resulting image was one of the closest I have ever obtained from such a young witness. The likeness to the offender was amazing,' says Paterson. As a bonus, the boy was able to remember the numbers on the registration plate.

One of the terrorists was killed in the blast. The second, Levon Demirian, who was arrested and convicted, bore a remarkable resemblance to the boy's Photofit.

In 1997, Mersina Halvagis was murdered in the Fawkner Cemetery while tending her grandmother's grave. Years later a witness provided a description of a suspect she saw leaving the cemetery at the time, having been struck by his sinister eyes. It was identical to serial killer Peter Dupas, later convicted of the murder.

Paterson spent more than two decades trying to move with the times, embracing computer technology and looking for the latest ways to identify crooks. Like many specialists he had to deal with two types of senior cops: the innovative, curious and open-minded; and the stubborn, old-school dinosaurs who saw change as an affront to their training. The latter didn't understand that by protecting the past, they were sabotaging the future.

Even when Paterson lobbied for and received government seeding money for world-first computer face recognition technology, it was knocked back by the woodenheads, more concerned about the chain of command than catching crooks.

Now aged 78, Paterson has written *Facing the Challenge: The Art of Identifying Offenders*, based on the history of the Criminal Identification Squad, which he feels many senior police did not give the credit it deserved. 'In my career I never worked with a group as committed as the CIS. We worked as a team.'

For a man who spent most of his career searching for tiny details that could unlock mysteries, it was only later in life that he found one close to home.

Only when his mother was frail and her health was fading did she share her secret: Adrian was adopted. The investigator searched for his past to find that he had four sisters and six brothers. He was born in November 1944 and his mother's husband was due back from the war the next month. 'That's why I had to disappear,' he says.

His adoptive father put his age up to fight in World War I and down to fight in World War II. Little wonder he would be regularly hospitalised with post-traumatic stress disorder.

While Paterson was working as a sign-writer and clerk, his adoptive father urged him to find a secure job, and so Paterson joined the Federal Police in 1964. After six years he moved to the Victoria Police. In his application under hobbies he wrote 'art and drawing' at a time when most were more interested in footy and drinking. Someone must have taken notice, because it was the main reason he would eventually transfer to the CIS.

As a young cop he learnt the need for thoroughness. After failing to search a seemingly harmless vagrant, Paterson went to remove him from the divisional van and he tried to stab Paterson in the face with a concealed glass, missing by centimetres – a lesson he would share with recruits when he was an instructor.

When he wrestled an armed offender to the ground while off duty, his wife said that as a father of three daughters, it might be a good time to go off the road for a while, so he accepted the move to CIS.

At different times there was a push to recruit non-police to fill the role of turning descriptions into images, but Paterson argued you needed investigators who could judge the credibility of the witnesses too.

Take the case of Drouin vet Mark Neilan and the 1988 murder of his pregnant wife, Kathryn.

On a Sunday in July, neighbours heard a muffled cry from the Neilans' sprawling property and found Mark locked in the boot of his Mercedes.

Worse was to follow. His wife was found shot dead at point-blank range.

Neilan gave an elaborate story of being confronted by three armed men. The property was trashed, as was his veterinary surgery down the road, with money and drugs stolen – a classic raid by ruthless thugs.

Paterson recalls: 'The "grieving husband" sat with one of the CIS members and methodically and in pedantic detail described all three offenders one by one. From years of experience, it became evident that the husband's detailed description of all three offenders was too good to be true. The grieving husband's credibility was immediately questioned and detectives notified accordingly.'

Police reconstructed the crime scene and established there wouldn't have been enough light to see the offenders in the detail Neilan provided. All the drawers in the surgery were left open as if rifled, except you could only search them by opening and closing them one at a time. The television was upturned, although residual dust marks on the stand showed it had been smashed before being placed on the ground. There were also breathing holes drilled into the floor of the Mercedes' boot.

When police concluded Neilan was lying, he doubled down. He reported to them that just by chance he had seen one of the offenders while shopping in Chadstone, followed him for a while but lost him before he could raise the alarm. Helpfully, he provided information for a Photofit.

Then one of the Neilans' pet dogs was shot dead with the gun used to kill his wife – a gun that was never found.

In 1990 Mark Neilan was convicted of murder and sentenced to a minimum of 15 years.

A picture – even a false one – can tell a thousand stories.

THE STUDENT, THE COP AND THE LONG ROAD TO JUSTICE

The serial child rapist teaching his class at Trinity College, Colac, could not possibly have imagined that one of the students in front of him would nearly 40 years later help launch an Australia-wide investigation that would lead to his conviction and eventual incarceration.

Kevin Wilmore Myers was a cool sportsman, conman, fraudster and fake teacher who molested children for 50 years. Every time he came close to getting caught, he moved to another hunting ground.

Too often, as was the way back then, those with suspicions dropped the matter, relieved he was now someone else's problem.

That is until 2020, when Myers, aged 74, was jailed for a minimum of 10 years for molesting seven Trinity students and two apprentice chefs. With ongoing health issues, he may well die in jail.

Pleading for mercy at his trial he told of a broken life, losing his child in a car accident and watching his sister die of bowel cancer. Just like his life, this was all lies.

Dean Paatsch was a Trinity student with a burning sense of injustice and a long memory. He wasn't one of Myers's victims but knew plenty who were. 'They were my friends,' he says.

Head of the Homicide Squad Mick Hughes at a media conference over the unsolved Tynong North murders.

Left: Joy and Roger Membrey with a portrait of their daughter Elisabeth.

Right: Carmel and Brian Russell, parents of murdered Natalie Russell – the last victim of serial killer Paul Charles Denyer.

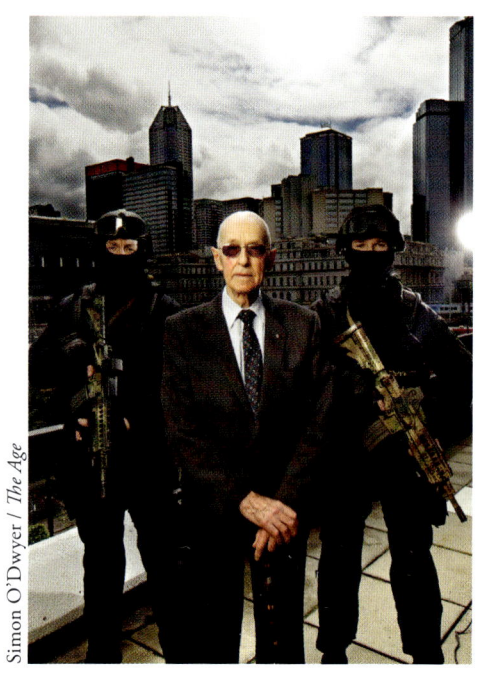

Former Chief Commissioner Mick Miller, flanked with members of the Special Operations Group. Mick was the brains behind the outfit.

Justice Frank 'The Tank' Vincent spent fifty years as a barrister and judge. Wise, witty and compassionate.

Former Queensland undercover cop Keith Banks.

Student turned sleuth Dean Paatsch and Detective Sergeant Nigel Freebairn.

One of the After Dark Bandit twins, Peter Kay Morgan (centre), led into court.

Leaders of the notorious cult The Family. Anne Hamilton Byrne and husband William (left).

Serial Killer Paul Charles Denyer created a public outcry when he applied for parole. He was knocked back.

Tony Mokbel (centre) with his legal team Nicola Gobbo and Con Heliotis QC.

Sergeant Brian Murphy with his daughter Geraldine, holding the Victoria Police Valour Award Medal.

Peter Mayoh / *The Age*

Bernie 'The Attorney' Balmer and knockabout lawyer.

Aaron Francis / Newspix

Left: Standover man turned bestselling author, Mark Brandon 'Chopper' Read.

Jake Nowakowski / Newspix

The very persuasive Mick Gatto.

Alex Coppel / Newspix

Left: Former police officer Ron Fenton suffered from PTSD and was rescued by Yogi, who was trained by a prison inmate.

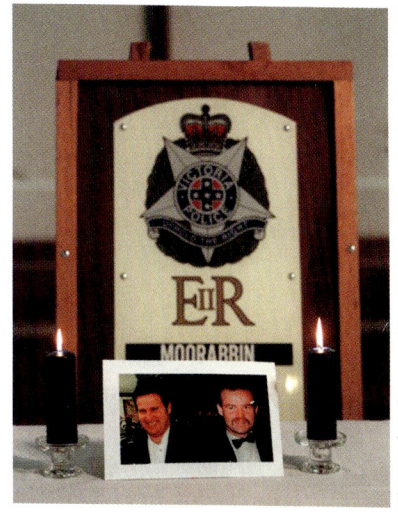

Right: Sergeant Gary Silk and Senior Constable Rodney Miller were ambushed and gunned down in Moorabbin in 1998. They will never be forgotten.

Left: Tony 'Kid' Currie and wife Michelle with Chief Commissioner Shane Patton.

Right: Gary Blair, partner of murder victim Debbie Fream, with their baby son Jake.

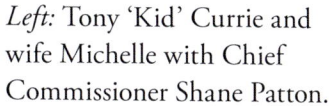

Silvester's first press pass at *The Sun*.

The new breed. Female reporters finally welcomed into the crime den. Georgie Malon (left) and Alison Puchy (right). Silvester is on the shoe phone. He thought he was funny.

The 'Hounds from the Round'. Police Rounds Christmas party at Russell Street, 1980.

You can never have too many friends. Silvester on the police headquarters roof with members of the SOG.

Silvester deep in conversation with Mark Brandon 'Chopper' Read. Red wine will do that.

Silvester pulls no punches. Archibald Prize entry by Mica Pillemer. It didn't win, proving the judges are idiots.

Terry Carlyon and John Silvester with the Logie for 'Most Outstanding Factual or Documentary Program' for *Conviction*.

Paatsch is talking to us for one reason. He knows of more than a dozen victims from Colac who have yet to come forward. 'My message to them is they can now take civil or criminal action. All the work has been done.'

He is not drumming up business for a slice of the compensation: 'I don't make a cracker out of this. I've made enough money in my life.'

Myers was 34 and a science teacher (he faked his CV) who was a rowing coach at surf lifesaving clubs. He would groom the kids at school, offer them the chance to learn to crew the Trinity surfboat then isolate and attack them in bunkhouses, his car, at the school and in private homes.

Paatsch learned his class teacher was a predator when two fellow students escaped after Myers attacked them in a bunkhouse in Lorne. When the news broke, he was at a friend's house. 'His mother was on the school board and another mother arrived saying her son had also been attacked.'

Yet nothing was done. Myers was allowed to quietly resign to travel Australia, finding his way into positions of trust to molest again and again.

Paatsch says the fact that Myers was a liar and a conman was common knowledge and he was once arrested in a classroom on fraud charges. He served time over school holidays and then was welcomed back.

One of the students at the school at the time (also not a Myers victim) was Peter 'Tommy' Hanlon, who went on to be a wonderful sports writer at *The Age*. Paatsch was a year ahead of him. '[Paatsch] was such a bolshie genius at school that he spent his HSC year in the library studying alone because he reckoned he could teach himself more than the teachers,' Hanlon recalls.

'In the old HSC system, the best possible score was 410. Dean got something like 403. He worked as a commercial lawyer before starting his own business dealing in governance issues and basically keeping the bastards honest at the top end of town.'

A qualified lawyer with a forensic nose for fraudsters, Paatsch has spent 20 years investigating companies and, as he puts it, 'uncovering corporate skulduggery'.

You get the feeling that if he were a ferret, there wouldn't be many rabbits left in Victoria. He could have left the events of Trinity behind him, but at his 10-year school reunion a drunken friend confided that he too was a victim: 'There was this dark cloud around our cohort.'

At the school's 50th anniversary he approached the vice principal to expose the institution's dark past and urge it to apologise. (It eventually did, though as is the modern way it had to be dragged to the line to compensate the victims.)

Paatsch used his investigative skills to pursue Myers. Using electoral rolls he traced his movements and found a trail of destruction – abused boys who became damaged men. When Paatsch was on holiday in remote Australia, he knocked on the door of a pub where Myers had worked. When he mentioned the name of the offender, he was introduced to yet another victim.

He even employed a genealogist to trace Myers's family, finding the sister the offender would tell the court had died of cancer very much alive.

Paatsch found not only that Myers was a prolific offender but that senior officials at two Christian Brothers schools had protected him.

One of his victims from Canberra, where Myers trained as a teacher, was among the first to blow the whistle and later took his own life.

In 1998, one of the apprentice chefs went to police and Myers was charged, but he was able to abscond to spend another 20 years free to assault kids.

As a teacher, he assaulted students, as an itinerant chef he molested young staff, and when he was finally arrested in 2018 in Brisbane's Fortitude Valley he was hiding out in a boarding house across the road from a boys' school.

In 2016, one of the Trinity victims made a complaint to the Sano police taskforce investigating child sex abuse.

Subsequently, Paatsch teamed up with Detective Sergeant Nigel Freebairn from the taskforce.

'Myers offended in just about every state in the country, and was chased out of town in NSW for targeting boys at surf clubs,' Freebairn says.

Many offenders target those kids who are isolated and lonely, stepping in as a trusted adult before betraying them.

Freebairn says Myers perfected a different method. 'He was a man's man, very sporty, and drove a panel van. He targeted sporty, popular kids offering to crew surf boats. He was the teacher who would let them smoke and drink.' These alpha boys, he says, felt 'shame and guilt, leaving them to blame themselves for decades'.

The detective met Paatsch at one of the criminal hearings. 'He was acting as a victims' advocate. I can't rate what he did more highly. He has this moral compass to right wrongs.'

Freebairn knew Myers was lying at his plea hearing, 'trying to mitigate his own horrendous offending, looking for the mercy he didn't show his victims'. When they left court, Paatsch told Freebairn he would chase down each lie, producing a dossier that condemned Myers with his own words.

Freebairn (who spent some of his teenage years in Colac) praises Myers's victims, who testified 'after suffering in silence for so long'.

Paatsch says Freebairn's meticulous criminal investigation provided multiple leads to pursue civil compensation for the Trinity victims. This case was aimed at Myers's enablers, who failed to protect the students in their care.

Paatsch didn't use a spade to dig the dirt but took to a bulldozer. He found four boys from Canberra who in 1969 were attacked on a weekend science excursion. He discovered the other adult present was a one-armed US exchange teacher who tried to protect the victims, then reported Myers to the school.

Myers resigned, yet returned to teach at the same Catholic school

10 years later. This time he quit when he said his property was vandalised by students.

Paatsch says Myers's victims rebelled and set fires at his house. 'One student tried to kill him.' Again Myers was moved on.

Trinity College's principal at the time, Ron Stewart, confronted Myers in 1980 over sexual assault allegations, then allowed him to continue teaching for two more years.

Paatsch says when stories of Myers's sexual assaults began to circulate, Stewart allowed him to resign and then 'systematically moved those kids out of the school. It was outrageous.'

'He was the crime scene cleaner for the Christian Brothers.'

For the civil case run by lawyers from Maurice Blackburn, Paatsch produced witnesses including the Canberra victims ('magic men who were prepared to relive the worst day of their lives'), nuns, fellow teachers and concerned adults. He even found a former professional basketballer who was friends with the US exchange teacher who could corroborate details of the 1969 attack.

Even with the overwhelming evidence Christian Brothers, Sisters of Mercy and the Archdiocese of Ballarat fought the case until they couldn't, settling in early 2023 with six Trinity victims for an undisclosed amount. (An educated guess is that it was truckloads.)

All because Dean Paatsch, the kid in the science class, had the memory of an elephant and a thirst for justice that the years would not diminish.

FAREWELL TO A GIANT AMONG MEN

The senior policeman's wife was sitting at the main table at the formal police function – two to her right was the man who had been chief commissioner for more than 10 years, the long-retired Sinclair Imrie 'Mick' Miller.

She turned to gain his attention and began to address him as 'Mick', but she couldn't manage it, choosing at the last second to call him 'Mr Miller'. Well into his 80s by then, he had lost none of his presence. He didn't have the title any more but to many in the room he would always be The Boss.

What made Mick so special? He was an innovator, but a respecter of traditions. A man with an eye to the future with a deep knowledge of the past.

He was the greatest policeman of his era and perhaps any era. Retired for more than 30 years, his presence looms large in Victoria Police's history and his legacy is still imposing. Not bad for a junior clerk from BHP who joined the police as a constable in 1947.

While not one to brag, he had a truckload of self-belief and backed himself no matter what the circumstances. This was the bloke with no trade experience who constructed the family home in Mount Waverley after reading a book called *How to Build a House*. Sixty years later the book has long gone and the house is still there.

In an organisation that rewarded mediocrity, where promotion was based on seniority rather than merit, Mick was identified early as one to watch, not always for the right reasons.

In the early days, more experienced cops saw that Mick wouldn't play the game – simply because he was too green to know the game was fixed. As a young, uniformed policeman who loved working on the streets, he couldn't work out why he was restricted to station duty at Richmond on Saturdays.

What was also frustrating was that, when let off the leash, he found plenty of SP bookmakers in pubs and lanes who were easy to charge.

He only understood when a local detective told him: 'Do you know you are being used?' It finally dawned on him he was let out not to make a mark against the illegal industry, but to drive up the protection price paid to police.

It was a tactic that backfired spectacularly. When he returned to the station as a senior constable following a stint at homicide, he began to organise his own raids using a few trusted colleagues. 'I thought, "It's my game plan now."'

The chief commissioner of the day was an outsider who wasn't part of the protection system. Major General Selwyn Porter decided he would set up a taskforce with junior men who hadn't been corrupted.

Local inspector Colin McPherson recommended Miller – a view supported by the *Herald*'s chief reporter Alan Dower, who knew Porter from their military days. As a senior constable, Miller was appointed head of the Special Duties Gaming Branch and given freedom to select his own staff.

Miller took his Richmond team and a squadmate who had run a baccarat school in the army to Russell Street, but McPherson insisted on one outsider – a senior constable from Wangaratta who also knocked over SPs. His name was Fred Silvester – my father – and they became lifelong friends. Mick spoke at his funeral at the Police Academy. Some time ago, he asked me to do the same at his. He was always a meticulous planner.

Dubbed 'The Incorruptibles', they carried out daring raids on fortified gambling dens and phone rooms, leading to the royal commission into off-course betting that found the SP network was worth $500 million, employed 100,000 people and had corrupted 60 per cent of general duties police.

As a direct result of Miller's team's work, the royal commission recommended the establishment of the TAB to destroy the illegal industry's monopoly.

In 1967 Mick was awarded a Churchill Fellowship to travel through Europe, Asia and the US looking at the latest law enforcement techniques. This was a time when police didn't even look interstate, let alone overseas, for better ways, preferring the known to the new, but that was never the Miller way. An open mind, a thirst for knowledge and a desire to innovate were his signature.

In 1971 he was appointed assistant commissioner (operations) and had to grapple with violence at anti-Vietnam War and anti-apartheid protests. The conventional wisdom was to use the most experienced uniformed police on the front line, but Miller saw the conflict was inflamed as many of the police were ex-military and pro-conscription. He removed them and sent in his youngest police, cops who weren't personally offended by the demonstrators. The violence was reduced.

Not that Mick would not use force when required. Asked why he authorised the use of horses at a demonstration, he replied that he would have used elephants if they were available 'and called it Operation Hannibal'.

He worked closely with education minister Lindsay Thompson when kidnapper Edwin John Eastwood abducted children and teachers from Faraday in 1972 and Wooreen in 1977. The children were rescued unharmed.

Asked what action would be taken with regard to the policeman who shot Eastwood in the leg during his arrest at Wooreen, he said he would 'give him target practice'.

He was appointed chief commissioner in 1977 and although he was the outstanding candidate, he was initially the long shot as the retiring chief, Reg Jackson, lobbied heavily for his reliable but unremarkable deputy.

Then premier Sir Rupert Hamer was frustrated with scandal involving police and wanted a new broom. Thompson suggested Miller, who had impressed him during the kidnap investigations.

For 10 years, Mick was chief. He was always there first, believing a 6 am start was a sleep-in, and was usually the last of his command team to leave. Yet every week he found time to slip away from work and visit every patient at the police hospital. Sometimes it is the little things that matter.

He introduced taskforce policing, the air wing, pushed for a national body to investigate organised crime (a move many of his wooden-headed and, in some cases, corrupt interstate peers tried to sabotage) and was the first senior policeman to advocate external anti-corruption bodies. He rotated police in corruption-prone areas, a practice abandoned by those who refused to learn the lessons of history.

One of his first initiatives was to place women on the general seniority list and promote equal career opportunities. Under him, Victoria had the greatest percentage of women of any force nationwide, an innovation not forgotten by those who lived through it. Former deputy commissioner Lucinda Nolan had two framed photos in her office: one of the Hawthorn team (she is now a club director) and the other of Mick Miller.

When a heavy-handed police minister mentioned that his lead-footed driver had been booked for speeding, Miller provided the politician with the officer's details and suggested he ring him personally to congratulate him on his outstanding work. That was the last time the minister tried to pull a string.

Mick established the elite Special Operations Group – a decision he would later admit was made on the spot. Appointed a few months earlier, he was called to a meeting with then police minister Pat Dickie and asked if we were prepared for a terror attack. Mick said he was planning a specialist squad of 15. Suitably impressed, the minister promised the appropriate funding.

Back in his office, he told Chief Inspector Harry 'Chippy' Norton – a former British Marine commando – that he was in charge of a counter-terrorism squad that didn't yet exist.

That weekend, while mowing the lawns, Mick decided counter-terror was a frightening name and changed it to the Special Operations Group. Norton, a religious man, later complained they had been dubbed the 'Sons of God'. Mick said the name was perfect and told Chippy to open his Bible to Matthew 5:9 – 'Blessed are the peacemakers, for they shall be called the sons of God.' It remains their motto today.

Retiring in 1987, he spent the next 30 years working for the community through Meals on Wheels, the Reclink Football League, the Football Integration Development Association and Bereavement Assistance, a group dedicated to providing dignified funerals for those who would otherwise end up in a pauper's grave.

Sinclair Imrie Miller was given the nickname 'Mick' after champion featherweight boxer Mickey Miller. But in all respects, he was a true heavyweight. He will never be forgotten.

ACT OF HEROISM ALL BUT FORGOTTEN

This is the story of a police killer armed with a bloodied knife, two young cops equipped with tiny rubber batons and big hearts, a pub drinker with a cold pot and a good arm, and an inspector with a woodenhead.

It is also about righting a wrong and acknowledging a couple of heroes whose acts of bravery brought down the killer on a summer's day in the middle of Melbourne nearly 50 years ago.

James Henry Patrick Belsey was profoundly mentally disturbed and repeatedly said he wanted to kill police. The trouble was, no one was listening.

In December 1973, he escaped from a Queensland mental institution and drifted to Melbourne, living rough with stray cats at the Queen Victoria Market.

Diagnosed with paranoid schizophrenia, he believed he was Jesus Christ (he also referred to himself as Robin Hood). He was also convinced police were persecuting him.

On 5 January 1974, he was sitting on the steps of Flinders Street Station with a group of young people when two police asked them to move, as they were blocking access.

Belsey responded: 'You will be sorry on Monday, mate. I have every cop's name in Melbourne in my book.'

The police understandably took the comments as the mutterings of a blowhard. He came back 30 minutes later and said to the same police: 'You will be sorry on Monday because I'm going to get a gun and kill you and also a few of your mates.'

He told a woman on the steps: 'I'm going to shoot them and if I can't do that, I'll stab them.'

He bought shotgun shells but on Monday he couldn't buy the weapon after telling a gun dealer he wanted it to kill police. Instead he walked down the road to buy a carving knife from Coles.

On Tuesday 8 January, Senior Constable Charles Norman Curson (known as Norm), 33, married with two children, was chatting with a newspaper vendor on the steps of Flinders Street Station. It was nearly 3.20 pm.

According to the book *In the Performance of Duty* by Gavin Brown, Gary Presland and Ralph Stavely, he had just finished his shift on traffic point duty at 3 pm. His colleagues said it was his habit to talk to retailers to kill a few minutes before jumping on a train back to his Nunawading home.

One of his replacements on the change of shift was a 19-year-old country kid, Constable Keith Pickering, who was standing on the road outside St Paul's Cathedral, directing traffic.

The 3.21 pm express would have had Curson at his home station in 18 minutes.

Curson was about to head up the steps to walk through the barriers when a woman spoke to him. He turned to reply when Belsey, wearing the shotgun ammunition belt and carrying a large carving knife, walked up behind to sever his jugular vein.

The newspaper vendor jumped out to grab Curson and lower him to the ground. He then yelled out to the point-duty police for help. An off-duty nurse worked on Curson at the scene, and a doctor was there within minutes, but no one could save him. He died in surgery two hours later.

Pickering ran from his post to see Belsey, crouched and muttering, while pointing the knife at the young constable. Asked all these years later how he felt, he says: 'I shit myself.'

He knew what he was up against when he saw the bloodied blade. 'My dad was a slaughterman, so I knew what blood on a knife looked like.'

Today a police officer would be wearing a stab-proof vest and be armed with capsicum spray, a long riot-style baton, a semi-automatic pistol and may have had access to a taser gun. The officer would have radioed for help, the incident would have been caught on CCTV on Melbourne Safe City network and the critical incident response team would have been minutes away.

Back then traffic police wore ties, often donned white pith-type helmets and were armed only with 14-centimetre rubber truncheons.

For Pickering and his fellow traffic cop, Trevor Pollock, waiting was not an option. 'I pulled my baton and wasn't really sure what to do,' he says, but then training and instinct kicked in. If Belsey moved towards Pickering he would back away, and when the man with the knife retreated, he would move forward.

Belsey calmly walked into Young & Jackson's Hotel, moving slowly through the crowded bar. 'I went in and Trevor followed,' Pickering says.

Knowing Belsey could turn his blade on drinkers, they wanted to force him through the bar to any area where he could be grabbed.

Pollock moved to the side and in a pincer movement they herded their target into a corridor. When Belsey put his knife down and Pickering went to grab it, the offender bent down and was about to pick up the blade. If he got there first it is probable the young cop would have been stabbed, as Belsey had planned to kill several police.

At that moment a drinker threw his beer over Belsey, creating just enough distraction for Pickering to pounce and handcuff him.

The two police marched him about 100 metres to the Flinders Lane police station, where he was thrown in the cells.

Belsey was not put on trial as he was found to be insane. He was committed to be kept in custody at the governor's pleasure until he died or was found to be no longer a risk.

According to *In the Performance of Duty*, Belsey had several stints in mental institutions and a long-held hatred of police. He once tried to rob a bank with a comb and in 1971 burst into the Bourke Street police station armed with two knives. Broom-wielding constables disarmed him. He told police then he wanted to slit a policeman's throat.

For the heroes of the day, Pickering and Pollock, there was no acknowledgment, no debriefing, counselling or even a cup of tea and a biscuit. They finished their shifts and were back on duty the next day.

Their inspector, it seems, held the view that all police were expected to risk their lives because it was part of the job. Easy to say from behind a desk.

The inspector was wrong. The prestigious police Valour Award is presented for 'exceptional bravery in extremely perilous circumstances'. Can you think of more perilous circumstances than confronting a homicidal, knife-wielding man who has just fatally wounded a colleague who lay dying across the street?

Today the police involved would receive psychological counselling, be monitored for their own wellbeing and would be able to take mental health leave if required.

Pickering says he thought of the incident 'every day' and it was one of the reasons he quit the city and headed back to Swan Hill to police his home town and raise a family. He retired in 2014 after a career lasting 43 years, five months and 11 days.

'Back then, there was no counselling. We just went home,' he says. But it has never left him. 'It is always in my head.'

In 1990, after years of treatment, Belsey was quietly released and lived a further five years without incident in the community. After he was diagnosed with inoperable throat cancer, an application to issue him with a pardon was fast-tracked to the Supreme Court so that he could die a free man.

He died three weeks before it could be heard.

Six years ago, Pickering took his grandchildren to the city in the summer holidays. When they stepped out of a jeweller's shop in Swanston Street, they saw a maroon Commodore drive past and turn into Bourke Street Mall to kill six people and injure a further 27.

The driver was James Gargasoulas, who moments earlier had been doing doughnuts without being intercepted at the very intersection where Pickering had chased and arrested Belsey.

Curson is honoured at the Police Academy, where the train platform used for training officers is named after him. But no one has acknowledged the men who caught his killer.

Jacqui Smith, who was just nine when her father was murdered, would like to see Pickering and Pollock recognised: 'They were extremely brave to capture the man who murdered my father.'

Police Association Secretary Wayne Gatt adds: 'Sometimes we need to review cases so that acts of courage can be acknowledged. We need to do the right thing.'

There is a precedent. For decades Special Operations Group members could not be awarded Valour Awards, as they were expected to display exceptional bravery. After a change of policy in 2002, six were retrospectively awarded VAs for acts of remarkable courage from 1985, 1993 and 1994.

Surely the acts of two young cops in Flinders Street 49 years ago should be reviewed by the police Honours and Awards Committee. They deserve nothing less.

[After reading this story, senior police re-opened the file and sent it to the Honours and Awards Committee for review to see if Pickering and Pollock should receive official recognition.]

THE CUTTING-EDGE SCIENCE OF SLEUTHING

A good cop knows how to dig up the dirt, but few did it better than Henry Huggins, one of the first to grasp that forensic evidence could be the jewel in any prosecution crown.

For years, while the cameras concentrated on stern-faced detectives in dark suits and porkpie hats, in the background a man in a grey dustcoat carrying his battered murder bag would be ferreting for clues.

We lost Henry, aged 90, in February 2022 and with him the last link to a time when you learnt largely on the road. He joined in 1959 and soon found himself in the Scientific Section, driving a former army Studebaker canteen van refitted as a mobile lab for some of Victoria's biggest crime scenes.

His son, Daniel, remembers family dinners when the phone rang and Dad was gone, meal left untouched on the table.

Victoria Police historian and former inspector Ralph Stavely says Huggins was 'extremely intelligent, patient and hugely thorough'.

Before computers simplified the most difficult forensic problems, Huggins used his trained eye and skilled hands to crack the case of the cracked skull. A man was found with fatal head wounds. A shattered vase was nearby. Piece by broken piece Huggins reconstructed the vase and found fingerprints on the neck that showed the offender used it as a weapon to bludgeon his victim. As well as the prints, Huggins found a button from the offender's shirt at the crime scene.

So respected was Huggins that he was called in to lead the 1986 crime scene examination when baby Azaria Chamberlain went missing near Uluru.

In retirement, he couldn't bear to watch Hollywood-style forensic procedural shows as he would solve the crime before the first ad break.

As a tribute to Henry and all the backroom experts, here are our top 10 contributions by the boffins.

1. Colin Campbell Ross was hanged in 1922, an innocent man, after he was wrongly convicted of killing 12-year-old Alma Tirtschke. The key evidence was hairs found on a mattress at Ross's home, declared to be from the victim.

In 1995, researcher Kevin Morgan traced the exhibit to an archive and pushed for the hair to be re-examined using modern technology. In 1998, a test by the Victorian Institute of Forensic Medicine found they were not from the victim's scalp and Ross was posthumously pardoned.

2. In September 1992, a man abducted a couple near the National Gallery. When chased by security guards the offender turned and fired, hitting one of the guards on the hip. He was arrested at the scene.

A ballistics expert saw similarities between the sawn-off rifle used and an unsolved triple murder in Burwood several months earlier. He took the gun to the Forensic Science Laboratory, test-fired it and proved it was the murder weapon. Ashley Mervyn Coulston was charged and convicted of the triple murder.

3. In 1990, Robert Tuddenham, 65, had been missing for six days from his home in the tiny Mallee town of Lascelles and police were convinced he had been murdered.

A sergeant from Search and Rescue was driving down a deserted road when he spotted a tiny piece of material stuck on the top barb of the fence. He stopped and saw it was a small piece of a rug. It was enough for him to call in the police helicopter. From the air it spotted a darkened piece of recently disturbed sand and fresh footprints where two killers had buried Tuddenham, wrapped in a rug taken from his house. The rip in the rug matched the piece on the fence.

4. On March 27, 1986, a gang detonated a bomb of 60 sticks of gelignite in a stolen Commodore parked outside the Russell Street police station, killing Constable Angela Taylor and injuring 21 people.

Slowly, experts rebuilt the bomb car – a massive task considering the size of the explosion, with debris found on the roof of the Queen Victoria Hospital, three blocks away.

5. In March 1985, Raymond Edmunds was arrested for indecent exposure in Albury, NSW and fingerprinted. The prints were instantly recognised by a police expert as a match to the Shepparton murder scene of Garry Heywood and Abina Madill from 1966 and a later rape in Melbourne.

6. It looked for all the world like a murder. The man was found with a fatal gunshot wound to the head, with the gun several metres away. Henry Huggins decided to test bite marks on the rifle stock, matching them to the dead man's dog – 'Macca' – leading to the conclusion that the loyal German Shepherd had dragged the gun away to try to protect his owner. The coroner concluded it was suicide.

7. The 1986 bombing of the Turkish consulate in Melbourne was one of those crimes where an offender's ambitions exceeded his ability, as he was blown up in the attack. Experts found a tiny piece of skin, the size of a five-cent piece, at the blast site. It was found to match a print on an invoice book from a Sydney suspect. The only other remains found was a pair of feet still sitting in the bomber's shoes.

8. It was a crime that would not have been reported if two Glen Waverley neighbours hadn't seen the young man being bundled into the boot of a car in the middle of the day in the middle of the week.

When police arrived, there was no obvious motive and only one obvious clue: a black baseball cap emblazoned with a red M. It was one of 150,000 promotional caps given away in duty-free outlets in the United States to buyers of cartons of Marlboro cigarettes.

One buyer grabbed four cartons from the Tom Bradley Terminal at Los Angeles Airport at 12.46 am on 20 April 1996, and produced his Cathay Pacific boarding pass for a flight to Hong Kong as proof he was a legitimate traveller.

From there he flew to Sydney and to Melbourne with his brother. They were here to abduct Le Anh Tuan, 21, because an international crime gang believed his parents owed $400,000. The abduction was ordered out of London, using US hitmen, on behalf of a Hong Kong-based syndicate. Once police became involved, the ransom plan was shelved and Le drugged and shot dead.

Once Victoria Police had connected the Marlboro cap to the brothers, Los Angeles detectives grabbed one from Long Beach City College to interview over bogus local charges. The man was nervous and asked if he could smoke. One cop said he could, as long as he spat on the butt to ensure it was dead. The butt proved a DNA match to the cap.

When the second brother was charged with heroin trafficking and was facing likely execution in a Vietnamese jail, Victorian detectives flew to the jail. After a lunch of pond fish, dog meat, rice and jail-made brandy, they offered him a deal to turn on the boss in exchange for a short sentence in Australia.

The brother declined because, he said, the syndicate would kill his family. He was executed by machine gun.

9. Drug boss Tony Mokbel had been on the run for more than a year after jumping bail during his cocaine trafficking trial. Police had no idea he had bought a yacht and sailed to the other side of the world to settle in Greece.

That is until, in May 2007, he rang a mate in Melbourne on a phone monitored by the police. 'Hey, buddy, what's happening?' he asked, saying he was at Starbucks at the Glyfada Piazza.

Sitting in the Purana Taskforce office was Jim Coghlan, who had married into a Greek family and knew instantly that Mokbel was hiding in an Athens suburb. It led to Mokbel's arrest and extradition.

10. Serial killer Paul Charles Denyer thought he had all the answers, sitting in the Frankston police station being interviewed about the 1993 murders of three women. At the same time pathologists conducting an autopsy on his last victim found a piece of foreign skin that must have been from the killer.

His interviewer, Detective Senior Sergeant Rod Wilson, had seen the fresh wound on Denyer's hand and waited more than 1000 questions to confront him. For the first time Wilson called Denyer out as a liar. It was the moment the killer knew he was trapped and decided to confess.

ABOVE AND BEYOND THE CALL OF DUTY

The death of four police on the Eastern Freeway was one of those awful events that brings a community together – it often takes a crisis to separate the mundane from the meaningful.

Apart from the usual cop-hating trolls, what happened touched everyone. Four people went to work and just didn't come home. Two experienced police, well respected by their peers, and two optimistic rookies just starting on their professional journeys. The city glowed blue in tribute as many of us reflected on how such a routine traffic stop could end so tragically.

All the police who attended had seen bodies before. None had seen them in uniform – their uniform.

What we saw in the aftermath of the impact was the best and the worst of the human spirit. Motorists on the busy freeway stopped and tried to help, providing dignity for the dead and comfort to the dying.

An official police review reported: 'In the immediate aftermath, civilian witnesses showed extraordinary courage to provide first aid to the victims among the chaos. They were followed by the attendance of emergency services personnel from all disciplines, that included local, specialist police and the Major Collision Investigation Unit, who performed their roles in extraordinarily confronting circumstances.'

There was the doctor who stopped and instantly knew he could do nothing to save the victims. Instead, he tried to comfort them. There was the firefighter heading to work who did what he could, knowing it could never be enough. And there were the ordinary commuters who stopped to help.

Fire Brigade units offered to free the bodies from the wreckage, but police said 'they are ours' and did it themselves.

Those who were there remember the silence. Specialist police going about their jobs without needing direction, as if the only way they could honour their colleagues was to rise above their grief and anger to gather every clue.

On 22 April 2020, a Connect Logistics truck driven by Mohinder Singh killed senior constables Lynette Taylor and Kevin King and constables Glen Humphris and Joshua Prestney.

The four police from two police cars were on the verge because they had pulled over a recklessly speeding Porsche driver called Richard Pusey. The only reason he is alive is that police allowed him to cross the crash barrier to urinate out of sight.

Pusey showed not a sliver of normal compassion, filming the scene – including the police – before leaving the site. He didn't get it then and doesn't get it now. His contemptible actions distracted us from important truths: Pusey didn't kill the police, and he didn't cause the crash. It was Mohinder Singh, drug-affected and sleep-deprived, who veered into the emergency lane and hit the police.

The scene was horrible and the cause obvious. In many ways it looked like a simple case – all the evidence was laid out for the investigators to see. But it was anything but simple for police wanting to find out not only what had happened but why.

Police formed the Paragon Taskforce, led by Superintendent John Fitzpatrick and made up of investigators from the Major Collision Investigation Unit, Homicide Squad, Counter Terrorism Command, the Heavy Vehicle Crime Investigation Unit and the Eastern Region Crime Squad.

Fitzpatrick has spent more than five years as the head of the Road Policing Operations and Investigations Division. He was on leave on the day of the collision. He was called in to take control, personally delivering the dreadful news to two of the four families. It was a job he could have delegated but believed was his duty. 'It was the right thing to do,' he says.

The investigation took 14 months and was split into three streams:
- The actions (or lack of them) from Porsche driver Richard Pusey;
- The actions and movements of truck driver Mohinder Singh;
- The actions (or lack of them) from Singh's employers, Connect Logistics.

Paragon interviewed hundreds of potential sources and conducted physical and electronic searches in Victoria, NSW and Queensland, seized computers and mobile phones and examined thousands of emails and electronic documents. 'It was like a complex fraud examination where you follow the paper trail,' says Fitzpatrick.

Police wanted to know where Singh bought his drugs, who knew he was a risk and who pushed him to keep driving when he was a danger to himself and others.

Fitzpatrick says investigators approached 'colourful characters' in the drug and vice worlds who would usually refuse to cooperate with police. Such was the level of public sympathy, he adds, that 'Only one was reluctant.'

Long-haulage trucking has always been a ruthless business. There have always been the cowboys (known as mile-men) who use drugs to stay awake and the owners who cut corners on safety maintenance to improve the bottom line.

The industry has worked hard to improve standards, developing a code called TruckSafe. Companies that pass a safety audit (that includes monitoring the hours and health of drivers) are given a top rating to show they are good corporate citizens. Late in 2021, Connect Logistics was given the TruckSafe stamp of approval, a decision that left many in the industry gobsmacked and led to the protest resignations of two long-term members of the review panel.

The decision is in direct contrast to Paragon's conclusion that 'If Connect Logistics had adhered to their lawful obligations with respect to safety, this collision would not have occurred.'

The police investigation identified more than 200 persons of interest: 'ranging from company employees who failed in their safety duty, to drug traffickers and users who were directly linked to the driver and his impairment'.

Singh pleaded guilty to four counts of culpable driving and was sentenced to 22 years with a minimum of 18 years and six months.

Fitzpatrick says: 'He pleaded guilty at the earliest opportunity, and he showed real remorse for what he did. His family was in court. They were shattered by what happened. There are no winners there.'

Pusey was charged with numerous offences, including outraging public decency and drug possession. In April 2021 he was sentenced to 10 months' jail and a community corrections order.

Unlike Singh, he has shown no remorse. He is an angry, self-obsessed and pathetic character destined to spend a miserable life feeling aggrieved, unloved and misunderstood. It will be a harsher punishment than any court could inflict.

The investigation didn't stop there, with Paragon using National Heavy Vehicle laws to investigate Connect Logistics's Sydney-based senior management.

Three Connect Logistics executives and the company were charged at the Parramatta Local Court with failing to adhere to 'chain of responsibility' standards by allegedly directing Singh to work when he had informed the company he was not in a fit state to drive. The charges sound rather innocuous but carry a serious punch, with penalties including up to five years' jail, $300,000 individual fines and

$3 million for the company. Each executive, however, was found 'not guilty' of any wrongdoing.

'In addition to holding individuals to account for their actions, the legacy of this investigation is anticipated to send a significant message regarding the safety obligations of employees and employers at all levels throughout the National Transport Industry.

'It is hoped that by shining a light on dangerous and deadly practices in these circumstances, it will affect positive change in preventing heavy vehicle-related road trauma, which historically accounts for 40 per cent of fatal and life-threatening injury collisions nationally.'

The taskforce was quietly honoured with Victoria Police's Mick Miller Outstanding Team Award. There was no media release or celebration. It was not that sort of investigation.

PART 3

THE CHARACTERS

There are the good guys and the bad guys, and then there are those in the middle. Larger-than-life characters who sometimes live in the twilight between the light and the dark.

Such as the international money launderer who carried his golf bag filled with black cash around the world. He didn't think he was doing anything wrong, believing governments were ripping people off by charging fees for money movement. He just cut out the middleman.

Or the TV star who had to deal with a drunken psychopath during her first interview on her national entertainment show.

And the always entertaining Mick Gatto, charged and acquitted of murder, who now has a contact book filled with the numbers of some of Australia's biggest celebrities and raises millions for charity.

For these characters, real life is often stranger than fiction.

A VERY PUBLIC MAN OF MYSTERY

For a bloke who is charming, friendly and a natural people-person, Mick Gatto certainly has accumulated more than his fair share of enemies. The Colombians were after him over a missing container, police apparently foiled a murder plot, the tax department wanted $10 million he may or may not have had hidden under the mattress and police have always wanted him back in the slammer.

He is banned from the casino and racetracks, can no longer act as a boxing promoter and appears at public commissions and secret law enforcement hearings so regularly he should get valet parking.

If the stories suggesting there are contracts out on his life are true, he is doing an appalling job of keeping his head down. First, Mick prefers al fresco dining in the Italian quarter of Lygon Street or the top end of Collins Street, which would make him a sitting duck while eating a roasted one. Second, he usually parks his super-shiny Rolls-Royce Ghost nearby, where it attracts admiring glances but few parking tickets. And third, his dining companions could double as extras in *The Sopranos*, with most having neck measurements similar to mature brown bears.

Mick, always the businessman, once considered writing his own cookbook, with the working title *Killing Them in the Kitchen*. Indeed, Mick Gatto is so into fine dining, he would make a first-class food critic, if he would accept the pay cut. (Warning: any chef stupid enough to serve him raw fish could end up sleeping with one.)

While Gatto admits to a criminal past, he says he is now a businessman and man of peace. However, his reputation would suggest the previous time he turned the other cheek, it was a slow-cooked beef one served with a red wine and rosemary jus.

It is virtually impossible to separate the myth from reality when it comes to Gatto. The question remains: is he a malicious mobster or maligned mediator? For decades he was well known in the world of illegal gambling but virtually anonymous to the wider community. That all changed during Melbourne's so-called Underbelly gangland war, when drug dealer Carl Williams organised the murders of many of Gatto's associates. Williams started the underworld extermination program after he was shot in the guts by Jason and Mark Moran, who were part of Gatto's wider social circle.

Gatto made it clear he didn't want to get involved. That is, until March 2004 when he ended up having a 'private chat' with one of Williams's hitmen, Andrew 'Benji' Veniamin, in the corridor of a Carlton restaurant. Benji ended up shot dead. Gatto emerged, not for the first time, having resolved a conflict in his favour.

A jury rejected the police case that Gatto shot Benji in cold blood, preferring his sworn version that it was an act of self-defence. 'If it was anyone else they would have got a key to the city,' he said. So, did he get away with murder? The jury said no, and that's all that matters.

After more than a year in custody waiting for his trial, it was a major upgrade to move into a 77-square mansion from his high security cell the size of the Lower Plenty ensuite.

As the underworld war was still ongoing, a big house on a gated property with plenty of security cameras made complete sense. It served its purpose, for Gatto is still breathing; many of his enemies are not.

Gatto may have planned to slip back into semi-anonymity but that was never a realistic option. The situation highlighted Gatto's natural skill for turning a disadvantage (his or someone else's) into a win. Unable to stay in the shadows, he used the spotlight to build a brand. He found himself a celebrity agent and wrote a book. His business portfolio is impressively wide. He has run a crane company, mediated industrial disputes, lobbied for union friends, settled financial disputes, dabbled in boxing events and supported favourite charities.

He is one of the few people who can appear in a newspaper on the front page (royal commission), business page (industrial dispute), celebrity spread (charity function) and sport (boxing) in the one edition. His advice in certain circles is considered so valuable that associates pay him a retainer for his counsel. And if a gangster dies, you will find his name in the obituary pages, as he always files a death notice.

When he was banned from the casino, he considered sending then chief commissioner Christine Nixon a diamond ring as a thankyou because 'She saved me a fortune.'

A Gatto function is always fascinating, with colourful characters and legitimate business types feeling an overwhelming obligation to buy multiple tickets at $1000 a pop. There are always elderly gentlemen who take much younger ladies (presumably visiting nieces). They have much in common; the men have deep pockets and the ladies deep cleavages. Many of both genders wear their hearts on their sleeves, most having been inked at Toby Mitchell's South Melbourne tattoo parlour. When Gatto arrives, he is kissed by more men than Liberace and stopped for selfies and autographs. As he once said: 'You never know who will be on a jury.'

When the word was out that Channel Nine had commissioned the *Underbelly* series on the Melbourne gangland war, Gatto wanted no part of it. However, when he realised there would be a Gatto character, his attitude shifted to one of cooperation. He agreed to meet the production team at his crane company, was charming as always but made it clear he would be saddened if he were portrayed as being involved in drugs. His constructive advice was welcomed and the TV Gatto was a stout opponent of the illicit trade. Gatto knows inside influence is more valuable than pointless hostility.

As an aside, when the Supreme Court banned the series, someone made a fortune from pirated copies, with the suggestion the first bootlegged DVDs turned up at Melbourne building sites.

In the media, he has been called an underworld figure and a crime boss. In court proceedings, he has been accused of being involved in at least three murders. But the record shows that his last conviction was in 1982, when he did about eight months over a burglary matter. He is known to be frustrated by the media portrayal of him as some type of mob boss, saying the unproved allegations against him are motivated by sour grapes of police who failed to jail him, and that the constant publicity harms his children. During the underworld war, other parents were so concerned at Gatto's presence, he was asked to stay away from his children's school. Could you imagine being the teacher assigned to give Mick the red card? He actually took it well, saying he understood how the others must have felt.

But back to Gatto's signature move – turning a disadvantage to a win. He uses the public image he denies to further his business interests. Put it this way; when Gatto rings for a chat, people listen. He doesn't need to utter threats to get attention. After all, a lion is just as frightening when it licks its lips as when it growls.

He told the ABC's *7.30 Report* a couple of years ago that his toughguy image helped in business. 'Oh, look, there's no doubt about that, you know, the reputation helps. Of course it does.' But he said it was all in the eye of the beholder, and that he didn't 'break legs or any of the other nonsense they carry on about'.

If Gatto is an active gangster, he is either brilliant or blessed. Crooks inside have been offered deals to turn on him, associates have been interrogated and his business contracts reviewed in courts and commissions. He must work on the belief that he is under surveillance, his phones are tapped, his bank records checked and he is constantly under investigation.

More than likely if he spills red wine on a tablecloth, it will be taken to forensic for DNA examination, which would be making a mountain out of a merlot.

The reality is that until he is charged and convicted, Gatto is entitled to the presumption of innocence, just like everyone else. Having said that, he continues to socialise with notorious characters who remain the subject of multiple police inquiries.

One thing is for sure; if he is a wolf in sheep's clothing, it would be premium ultrafine Merino.

THE LIFE OF BRIAN: SAINT OR SINNER?

If there is a human version of Winston Churchill's description of Russia as 'a riddle, wrapped in a mystery, inside an enigma', then it would be former Victorian detective sergeant Brian Francis Murphy.

Just about everyone who has met him (and plenty who didn't) have an opinion of him that covers the spectrum from hero copper to corrupt bastard.

Murphy, 90, died on Anzac Day 2023, having outlived nearly all of his enemies – no doubt to his immense satisfaction. His family joke that he hung on a little longer so he wouldn't arrive in heaven at the same time as Father Bob Maguire because the Pearly Gates would not have been big enough for the two of them to enter at the same time.

The winner of the Valour Award, the target of what was at the time Victoria's most expensive corruption probe, charged and acquitted of homicide, falsely accused of an underworld murder, and the subject of taunts during mass demonstrations, Murphy was a central figure in creating the Costigan royal commission into the Painters and Dockers Union that became a quasi-national organised crime investigation.

A family man with five children, 12 grandchildren and seven great-grandchildren, he prowled Melbourne at night, a teetotaller who could often be found in pubs and a policeman feared on both sides of the law.

In later years, when I visited him at his bayside home, he was in his workshop, listening to classical music and making furniture for the grandkids while Margaret, his wife of more than 60 years, was inside with a cup of tea.

We talked about the old days. He swore, defamed the dead and the living and told the most outrageous stories – including attempting to bite the nose of drug dealer Alan Williams inside a court.

Williams had paid for the 1984 botched hit on NSW undercover policeman Mick Drury. Murphy later warned Williams not to go home one night, as he was certain to be knocked (murdered). Williams's brother-in-law, Lindsay Simpson, was killed in Williams's driveway in a mistaken identity murder.

Williams's gratitude was short-lived. When he was dying of a drug-related blood disorder, his bucket list included killing Murphy. I rang Murphy to warn him Williams was checking Murphy's known haunts and had nothing to lose.

Murphy, then retired, says when he took his grandchildren to a Carlton restaurant, the owner said: 'Williams has been in here, he's got a gun and he's asking everybody where you are.'

A few days later, I told Murphy that Williams was in hospital and wouldn't be coming out. It was one of many close shaves for the man known as 'Murph' to his friends and 'The Skull' to the rest.

Some colleagues loathed him, while others loved his irreverence. He once (for reasons known only to himself) completed a full shift in a monkey mask. Another time, he doffed his cap to an officer only to reveal he had written in lipstick 'Get Fucked' on his bald head.

It was impossible to know when Brian was the real Murph or playing the role of The Skull. Dealing with a couple of street crooks Murphy's eyes started to roll in his head as he began to rant with spit frothing at the sides of his mouth. His young police partner stood open mouthed, fearing for both the crooks and his career. Then Murphy turned away from the suspects to give his partner a wink. It was all an act.

He told me once that cold water was the best way to cleanse a suspect of lies. It was as if the deeply religious detective was trying to christen the sinners as born again do-gooders.

He said that if you placed a suspect up to his neck in freezing water, nominating Lake Eildon as a perfect spot, it would give them a chance to reflect.

On one occasion, when the cold fellow began to wade out of the water uninvited, a few shots over his head dissuaded him of the notion. Meanwhile, Murphy and his associates had built a small campfire and started a BBQ. 'When I let him out, he sat next to me at the fire and I put a blanket around him. He put his head on my shoulder and started to cry. After that he told me everything we wanted to know. I gave him a sausage.'

Was he having a lend? Who knows.

Murphy dismissed most officers as hopeless career climbers, yet had respect, bordering on hero worship, for former chief commissioner Mick Miller. At least two chief commissioners had a private policy: if they needed an ugly problem solved, call Murphy.

When he appeared on page one of the paper rescuing a baby (naturally), he pulled up next to me on the street, brandishing the paper, yelling: 'Now this is the Murphy we want to see.'

He joined the police force in 1954, aged 22, and while he built a fearsome reputation amongst police and criminals, he was unknown to the public until 1971, when police stopped a car containing three suspects and two sets of golf clubs believed to be stolen.

In the car were underworld figures Neil Stanley Collingburn, Ian Revell Carroll and Thomas Connellan.

They were taken to the Russell Street police station, where Collingburn received fatal injuries.

The police said Collingburn attacked them and he was injured while the detectives defended themselves. Connellan and Carroll said Collingburn had been bashed.

Murphy and fellow detective Carl Stillman were charged and acquitted of manslaughter, leaving demonstrators to chant 'Who killed Collingburn?'

Connellan was shot in the back as he walked to his Preston home on the first anniversary of the Collingburn incident.

Carroll became a prolific armed robber and in 1983 was killed in a gunfight with NSW prison escapee Russell Cox in Mount Martha.

Standover man Mark Brandon 'Chopper' Read wrote a poem about Murphy, with special reference to the golf clubs in Collingburn's car:

Murphy was the master of the bullshit and the baffle,
He'd be in anything from a gunfight to a raffle,
From a gun-butt to a headbutt, he dropped a hundred men,
He'd fight them 'til they couldn't stand,
Then he'd do it all again,
He loved to go a round or two,
This tough old Melbourne jack,
He lost his golf clubs down the Docks,
But by God, he got them back,
Love him or hate him, they could never call him dull,
A bloody Melbourne Legend,
Was the cop they called 'The Skull'.

Back working as a detective, Murphy built a network of informers. One – killer and drug dealer Dennis Allen – caused deep concern among Murphy's bosses.

Many thought Allen (part of the notorious Pettingill clan) used Murphy to keep himself out of jail, while Murphy argued that information from Allen had led to hundreds of arrests.

In 1979, the mastermind of the Great Bookie Robbery, Ray 'Chuck' Bennett, was shot dead while in the custody of police inside the courts building, about to appear on an armed robbery charge.

The whisper was that the gunman was Murphy. He told me: 'It was Brian, but not this one.' He was referring to criminal Brian Kane. Chuck was one of three men acquitted of killing Kane's brother, Les.

Murphy said rogue police were involved, facilitating the escape route for Kane and smuggling him into the court for a dry run the weekend before the hit.

In November 1983, Murphy, who had just given up smoking, smelled cigarette smoke over his back fence, and knowing his neighbour was a non-smoker, went to investigate.

There was an intruder who, when challenged, dismissed Murphy as an old man, before (allegedly) lunging at him.

Bad move. Murphy shot him in the foot. He said he was allowed to carry a gun off-duty for protection, although the appropriate written authority had (apparently) gone missing.

He had a strong relationship with convicted killer, Painter and Docker Billy Longley, and helped *The Bulletin* magazine expose corruption on the docks that led to the Costigan royal commission. Later, Murphy and Longley formed a mediation business with the motto: 'Everything is negotiable'.

In the early 1980s, Murphy was investigated by a team of anti-corruption detectives. One reported: 'Throughout my research into Murphy, it became apparent that there were no real hard facts relating Murphy to criminal offences. The majority of information was from good informants passing on third-hand information.'

The consummate actor, Murphy could talk his way into a private meeting pretending to be a priest, a patient or a politician, and could talk his way out of (most) ugly situations.

When senior police wanted to check his official diaries, he said they had been stolen. When a cop buddy was in a smash after running a red light, he suggested the driver had had a sneezing fit.

In 1986, police launched Operation Cobra, a seven-year corruption investigation, with Murphy the main target. Cobra interviewed 805 people and found 170 witnesses to give evidence of bribery and detectives perverting the course of justice.

In April 1987, Senior Sergeant Paul William Higgins was charged and suspended. Higgins was a highly decorated member of the force with 11 commendations. In April 1992, he was found guilty and sentenced to seven years' jail with a minimum of five.

The investigation and prosecution cost $33 million. The exhaustive probe found insufficient evidence to justify interviewing Murphy, let alone charge him.

He retired in 1987 after 33 years because he knew he would be kept on such a tight leash that he would never be allowed to chase crooks.

If Murphy was bent, where's the money? He worked into his 70s, painting houses, mediating and doing paperwork for a meatworks.

He loved living on the edge, advising me that in the world of cops and robbers, 'You have to be shifty to survive.'

Brian Francis Murphy – there will never be another like him.

HAVE SOME CASH? CALL MR CLEAN

For a man who wanted to be a professional baseball player, it was the world of golf that helped place millions of dollars at his feet, and without him ever having to step onto a course.

When Bruce Aitken headed to an international airport for one of his hundreds of overseas trips, he would always take his golf bag, a fairly normal piece of luggage for a globe-trotting businessman. But in all those trips (he would fill a 48-page passport every six months) and in all those countries, not one customs officer ever wondered why there were only four clubs in the golf bag (made to order in the Philippines). Also inside Aitken's bag was a secret compartment to hide up to $500,000 in cash that his clients, ranging from legitimate business types to drug dealers, wanted to be moved discreetly around the world.

Asked how much cash he carried onto international flights over his career as a prolific money launderer, he pauses and says: 'Twenty to 25 million [US dollars].'

In Australia, Bruce Aitken was dubbed Mr Clean. 'I really like Australian wit,' he says from Hong Kong. 'They had an expression: "Have some cash? Call Mr Clean."'

Aitken and his colleagues had a strict no-questions-asked policy but over the years police, international security authorities and Australian royal commissions began to ask plenty of questions about him.

His autobiography, *Mr Clean: Cash, Drugs and the CIA*, places him in an international world of organised crime, mysterious deaths, widespread corruption and shadowy intelligence agencies.

It was a long way from the small town of Hasbrouck Heights, New Jersey where he was raised in the 1950s before moving to study at the Florida Southern College on a baseball scholarship. Having made the 1965 All-American College Baseball team, he was about to sift through professional rookie offers when his knee gave way, ending his sporting dreams.

With an economics degree, he landed a job with American Express and was stationed in Saigon during the Vietnam War. There he learnt how to use backyard money exchangers to double his money. It was his introduction to money laundering. He also saw there was a giant club of military and business people who were there not to fight a war but to make money on the black market. 'They turned Vietnam into a business,' he says.

Back in America, he was recruited by the charismatic Nicholas Deak, founder of financial house Deak and Company. Deak had been a US spy and his company acted, at different times, as a front for CIA operations. 'He was a brilliant guy from Hungary who spoke many languages,' says Aitken. 'His philosophy was: "Have cash, call Deak, no questions asked."'

When a new client asked Deak to move black money, the launderer would cut a $2 note and give half to the budding business partner. When Aitken or one of the other field officers arrived at the pick-up point, they would be carrying the other half. If the halves matched, the deal was on. If not, they would walk away.

Aitken was now based in Hong Kong, and says Deak moved vast sums for the CIA and was known as the 'James Bond of money laundering'. The company's reputation was well known to those who needed its special skill – until all hell broke loose.

One of America's biggest aviation companies, Lockheed, was drowning in debt and embarked on a program of targeted bribery to influence governments to buy its civilian and military aircraft. Deak's company moved more than $8 million (US) into Japan for officials (all the way to the prime minister) to pocket. Although they were the outsider to sell their TriStar passenger planes: 'Somehow, Lockheed won the contract,' Aitken says.

Prime Minister Kakuei Tanaka was later convicted of bribery and the Deak company was exposed as a massive cash launderer for large companies and drug cartels, including cleaning $10 million for the notorious 'Grandma Mafia', a cocaine syndicate in the US run by elderly women. According to Aitken, the publicity led Deak to 'fall out of favour with the intelligence people'.

In 1984, Deak was shot dead in his New York office by a mentally disturbed woman. Aitken queries why a woman would fly across the US to kill a man she had never met. 'It is still speculative what happened and if other people will be involved.'

One of Mr Clean's clients and close friends was Ray 'Cito' Cessna, a businessman/hippie/drug dealer from central casting. An American who settled in Australia via Iran, Pakistan and Afghanistan, he lived in a sprawling home protected by two great Danes in the prestigious Sydney suburb of Lane Cove. A vegetarian with a love of Persian culture, he was an importer, particularly of Thai cannabis, along with his business partner, UK-born Tim Milner.

Milner and Cessna were arrested in 1979 over the importation of 110,000 Thai buddha sticks weighing 137 kilos, a serious charge that could have attracted a jail term of about 10 years. Police announced the value at $1.5 million.

Aitken was to see how the NSW justice system worked. At a farewell dinner for retiring chief magistrate Murray Farquhar, a group of cronies that included solicitor Morgan 'The Magician' Ryan, police commissioner Merv Wood and High Court judge Lionel Murphy discussed the case and the fix was in, lubricated by fine wine and a $50,000 bribe from Milner.

Wood agreed to reduce the weight of the haul, which meant the case could be heard at magistrate level. Guess what? Farquhar decided to hear the case as the last before his retirement. Milner received an 18-month sentence and served about six months, while Cessna was fined $1000. This and other cases, recorded on illegal phone taps known as 'the Age tapes', sparked police interest in Aitken, who had visited Sydney 15 times in less than three years.

In the dying days of Deak and Company, another, more sinister group moved in, the Australian-based Nugan Hand Bank. The partners were American Mike Hand and Australian lawyer Frank Nugan. Hand, a Vietnam veteran recognised for his bravery, was immersed with the CIA.

'I didn't like him,' Aitken says. 'You got the feeling if you got involved with him, there would be no turning back. They considered themselves CIA bankers. When they opened a branch in [Thailand's drug centre] Chiang Mai, they gave the game away.'

Eventually, the bank collapsed. Hand disappeared to the US (living under an assumed name in Idaho) and in January 1980, Frank Nugan was shot dead in country NSW. Nugan's death was declared a suicide, although Aitken and many others suspect the lawyer was murdered because he was seen as a weak link. In his Mercedes was a list of names which included Bob Wilson (a member of the US House of Representatives Armed Services Committee) and former CIA director Bill Colby.

Another of Mr Clean's clients was Howard Marks, the Oxford graduate son of a Welsh tugboat captain and, at that time, the world's biggest cannabis trafficker. He owned a 30-metre trawler (the *Axel-D*) which he used to distribute up to 30 tonnes of cannabis around the world, and formed a bogus rock band, importing weed inside giant speakers that were to be used for non-existent outdoor pop concerts.

The authorities should have read the fine print. The band was called Laughing Grass. Typical Howard.

Marks wrote in the foreword to Mr Clean's book: 'He was a master of his chosen trade.'

Aitken recalls: 'He was a soft-spoken guy. The first time I met him, he gave me a suitcase full of money [$US150,000] and asked me to look after it.' All Marks wanted was a handshake agreement the money would be there when required. 'That's how we did business back then,' says Aitken.

Aitken knew he had become too well known for his skills and was in the process of trying to leave the business when in 1989 he was grabbed in Bangkok and bundled back to America, kept in a detention centre and pressured to turn on his clients. Instead, he finally agreed to plead guilty on the relatively minor charge of aiding and abetting money laundering and was released with time served.

He returned to Hong Kong, where he has a weekly Christian-based radio program. He no longer takes his golf clubs when travelling overseas.

WHEN CRIMS AND LAWYERS COLLIDE

Graeme Alford was a smart, cunning, hard-working criminal lawyer with a loyal and regular client base all connected to the feared Painters and Dockers Union, a union that proved a perfect front for organised crime. It was a licence to print money (no doubt some of his clients would have tried that).

For years he was the private school, top-of-the-class-type student who won a Commonwealth scholarship, excelled at Melbourne University and breezed his way into a city law firm. He was also a heavy punter and prodigious drinker – both vices that are not unknown in the legal fraternity.

As he would write much later in his book, *Never Give Up*: 'Booze, gambling and the law, I was under the spell of all three and they would influence my life for years to come.'

It was when those worlds collided in a bar near Geelong that Alford started a descent which took only a few years to destroy his marriage, career and reputation – and decades to rebuild.

In 1975, after a routine .05 case at Winchelsea, he stopped off for a beer on the way back to Melbourne and ended up chatting with a couple of blokes. They were members of the Painters and Dockers and when they discovered Alford was a knockabout lawyer who thought the art of drink driving was not getting caught, they saw a kindred spirit and asked for a business card.

It turned out to be a pivotal, lucrative and ultimately disastrous move. He ended up with a group of habitual criminals on his books – the type that were likely to provide repeat business – with the union underwriting his fees so he was always paid.

He was able to roll his two great pleasures – betting and drinking – into a networking opportunity. Alford crossed the line and began socialising with his underworld clients. 'I was warned about socialising and drinking with my clients – in legal circles, an absolute no-no – but I thought, "No, I'm cleverer, this is how I will build my practice".' Every day he would down 20 to 30 beers, sometimes topped with half a bottle of Scotch. At night he would drink in pubs then head to the illegal two-up and baccarat games until about 2 am, drive home drunk and be back in the office at 7 am. Add some 60 cigarettes a day, fast foods, crushing work hours and a pathological desire to prowl Melbourne at night, and it was always going to end badly.

Alford quickly stopped being a lawyer acting for criminals and became a criminal acting as a lawyer. He laundered money at casinos for select clients, organised bail at any time of night, was available to crooks 24 hours a day and saw many of them as his closest friends. He washed money through the TAB and would buy winning tickets above their market rate. He knew 'a couple of TAB managers who would arrange for me to acquire winning tickets'.

He also had a kickback system with some police where if they recommended him to arrested suspects, he would sling 10 per cent of the final fee back to the officer. Sometimes he would bribe police to remove prior convictions from his client's file so that if they were convicted, they would receive a lighter sentence.

Eventually, facing huge gambling debts, he stole from his legal trust account and was short $80,000. He was charged with multiple counts of fraud and handcuffed in the Russell Street Police Station lift when one of his clients, who was also under arrest, stepped in. He looked his lawyer up and down and said: 'Well, Graeme, there's not much point ringing you, is there?'

He was sentenced to five years with a two-year minimum. Out in 16 months – fit for the first time in years but still in denial – he applied for a series of jobs requiring a legal background and failed each time. He drifted back to crime because, he says: 'The money is good and the hours are short.'

It was 15 October 1982 when a half-drunk Alford donned a balaclava, grabbed his shotgun and, with fellow armed robbers, burst into the Chapel Street Prahran branch of the National Bank.

It was just after 2 pm when two junior police in plain clothes patrolling Armadale in an unmarked Datsun 200B cruised down Chapel Street, looking for a park to grab a late lunch. Phil Bogle, 20, and Craig Gye, 23, may have been inexperienced but they already knew cops can park where they like when on duty, so they mounted the curb and parked with two wheels on the footpath.

Meanwhile, the manager of an adjacent food bar saw the bandits park at the rear of the bank. She rang the police, saying there was a robbery in progress and used her own car to block the getaway vehicle.

Bogle, who is now the senior sergeant at Lakes Entrance and about to retire, recalls: 'We were parked illegally, of course, but we were on the Queen's business: buying our lunch. A radio call came in that there was a hold-up at the NAB in Chapel Street. I said to Craig, "I think that's here."

'In plain clothes we wandered in and there was a full-on stick-up in progress. There were three blokes disguised in masks, they had sprayed over the cameras and were emptying the tills. All armed with sawn-off shotguns. One of us yelled out: "Police!" and we pulled out our [undercover] five-shot Smith & Wesson revolvers.

'One of them ran off down a lane. He was carrying a shotty and a bag of money. Money was flying everywhere and people were taking cover. He turned around, raised the barrel and pulled the trigger. We were too scared to shoot him so we yelled: "Police, don't move, drop it or we'll shoot" and he dropped it.'

The bandit was Graeme Alford. 'How lucky was I? They were young coppers who still believed in "stop or we will shoot". Thank God it wasn't the Armed Robbery Squad.'

Two sergeants from Prahran, Peter Steele and Ray 'Dingo' McLeod-Dryden, were nearby on an important mission – heading to the Station Hotel for a long afternoon – when they saw 'the divvy van scream by'.

Unarmed and in civilian clothes, they saw bandits scarpering from the bank. Dingo tracked one, Lawrence William 'Chocka' Rowley, as he tried to disappear through a car park. 'He produced this big shooter from his tracksuit and I thought: "Jesus, what's going on here?".'

The policeman backed off for a moment as Rowley walked away, but cut back to Chapel Street where the gunman again took aim at his pursuer. He watched as Rowley walked down the middle of the busy road, trying to carjack a motorist.

'I thought: "I can't have this" so I ran up and grabbed him around the guts, but I had new shiny boots and slipped on the ground. He pointed the gun at me again and I thought it could be third time unlucky.'

McLeod-Dryden crawled under a car and Rowley jumped in another vehicle, put his gun to the female driver's head and ordered her to drive to Canterbury Road, Middle Park. He was arrested months later and convicted. Instead of receiving first-aid or counselling, Ray McLeod-Dryden continued to the Station Hotel. 'I think I had 20 pots.'

Meanwhile Alford was in jail with broken ribs (care of a robust police interview). He was sentenced to five years' jail and was released in 1986 after serving just over three, determined to rebuild his life. He gave up cigarettes and the booze, dropped weight, ran marathons and set himself mental challenges to improve his alcohol-damaged memory.

The turnaround has been remarkable. He has written three bestselling books, set up several successful businesses, is a sought-after motivational speaker and now works in drug rehabilitation.

Alford says drugs had changed the underworld. 'Drugs have changed everything. Once it was all about tough, hard people like Les Kane, Brian Kane and Ray Chuck. Now with drugs it is about how much money you have. People like Carl Williams would have been chopped up back then.'

THE TRAGIC TALE OF A MAN WHO WANTED TO BE A FISH

Nobody knows why Neil Gordon Wilson, 49, liked to pretend to be a fish. When Mr Wilson was found dead in a meticulously made fish-suit near his family's Toolondo holiday home, 390 kilometres west of Melbourne, it opened a case that police say remains one of the most baffling. It has also become a case study of the life of an eccentric personality in a small country town, and the ability of its residents to show sympathy and understanding of his plight.

Police believe he spent at least four years developing prototypes of the fish-suit before he finally died wearing one. He photographed himself in an early version on the banks of the local lake a year before his death.

The coroner, Mr Graeme Johnstone, officially closed the file without getting close to finding why Mr Wilson chose to hop about in a vinyl fish-suit in a deserted paddock near his home.

Mr Wilson was a quiet, gentle man who suffered brain damage after a motorbike accident in the 1970s. He was placed on medication to control epilepsy but, according to his family, he would often fail to take it.

Mr Wilson lived in a world populated by one. He foraged in the local tip, hanging items he found in a tree in front of his holiday house. The people of Toolondo knew Mr Wilson was different, but they also knew he was harmless. They grew used to his strange ways and were rarely shocked by his behaviour.

Local resident Mr Graham Bedford told police he remembered seeing Mr Wilson near long grass in Toolondo swamplands in 1991. 'He was totally naked except for a number of Coke cans tied to a piece of hay band around his chest like a bandido. He said good day to me and then started to get dressed,' he said. 'Most of the people who lived in Toolondo knew what he was like, but after so many years of strange behaviour, Neil was accepted. There was never any incident where Neil posed a danger to anyone else that I know of.'

Around the same time, duck hunters found a green, plastic bodysuit on the edge of the Toolondo Lake. 'We knew it was Neil's because it was in one of the spots where he used to go regularly and there were items of clothing around it,' Mr Bedford said. 'Neil seemed to avoid people and go about his business. It was not uncommon for Neil to run and hide on the approach of anyone.'

In 1974, a tourist told local police he had found Mr Wilson in the Toolondo Channel, attached by a rope to a bridge railing. After the tourist pulled him from the water, naked, Mr Wilson explained he 'was playing (pretending to be) a fish at the end of the line'.

In November 1995 Mr Wilson was driven from Melbourne to Toolondo, where he expected to stay three weeks. He was reported missing on 27 November. Police found his medication in the house and, from the number of pills, were able to deduce that he had stopped taking his tablets 10 days earlier.

Just after 4 pm on 27 November, the police helicopter spotted the body of Mr Wilson in a green fish-suit in an open paddock, about a kilometre from the lake.

Senior Constable Kerry Allen from Natimuk pieced together what he thought had happened. He believed that Mr Wilson spent hours in the garage of the holiday house fashioning versions of the fish-suit using plastic recovered from a local tip, including a vinyl, queen-sized waterbed mattress and a brown vinyl mattress protector. Police found a sewing machine and plastic offcuts from the fish-suit in the double garage of the home, as well as an identical spare fish-suit.

Senior Constable Allen said that on about 20 November, Wilson placed a bodysuit and other items into a wheelbarrow and walked more than 100 metres north into the paddock opposite the holiday house. He said Mr Wilson covered himself with soap and water from a container so that he could slip into the tight-fitting suit. He then used a padlock and wire to pull up the back zip of the suit. 'It would seem that Wilson has then hopped 52 metres back south, where for some reason he collapsed,' Senior Constable Allen said in a statement to the coroner.

The suit contained two vinyl layers separated by carpet underlay to act as insulation, four zips, a padlock, mittens, a headpiece with eye holes and a mermaid-type tail made of a tyre inner tube. It was carefully double-stitched and waterproof.

Detective Sergeant Graeme Arthur, who oversaw the investigation for the Homicide Squad, said: 'It was probably the most bizarre case we have ever seen.'

Senior Constable Allen put forward a likely cause of death. The combination of lack of food, lack of medication and the exertion of hopping about in the suit brought on a seizure and subsequent loss of consciousness. Caught in an open paddock and unable to move, he would have been killed by the heat.

Mr Johnstone found there was no evidence that Mr Wilson took his own life but while a cause of death could not be found, there were no signs of foul play.

'MACHINEGUN UNDER THE APRON': LIFE FOR A GANGLAND WIDOW

For a notoriously hard woman, gangland widow Wendy Peirce is a soft target for media types whose idea of jolly good sport is to shoot slow fish in shallow barrels. Like Judy Moran and Roberta Williams, her high profile and apparent lack of remorse for a life spent in a crime web has made her a headline writer's dream. Too poor to sue and with no reputation to defend, she has been roundly pilloried on radio, television and in the papers.

And with good reason. This is a woman who did not fall into crime so much as ran open-armed towards it. To her law-abiding parents and siblings, her life choices must have been a constant embarrassment ever since she fell in love with armed robber and killer Victor George Peirce while still a business college student.

'I was 17 when I got into this. I should be in a mental home,' she once stated.

For three decades Wendy's life has been beyond bizarre and almost beyond description. During one of Victor's many bail applications, she rose to her feet and deliberately wet herself, claiming her waters had broken and she was about to have a baby. If Victor was grateful to her, he had a strange way of showing it. Once when they ran out of marijuana he fired two shots between her legs, Wild West style, to encourage her to dance. She refused.

She lived with Victor in the same street as Peirce's half-brother Dennis 'Mr Death' Allen, a man police maintain was responsible for 11 murders. It was a horror show. In November 1985, Allen killed Melbourne bikie Anton Kenny and, with the help of Victor, used a chainsaw to dismember the body. Before dumping the body, secure inside a 44-gallon drum, in the nearby Yarra River, the impish Peirce chased his wife around the house with a severed big toe.

When Peirce was in jail charged with drug trafficking, Allen suggested he could shoot the then heavily pregnant Wendy in the foot so her husband would be granted bail on compassionate grounds. The spookiest thing is that Wendy actually considered it.

Allen was turning over huge amounts in drugs and his vicious streak was magnified by his prodigious appetite for his own products. Aged only 35, he died suddenly from drug-related heart disease in 1987.

In this toxic environment, where violence was mundane and murder a viable option, Wendy Peirce chose to have an affair with Victor's best friend, armed robber Graeme Jensen. It could have got her shot, and yet it was Jensen who died, killed by police during a botched arrest bid at Narre Warren on 11 October 1988. Police have always maintained that Peirce and his crew set up the Walsh Street ambush as payback for Jensen's death 13 hours earlier.

Wendy Peirce was in witness protection for nearly two years after she implicated her husband in the police killings. She gave first-class evidence at the committal and when all four were sent to trial, she was so excited she wanted to host a party (complete with dip and vegetable platters) with some of her minders. They declined the invitation.

But during the pre-trial hearing, she changed sides and even denied ever seeing her armed robber husband with a gun – those who knew him said they rarely saw him without one – and without her testimony, police could not link Peirce to the murder weapon.

Now she knows she can't hurt her husband, murdered in 2002 while sitting in his maroon Commodore in Bay Street, Port Melbourne. In 2005, Wendy finally agreed to go on the record with her version of the truth: 'It [Walsh Street] was spur-of-the-moment. We were on the run. Victor was the organiser.' She said her husband later gloated: '"They deserved their whack. It could have been me."'

Even though she wants a new start, there is still a little of the old Wendy on display. When ace photographer Craig Abraham took her to Station Pier for a snap, she pleaded: 'Don't make me look like a slag.'

Abraham, who thinks hyperbole ran second in last year's Warrnambool Cup, assured her she would be made beautiful through his lens.

Peirce responded: 'You better, or I'll fill your pockets with rocks and throw you off the fucking pier.' The smooth Abraham refused to lose focus.

Wendy is a walking contradiction: cunning and naive, vicious and vulnerable, exploited and an exploiter. She has inflicted more pain and suffered more tragedy than anyone should in a lifetime. She knows her life has been a disaster yet lacks the resolve to change.

Her daughter, Katie, died in 2009, the victim of a drug overdose. Hers was a short and unhappy life. Even in primary school her father's reputation dogged her. Back then, Wendy told us: 'Parents don't want my kids mixing with theirs. What do they think, I've got a machine-gun under the apron? I'm just a housewife. Katie's a good kid, but she hardly ever gets invited to a birthday party. Another kid said at school the other day: "At least my dad isn't in jail".'

At the time, the schoolgirl wanted to be a policewoman but soon learnt her surname would block her dreams. There were daily reminders of her family history; she was even taught to drive in the car her father was killed in.

Eventually, her environment weighed her down like a pocketful of rocks. She was facing serious criminal charges at the time of her death.

Wendy was in jail when her daughter died and the funeral was delayed three months until she was released.

If the prosecution of the surviving suspects accused of murdering two police officers in Walsh Street had been reactivated, she would have been asked to testify for the prosecution. Even as a hostile witness, she would have been valuable because the video record of her interviews can be played to a jury. They show her implicating her husband and others as the killers who lured Steven Tynan and Damian Eyre to Walsh Street on 12 October 1988.

Attorney-General Robert Clark stated that under changes to the double-jeopardy rules, another trial could be ordered after an acquittal if a major witness committed perjury. Wendy Peirce was found guilty of perjury after four men – Victor Peirce, Peter McEvoy, Trevor Pettingill and Anthony Farrell – were acquitted in 1991.

One of the detectives who worked on the Ty-Eyre Taskforce Jim O'Brien maintained an understandable dislike for the witness who helped scuttle their case. She was frightened of O'Brien and wouldn't deal with him when she was in witness protection. When Victor Peirce was shot dead, Wendy believed police would never really try to find his killer. And yet it was O'Brien's team at Purana that would make the arrest.

Wendy originally stated she would cooperate with a new coronial inquest into the Walsh Street murders. 'I will tell the truth. I have nothing left to hide. I feel a great weight has been lifted off me. I can finally walk down the street with my head held high. I feel so sorry for the [Tynan and Eyre] families. I didn't back then but I do now.'

But already you could sense she was wavering. And then she declared she would not give evidence. She kept changing her mind, telling police she would give evidence at a Walsh Street inquest and is believed to have signed a statement saying her original video confessions are true.

In the end, the point was moot, with Victorian State Coroner Jennifer Coate ruling there was not enough evidence for a new inquest. Of Wendy Pierce, the coroner said: 'The credit of Ms Peirce is so damaged by her history, it would be against common sense to describe any one position she may state she holds at any given time as sufficiently cogent to render it appropriate to reopen the coronial investigation.'

THE CUT-THROAT WORLD INSIDE PRISON

You don't need to know his history to sense that Paul O'Sullivan has been a hard man who has lived a hard life. It is not just the tattoos, the long scar on his neck and the boxer's gait, but the eyes that reflect a life where violence was a natural part of his daily routine.

He spent nearly 20 years behind bars not as a prisoner but as a guard, assigned to deal with the worst inmates in the state. Like the fight game, working inside a prison comes at a cost and O'Sullivan saw, inflicted and was subjected to more brutality than is conceivable to anyone outside the system.

It was late 1999 when he applied to be a prison officer at Port Phillip Prison, attracted by a steady income, four-day weeks and generous leave entitlements. As a boxer and a man who had mixed with a few crims on the outside, he was confident he wouldn't be intimidated on the inside.

That confidence took a hit on his first day. 'There were tennis courts and a swimming pool. There were prisoners sunbaking and it looked like a holiday camp. I thought: "This is a jail?"'

The prisoners lined up against the wire to yell abuse at the new officers. He knew then that respect would have to be earned.

A few months later, on a Sunday shift in April 2000, an inmate wanted to see the psychiatric nurse, saying he planned to self-harm or hurt someone. True to his word, when he came back to the division, he grabbed O'Sullivan from behind and cut his throat from the right ear to the windpipe.

'They would melt the end of a toothbrush and attach a blade to make a Stanley knife,' he says.

O'Sullivan chased his attacker but other prisoners blocked his path. Convicted murderer Lewis Caine (himself murdered in 2004 as part of the gangland war) followed the wounded prison officer with a mop to clean up the spurting blood before finally persuading him to stand still.

Eventually, senior officers demanded he go to hospital – although he wanted to return to work the next day for his overtime allowance. 'They promised I would get it. I never did.'

Once the 12 stitches were removed he went back to work, winning the respect of the hard men in Charlotte division. 'It became an urban myth. Eventually they said I chased the guy who slashed me and flogged him. It didn't happen.'

Prison officers were told they must always act lawfully but inside the jail, there were different rules. 'If a prisoner played up, he was told he had a visitor. When he went to the visitor's room he would be bashed.

'There were some who only understood violence – jail is a jungle and only the hardest survive. You give a heavy a lecture and he won't listen. Take his TV as punishment and he will just take someone else's.'

O'Sullivan learnt inside prison that the heavy inmates helped maintain order. Lewis Caine, he said, controlled the billets, bashing one when he wasn't up to standard. When the imposing Richard Mladenich was in a cell under Caine, he made the mistake of playing his music too loud. Caine walked in and beat him senseless even though 'Mladenich was one of the most dangerous in there.' (Mladenich was shot dead in 2000 in a St Kilda doss house.)

'The bikies ran their unit and they were well-behaved,' O'Sullivan recalls. 'The Mokbels were never a problem.'

When one prison officer mentioned his holiday at Rosebud, Milad Mokbel said he preferred Sorrento. 'He was talking about Sorrento in Italy.'

Prison officers learn when to see and when to look away. On the bottom level of the Scarborough North division was a large three-bunk cell known as the Boxing Ring. 'That's where prisoners went for a fight or a bashing. They would turn up the music to drown out the screams. We appreciated that they didn't do it in front of us.'

O'Sullivan says prisoners were inventive when it came to weapons. A tiny piece of wire or a sliver of veneer from a table could be sharpened into a shiv. Jam could be heated in a kettle and thrown at an enemy to stick and burn: 'It was like napalm.' Tinned food in a sock could crush a skull. 'It was called being bake-beaned. They'd pour boiling water on the legs to distract and then whack them on the head.'

Major drug dealer Dragan 'Machine Gun Charlie' Arnautovic took O'Sullivan under his wing, explaining that if you were having a dispute with a prisoner, it could be resolved in the cell. 'He said: "If you walk in and the guy sits on his bed, he is saying sorry – if he stands up, it's on, so hit him".'

Sometimes the fights were more open. Tony 'Mad Dog' Loguancio challenged O'Sullivan to a bout in the prison boxing ring. The inmate had his mates screaming: 'Kill the Dog.'

'I knew exactly what he would do. He was going to charge at me. I slipped to the side and smashed his head into the wall then hit him once. That knocked him out.'

It didn't knock any sense into the serial rapist. Loguancio killed himself in 2013 at the end of a two-day siege in Glenroy.

O'Sullivan says it is the prisoner's behaviour inside jail that defines his long-term treatment, not his crime on the outside. 'If you want to be a prison officer, you can't be a judge.'

Here are his observations on some of the most notorious inmates.

Hoddle Street killer Julian Knight: 'I had a lot to do with him in the gym. He didn't ever show the slightest remorse for what he did.'

Russell Street bomber Craig Minogue: 'He says if he ever gets out he will change his name and, because of all his qualifications, get a job. He has cleaned up, given up smoking and doesn't even swear. I know police hate him for what he did – I would too – but I take people as I find them.'

Armed robber and master escapee Christopher Dean Binse: 'I liked him. He hated Julian Knight and would have killed him if he ever got near him. He spent most of his time in solitary and when finally moved into mainstream, he didn't bother unpacking. He came out of his cell with magazines under his clothes to protect him from a knifing, found an enemy he was stalking and bashed him. He was taken straight back to solitary.'

When Binse was released he tried to leave $600 for the prison officers to have a drink. Police wanted to know when he was released so he could be followed. According to O'Sullivan, it wasn't hard. 'He had a stretch limo filled with prostitutes.' After another armed robbery and a siege, Binse was back inside. 'Whenever he was in a new division, you would see him looking up, always calculating how to escape.'

Stephen John Asling, armed robber convicted of the 2003 contract murder of Graham 'The Munster' Kinniburgh: 'He told me they called him "The Magician" because he could make people disappear.'

Triple killer Greg 'Bluey' Brazel: 'He was the most manipulative person you could ever meet. He was so intelligent with an amazing memory and he was hated in the mainstream.'

O'Sullivan says when Brazel was allowed to socialise with other inmates, he swindled one out of $60,000. He found personal details of inmates to use against them and discovered the home addresses of senior prison staff. Realising prison officers hated to clean the kitchen, Brazel offered to take over so he could steal food. 'We found eight tins of coffee and a year's supply of sugar under his bed.'

Gangland killer and drug boss Carl Williams left O'Sullivan less than impressed. 'David McCulloch [a convicted drug dealer] was the heavy who called the shots. Carl was nothing but a clown.'

O'Sullivan says major drug dealers saw jail as 'income tax' – the cost of doing business. He was respected by most of the inmates. 'I'd challenge bad behaviour and tell them to act like men.'

But he adds that it could be like working in a war zone. 'You can never win. By the time you win them over they move out and you get new ones and the threats start again – "You are a dog, I'll find out where you live, I'll kill your wife, you're a maggot".

'You work four days. Day one you are full of fight, day two you are tired, day three you are looking forward to the end and day four you just give up.'

During his working life he saw two murders, including a mafia hit, and 10 deaths from various causes, more than 30 stabbings and countless bashings.

O'Sullivan has now left the prison business, diagnosed with post-traumatic stress. Some days are better than others. 'All the fight has gone out of me,' he says.

His wife, also a prison officer, has been diagnosed with cancer and continues to battle on. 'I'm not the fighter in the family; she is.'

THE ATTORNEY'S SCHOOL OF HARD KNOCKS

Big, loud, funny and a natural showman, legendary lawyer Bernie Balmer is instantly recognisable as he sips on a Victoria Bitter ('Vitamin B') in Melbourne's Hardware Lane. Judges, restaurant staff and fellow lawyers stop for a chat and it is immediately clear that Bernie the Attorney holds court both in and out of the judicial quarter.

But it doesn't take long to realise this is part of a well-crafted professional act – that of the knockabout, wrong-side-of-the-tracks boxer and bouncer turned legal street fighter who has built a reputation as the gangster's last resort.

A career in the criminal courts has taken its toll but it was an event just outside the precinct more than 30 years ago that even now brings him to the brink of tears.

It was 27 March 1986, when Balmer, then a youngish solicitor, walked out of the Magistrates' building to slip around the corner to his office in Latrobe Street, just as the Russell Street bomb detonated. He was the first at the scene, and the first to try to help the fatally injured Constable Angela Taylor.

'The blast had ripped her clothes away and she had shocking burns. Her shoelaces were still on fire and I bent down to put them out.

'She was able to talk. I asked her name and where she worked.'

He carried her back across the road, well away from the smouldering wreckage of the car bomb. 'She was such a tough girl. She lasted 24 days.

'There are smells, tastes and noises that never leave you. They take you back. I was walking down the street when a truck backfired and I dived on the ground, took the knee out of my suit pants. People must have thought I was a fruit loop.'

In 2022 Balmer received a Citizen Commendation, the highest civilian honour that can be awarded by police for his actions on the day of the Russell Street Bombing.

If Bernie wasn't born with a keen sense of justice, he developed it while still a teenager when he became the victim of a stitch-up that has left a scar.

In Year 11 at Assumption College, the students complained the milk tasted off. 'The cows were feeding on capeweed, which makes the milk bitter.' Already known for his gift of the gab, Balmer's fellow students elected him to raise the subject, so he suggested to a Brother he take a sip to find out for himself.

Rather than agreeing to what seemed a perfectly reasonable request: 'He punched me, putting me teeth through my lip.' It was a major mistake. Balmer was a big lad who could hold his hands up (he would later become Australian University Heavyweight Boxing Champion) and he dropped the bully Brother.

While he was only defending himself, he was forced to leave under threat of expulsion. It still burns that some who knew the truth failed to stand up for him. Perhaps that is one of the reasons he became a seven-day-a-week defence lawyer, often giving a voice to those who desperately need one.

(The wheels of justice move slowly, but they do turn; the Brother in question has now run into legal troubles of his own.)

Balmer's road to a law degree was a winding one. He bounced at Fitzroy's Champion Hotel (a notorious bloodhouse), worked as a galley rat on a fishing boat and then in a bank (later defending bandits who robbed them), went to uni part-time and learnt the legal rules of engagement in his years as a clerk of courts.

In November 1979, he was uncomfortably close when Ray Chuck was shot at point-blank range inside the Melbourne Magistrates' building: 'I could have won the Stawell Gift that day.'

He hid in the law library, reasoning the killer was unlikely to wander in to examine old statutes, for he would be the type who thought jurisprudence was a Beatles cover band.

At any one time Balmer and his team have several hundred clients, with thousands more on file (in criminal law, sadly, many become repeat customers). The firm covers everything from traffic offences to murder, and he has often represented the underworld big guns.

Many of his clients have come on the recommendation of police, who have known him since the clerk-of-court days.

Working in his firm has been the ideal finishing school, with three magistrates, a County Court judge and a silk going through the business.

His training is simple: 'Prepare, do your job well and don't use tricks. We don't win cases, the coppers stuff 'em up.' In boxing terms, learn to be a counter-puncher and don't hit below the belt.

He quietly tries to help kids through his work experience program, where students with an interest in the law get a real taste, heading to court rather than sitting behind a desk, shuffling papers and listening to war stories from blowhard barristers who have, apparently, never lost a case.

(He knows how to look after kids. After all, his four daughters have all worked for the firm.)

He recalls when one student from the north-west fell silent as they were heading to Frankston Magistrates Court. 'She was staring out the window and I asked her if there was anything wrong. She said: "I have never seen the sea."'

Later at a restaurant he asked why she wasn't eating her meal. 'She said she was not allowed to start until the men at the table had finished. I was blown away.

'I think I learn more from them than they learn from me.'

Like many who have built a successful business, he wonders about the cost. For years it was a seven-day-a-week job – Monday to Friday was in the courts and the weekends spent visiting clients in prison. 'Dealing with people's problems every day can wear you down. I suppose we use black humour to survive.'

He always carried a beeper and later a mobile phone. 'Crooks don't work nine-to-five.' Which meant his wife Mary – herself one of 12 – had to do the bulk of the parenting.

The hard work, the gangland clients and the headlines left a mark. 'I didn't know it at the time but the family was concerned for my safety during the underworld war.'

Daughter Anna, who now works as a lawyer in the family business, recalls that with her mother working as a nurse, she would go to work with her dad when not going to school. 'I remember going to the Dandenong court and the magistrate (the legendary Darcy Dugan) told me to stand up and introduce myself. I was nine.'

At 15 she went to Barwon Prison with her father as work experience. She was with two killers when she asked one what he was hoping for in the future. 'He said: "I'd kill for a piece of meat."'

When she eventually joined the firm, she tried to teach her father about the use of computers. 'I failed. You have to let Bernie be Bernie. He uses the same type of pen and the same notebook he always has. It just works for him.'

His love of boxing led him into the sport, and he only recently stood down as chair of the Professional Boxing and Combat Sports Board after 17 years. That too has come at a price. When he controversially granted the colourful Mick Gatto a promoters' licence, some thought he was running on the wrong side of the tracks.

'I acted according to the law,' he says. 'The legislation was stuffed up.'

Then at a legal function, someone of influence told him he would never be appointed a magistrate because he was seen as too close to notorious crime figures. If this is true, then it is Victoria's loss. Balmer has more practical legal sense in one of his sausage-sized fingers than some who now occupy the bench.

Balmer is a practical man who knows the limitations of the law and says drugs now drive crime. 'When I started I thought snorting cocaine was a heavyweight boxer.'

Like some of his more notorious clients, he has a reputation as a straight shooter, saying many decision-makers are impractical 'tofu-chewing tree huggers' and too many politicians 'act out of self-interest rather than looking for results'.

He says too many parents are not taking responsibility for bringing up their children, courts are swamped and unrestricted computer search engines are allowing the vulnerable access to dangerous information.

'Kids have access to everything from ice recipes to how to make a bomb. Police tell me primary school children are engaging in sexual practices they have seen on the internet.

'Google has no moral police. We have a bandaid approach to our problems. Too many people are falling through the cracks with legal, drug and mental health problems. I just hate seeing where our kids are going.'

THE TV STAR AND THE INTERVIEW THAT 'CHOPPED' HER CAREER

This is the story of three Australian entertainers: one whose career hit a brick wall after the first guest on her brand-spanking-new TV show turned up profoundly drunk; the next who won a Walkley Award for interviewing the same guest in entirely different circumstances; and the third – the guest himself – who cheerfully admitted to being a homicidal maniac.

Libbi Gorr, under her stage name, Elle McFeast, stood in front of a live TV audience to welcome her guest, career criminal turned bestselling author Mark 'Chopper' Read.

Five weeks earlier, Read had been released from his latest (and last) stint in prison. Many media groups had reached out to interview him. Gorr won the race, and it would cost her dearly. She is living proof that the industry of confected outrage was up and about long before social media.

Gorr (or McFeast) was a budding star. Brassy, bold and unafraid, she progressed from a character to host of the satirical ABC sports program, *Live and Sweaty*, along with another new-generation star, Andrew Denton.

In 1998, she was the first Australian woman to be given her own national night-time variety show, *McFeast Live*. She was part of a generation of Spice Girls feminists, she says. She felt she could handle just about anything.

That was until she was confronted on national television by an earless killer left legless from the free grog in the green room.

Around the time of Read's release, I received a call from a *McFeast Live* staffer asking if I thought Chopper would be a good guest for the program. I said it was a particularly bad idea to fly him to Sydney from Hobart, where he was living on a farm having just served nearly six years for shooting bikie Sid Collins in the guts. (Collins later disappeared and his body has never been found.)

'It's been 25 years [since the interview], and that's the first I've heard of that,' Gorr told me.

Respected journalist Andrew Rule, Read and my good self conspired to publish a series of crime books that, while an affront to good taste and grammar, became bestsellers. Read delighted in referring to well-known Sydney crooks as hoons and pimps who were protected by crooked cops.

I liked Read and always found him engaging company, but a live interview would be as risky as a high-wire act over a pool of sharks. If nothing went wrong, it would be entertaining. If something went wrong, it would be deadly.

I told them that if he was left to his own devices in Sydney, it could end badly.

The McFeast team decided to press on. They hired some form of security to protect Read and to protect people from Read. What they didn't do was protect Read, which meant he committed grievous bodily harm on the beer fridge.

When he staggered on stage, he leered at the host's breasts, joked about killing people and told a story of the dangers of putting a victim in a cement mixer.

I remember thinking how game Gorr was not to flee from the stage.

As the interview started, a floor manager madly gave the wind-up sign but Gorr, unaware Read was hammered, continued. 'I was taught the show should go on.' It emerges now there was an emergency guest in the green room and if anyone had known how drunk Read was, they could have made a switch.

When he moved in for a grope, she knocked his hands away and continued the interview. 'That's what you did back then. It was a long time before the MeToo movement.'

Gorr did slap a man's face for copping an unsolicited feel of her bottom. He was a captain of industry, once touted as a possible prime minister.

With Read, she pushed through, leaving him to sit in the corner dozing and occasionally interject for the rest of the program.

After the show, Read made an unusual offer, telling Gorr: 'I don't know anyone in Sydney, but if you ever need anyone knocked off in Melbourne . . .'

The response to the program was immediate. She wanted to ruffle feathers, but the interview left her show a dead duck. There were more than 100 complaints, and the ABC apologised, conceding it was 'an error of judgement'.

Communications Minister Richard Alston blasted: 'I think it is appropriate for the government to express its outrage at the appalling way in which this episode has been conducted.'

Gorr and Read were to pay a price. She was commissioned to host 32 programs, but the show was shelved after 16. 'I was cancelled before they invented cancel culture,' she says.

Many who had been in her corner disappeared after the Read interview. She was brave and a natural risk-taker, but the aftermath to the Read interview shook her confidence with a microphone. A comedian/interviewer requires split-second timing, and if you second-guess yourself, the moment has passed.

NAKED CITY

The Read interview was big news, and *The Midday Show* and Kerri-Anne Kennerley wanted a piece of the action, believing it was a perfect subject for a blast from broadcaster Alan Jones. Trouble was, to invite Read in for a chat would open them up to the very criticisms they had planned to make of the ABC.

In fact, more than a month before the Gorr fiasco, the day after Read was released from Tasmania's Risdon Prison, *Midday* had written to him, asking him to come on the program: 'We can put you on the telly [and you can] hold your books up while Kerri-Anne asks you relatively mild questions.'

Then the backroom boys hatched a plot: drive Read to the Nine studios in Hobart, where he would 'just happen' to ring in as Jones was condemning the already infamous interview.

Read rang to tell me of the plot and his plan to rebut Jones by raising an incident when the broadcaster was arrested (and later released) in London. (Read rang again from the television station to complain that the fridge was locked and that he had broken into a cupboard to steal a couple of beers.)

Sure enough, right on cue, Read was on the phone to Jones, informing him that people in glass houses shouldn't throw stones and recalling the unfortunate events of London. It was the television equivalent of a drive-by shooting. An outraged Kennerley terminated the interview. Jones remained silent.

Five years later, Denton, Gorr's colleague on *Live and Sweaty*, hosted an interview program called *Enough Rope*. He interviewed Read, but it was not a light chat about his life in crime. It was a deep dive, taking Read to places where he was not comfortable, including his brutal childhood. It was compelling and part of a package that won Denton the 2003 Walkley Award for Broadcast Interviewing.

Reflecting on the interview, Denton said: 'There was a lot of debate within the *Enough Rope* team about putting someone with this sort of record on television. Initially, I wasn't sure, but remembering the Elle McFeast fiasco, Chopper's last TV appearance, and the way in which many interviewers tended to giggle at the violence of the stories rather than addressing it, I thought it was worth a try at a different approach.'

Denton's attitude had changed markedly from 12 February 1998, when he wrote to Read (the same day as *Midday* did) with a different proposal. Then on FM radio, he offered Read the chance to 'shamelessly promote your latest book and take Sydney listeners inside your humour-filled world'.

For a while, Gorr felt her career was destroyed. Since then, she has come back as a successful writer, broadcaster, radio host, lawyer and performer.

'I'm still up for taking risks, but they need to be considered,' she says. 'If you plan to hang out the window, be sure of who is holding your legs.'

For Read, it was an expensive exercise. Production for the movie *Chopper* was just getting off the ground, but the government made it clear that if Read was paid, any funding would disappear.

Read donated his payment of $22,000 to the Royal Children's Hospital. They refused to accept it, so we slipped it through a police charity that sent it onto the hospital. It amused Read that the police were laundering his take.

Much later, when Read surrounded himself with bottom feeders, he was convinced he had been ripped off, to the point he sent heavies around to co-producer Michael Gudinski's home. As the character Neville Bartos said in *Chopper*: 'There's no cash here. Here, there's no cash. All right? Cash? No.'

Read died in 2013, a household name.

PART 4
THE CRIMES

Crime should be pretty simple. There is a victim, an offender, an investigation and hopefully a conviction. But the crimes within these pages are anything but simple.

One of the first crimes I covered was the murder of the notorious Ray Chuck Bennett, organiser of the Great Bookie Robbery, and one of three men who killed an underworld enemy. It was no surprise Chuck was eventually killed. What *was* surprising was that it happened in a court building and almost certainly, at least partially, organised by police.

One of the most recent stories to be covered was a double murder/suicide in a small country town where one of the victims was seen as the villain, and the killer (who took his own life), was seen as the hero. A story of what happens when someone feels the need to take the law into their own hands.

With changes to the law and advancements in technology, crimes and convictions can evolve – for better or worse.

Serial killer Paul Charles Denyer killed three women in seven weeks, leaving the Melbourne district of Frankston with permanent scars. Now, he has asked the parole board for a second chance – something he denied his victims.

Then there is the murder of a young woman, whose parents fought for decades to pursue the truth; a case where police twice concentrated on the wrong suspects. When detectives finally find the right man (confirmed by DNA), it is too late to provide any peace for the father who would die just days later.

MURDER, THEY WROTE

In the days before security metal detectors, luggage X-ray machines, (legal) phone taps, widespread CCTV and armed Protective Services Officers, court security hadn't really changed since they hanged Ned Kelly. You could wander around the courts, slip inside police stations and stroll the halls of power unchallenged.

Which is why when notorious standover man Brian Kane planned the revenge killing of one of the men who murdered his brother, he chose to carry out the shooting inside Russell Street's Melbourne Magistrates Court. His target was Ray Chuck Bennett, the mastermind behind the 1976 Great Bookie Robbery and one of three men who, on 19 October 1978, burst into Leslie Kane's Wantirna home and shot him dead. Kane's body was never found.

On the surface, it was insanity to kill a man surrounded by cops, but they would be unarmed, he would have the element of surprise and – almost certainly – inside help.

In November 1978 a man in a dark blue suit, a beard and gold-rimmed glasses stepped forward, brandishing a snub-nosed revolver and said: 'Cop this you motherfucker' before firing at point-blank range. Within hours of the hit at the Magistrates Court, the whisper was that a group of police not only green-lighted the Chuck murder but also helped Kane set up his getaway.

Now, for the first time, we can reveal an insider's account from one of the detectives who worked in the Russell Street crime squads at the time and knew the players on both sides of the law.

First, the backstory.

While serving a jail sentence in England, Chuck learnt military-style armed robbery tactics from a prolific gang known as the Wembley Mob. In April 1976, he used those techniques to raid the Victoria Club. Chuck's team of six hit the club on settlement day for Melbourne bookies, who were carrying massive cash holdings inflated by the Easter races. The official haul was declared as $1.4 million, although it is believed the real figure was three times higher.

Usually members of the hard-nosed and armed consorting squad would have been at the club to add a layer of security, but mysteriously they were called away on the day of the raid.

In the days, weeks and months that followed, not only were police looking for the bandits but so were the Kanes. As the established standover team they wanted a slice of the new boys' profit, but Chuck (known as The General) hadn't planned a masterful stick-up only to give it away to the first wolves prepared to huff and puff outside his door.

It came to a head when one of Chuck's crew, 'the third man', refused a drink from Brian Kane in a Richmond hotel. To add injury to insult, the third man won the subsequent fight.

The Crown would later allege Chuck, Laurie Prendergast and the third man thought the Kanes would strike back and decided to get in first by murdering Leslie Kane. A jury found the three innocent – only for Prendergast to be abducted and murdered in 1985. His body has never been found. The third man moved to Western Australia for many years, while Chuck remained in custody as he was still facing armed robbery charges.

For Kane, if Chuck was convicted, he would be hard to reach inside prison. Hence the plan to shoot him in the courts.

Remarkably, our insider admits police took sides, backing the Kanes against Chuck's team. 'We decided to stick with the Kanes, not because of the Kanes themselves but because they were more predictable, because they had rules. They caught and killed their own and looked after their own.

'Brian Kane kept to himself and trusted no one. He was only concerned about staying alive and avenging the murder of his brother. He would never make an appointment because he didn't want anyone to predict his movements.'

In those days, interstate detectives came to Melbourne during racing season, ostensibly to look for professional pickpocket gangs but really to party with the racing crowd.

'It was on the Monday after the Cup carnival had finished,' the insider recalls. 'On the Saturday and Sunday there had been barbecues and farewells after a month of solid entertaining. We were happy it was over so we could give our livers a rest and get back to our marriages and work. Everyone worked day shift that day.'

That morning some of the consorting squad went to the police canteen for milkshakes – the first non-alcoholic drinks to pass their lips in weeks.

Armed robbery squad detectives requested help to escort Chuck upstairs to Court 11 to face a committal hearing for a $69,000 armed robbery.

'They [two consorting squad detectives] grabbed him – there was no conversation. They were to take him up the stairs but he said: "I'm not going up there. There are witnesses up there and I don't want to be seen by them." He was kicking up a stink.'

A detective went ahead to clear witnesses. He apparently didn't notice the man in the dark blue suit, or thought he was an on-duty solicitor.

'Then someone opened a door and fired three shots. What happened then was a real panic. No one actually believed he had been shot. Later we found he had been shot through the heart and twice through the hands as he put them up to protect himself.

'He managed to run back down the steps and then collapsed. People thought he was trying to escape – it was so unexpected, people weren't thinking straight. People came from everywhere, jumping over blood and running through the crime scene.

'The police were unarmed and someone grabbed the gun that was the exhibit in the court case [Chuck was supposed to have used it in the armed robbery]. The funny thing is not all the bullets fitted the gun, which meant Chuck probably would have beaten the charge.

'About two in the afternoon an informer told Angus [Detective Senior Sergeant Angus Ritchie, chief of the consorting squad]: "It was an inside job from your office".'

'That night at the Police Club we couldn't buy a drink. At first that was fantastic, until the sobering reality hit us that 50 per cent of the police force thought we had done it.'

Kane made his escape through the rabbit warren of the court building, running out the back where two corrugated tin fence sheets had been prised apart to allow him to run into RMIT and catch a tram out of the city to his car parked in a suburban street. It was a prepared escape route.

Brian Murphy was then a colourful detective whose name was mentioned in connection with the Chuck murder. 'Yes, it was Brian, but not this one,' he said. 'It was Brian Kane.' Asked if it was an inside job, Murphy replied without hesitation: '100 per cent.

'Brian Kane came to me after the three were acquitted of murdering his brother. He wanted me to get him police records and photos. I knocked him back.'

Murphy said he saw Kane in Lygon Street days before the killing: 'He had grown a beard.'

The rumour, never confirmed, was that the day before the murder, Kane was smuggled into the court complex hidden in the boot of a cleaner's car by two detectives for a dry run.

The events of those turbulent years still echo through the underworld today.

Brian Kane was shot dead in Brunswick's Quarry Hotel in 1982. The prime suspects were underworld heavies Russell Cox and Rod Collins. In the death notices there was one to 'Uncle Brian' from 'Your little mate, Jason'. This was Jason Moran, who married Les Kane's daughter.

A prominent mourner at Moran's funeral was Graham 'The Munster' Kinniburgh, also a great mate of Brian Kane's. Kinniburgh was later the victim of a paid hit, carried out by Stephen Asling and Terrence Blewitt, on the orders of Carl Williams.

Normie Lee was the only one charged over the Great Bookie Robbery. After he was acquitted he seemingly dropped out of the underworld, resurfacing in 1992 when he was shot dead by police during a $1 million armed robbery at Melbourne Airport. The getaway driver in the failed armed robbery was Stephen Asling.

Williams was the middleman who in 2004 employed Rod Collins to kill police informer Terence Hodson and his wife, Christine, in their Kew home. When Williams became a prosecution witness in the Hodson murder case, he was bashed to death inside Barwon Prison.

Just like Ray Chuck, he was killed while in custody – and just like Chuck, those complicit have never been called to account.

VIOLENT SHADOW LAY OVER TINY TOWN

In death, even the most violent of crooks can be sent from this earth with a volley of compliments, often from those who organised the volley of shots that stopped them breathing in the first place.

The 'rough diamond with a heart of gold' will have been a bash artist, 'nature's gentleman' a standover man, and 'generous to a fault' a drug dealer. The more notorious get pages of death notices, and police will sometimes be needed to control traffic at churches surrounded by limousines carrying men who feel the need to wear sunglasses in the middle of winter and overcoats on a sunny day.

Kevin Knowles was not that sort of crook. If it wasn't for the manner of his death, few would remember him outside the tiny town of Kirkstall, a place he terrorised for a decade.

Since his violent death thousands of words have been written about his bloody life and grisly end, with one of the few positive comments coming from a girlfriend who told *The Warrnambool Standard*: 'He made the best poached eggs ever.'

The killer, hippie and part-time gold prospector Travis Cashmore, 45, lived in the town for 15 years and had grown up in the region.

Often barefoot and recognisable from a distance by his dreadlocks, he was always up for a chat.

Unlike Knowles, he was well-liked. What pushed him over the edge that Friday morning may never be known but what is known is he chose to take the law – and a shotgun – into his own hands.

It has been reported Cashmore had a dispute with a neighbour over giant gum trees encroaching on his land, blocking the sun and his gutters.

Knowles threatened Cashmore with a knife and launched a campaign of terror against a local woman. This was Knowles's way – to take a dislike to someone and make their lives miserable with a dogged determination he failed to replicate in any lawful activity.

Jailed for a short time for threatening her – 'I'm going to kill you and your kids, your days are numbered,' he said – once released, he began again.

With no local police, Knowles could make his threats and disappear before patrols from the 24-hour Warrnambool station could drive the 25 kilometres to Kirkstall. Cashmore went to police complaining that on 20 July, Knowles breached an intervention order (yet again) against the woman. There was no immediate response, perhaps because Knowles was due at Warrnambool Court on Monday 25 July to answer similar charges. On Friday, 22 July, less than 48 hours after reporting Knowles's latest breach, Cashmore took a chainsaw to the neighbours' trees in Chamberlain Street, hopped in his white van and drove until he found Knowles, 49, and his sidekick Ben Ray, 48, walking about six kilometres to Koroit.

Cashmore blasted Knowles in the back of the head with a shotgun before reversing over what remained of the dead man's skull. He ran over Ray before shooting him twice.

Cashmore then drove home, walked into his backyard and ended his life with the same gun.

In many ways, Knowles's death freed his small community. 'We have lived in fear for 10 years. People talked of selling up and moving,' says one resident.

A resident holding a small party heard Knowles yelling: 'I hope you die' from the street. Locals drove and walked different streets to avoid him. Garage sales stopped and functions were planned to avoid the local powder keg.

In 1991, career detective Col Ryan transferred to Warrnambool and made it his home, serving 12 years as a shire councillor and two stints as mayor. As a policeman in Richmond he had confronted drug dealer and killer Dennis Allen; at the Armed Robbery Squad it was bandits with guns, and he was part of the taskforce that investigated the 1988 Walsh Street murders of police officers Steven Tynan and Damian Eyre.

When he first arrived Kirkstall was not much more than a pub and a bus stop, he says, but 'In the early 2000s sea- and tree-changers began to discover the quaint little location, five kilometres from Koroit and 14 from Port Fairy.'

The 2016 census showed Kirkstall had become a family community, with a population of 366 that included 69 children under 10 years old.

'The sense of community was strong, with the local progress association developing a park with tennis courts, playgrounds and barbecues,' says Ryan. 'They also renovated the local hall, which was the venue for community functions. Over the road is the local pub, fondly known by locals as the "Kirky".'

But Kirkstall 'had a shadow cast over it when evil arrived, in the form of Kevin Knowles, who purchased a house in town . . . Knowles, a criminal, bully and thug whose many victims were usually female, soon became well known and almost immediately was banned from the pub.' Knowles, who had over 40 pages of priors, arrived in Warrnambool in the early 90s after a quick exit from Melbourne following the death of his then partner.

Ryan said when a local magistrate refused Knowles bail he 'stacked on a turn in the court, which took five coppers to forcibly remove him but not before capsicum spray was used like fly spray'.

As a criminal Knowles was an abject failure because he was invariably caught. His police record listed 300 offences.

These are the offenders police hate. Their convictions don't justify long jail terms but they are vicious enough to damage a community. There are three reasons most of us obey the law: We don't want to hurt people; we don't want to be arrested; and we don't want to go to jail. Knowles wasn't concerned with those consequences, which made him impossible to control. Which may be why that quiet Friday morning Cashmore (known in Kirkstall as 'Trav') snapped.

Cashmore murdered two people, yet many locals see him as a victim. 'As far as I am concerned, he is a hero,' one says. On the night of Knowles's death, a local band played at the Kirky and they served around 150 meals – three times more than usual.

Ray, who had returned to the district a few days earlier, was with Knowles when he threatened Cashmore's female friend. Intellectually disabled, Ray was caught in a dispute beyond his comprehension.

Knowles subjected women to unrelenting family violence. One relationship resulted in 35 police reports, with his partner finally stabbing him in the face with a wooden stool leg. In another, a woman smashed him in the face with a kettle. He threatened people with knives, turned up for a court appearance in a stolen car, trashed cells, stole someone's beloved dog, and sped from police at 150 km/h.

When locals saw flashing blue lights they knew police were heading to Knowles's house. On the police computer his name raised flags for assaulting police, weapons, family violence and drug use.

He was also a killer who was not charged with homicide as the only potential witness died in circumstances that still have some wondering. On 7 December 2016, Knowles and partner, Amanda Bourke, had a giant drinking session with Stephen Johnston in his backyard in Suzanne Crescent, Warrnambool. Johnston was later found dying with 101 wounds, including a fractured skull.

The couple took Johnston's credit card to buy cigarettes and Bourke destroyed the CCTV hard drive that probably showed Knowles beating the drunk and defenceless Johnston.

JOHN SILVESTER

Crime Stoppers received a tip the fatal injury was inflicted by Bourke, who hit Johnston on the head with a vase. Police believe Knowles organised the call – which came from the home of one of his best friends – throwing his girlfriend under the bus to save himself.

On 12 February 2020, Coroner Simon McGregor found Knowles responsible for Johnston's death, asking the Director of Public Prosecutions to consider charging him. The only way to build a case against Knowles was for Bourke to give evidence. That option disappeared when Bourke and Knowles went swimming at a poorly signposted local beach on 18 January 2018. Even though the temperature was bumping 40 degrees, there were no swimmers because the beach was notorious for rips and shifting sands.

The evidence was that the couple were about 30 metres from shore, with Bourke affectionately climbing on Knowles's back. Two weeks earlier she told police he had punched her, leaving her with a black and swollen eye.

They stepped out of their depth and were caught in a rip. Knowles said he tried to grab Bourke's hand, but she slipped free. A man walking on the beach jumped in and battled strong currents to reach her. It took him 10 minutes to swim the 50 metres to bring her back to shore. She could not be revived.

Coroner Caitlin English said: 'While I am satisfied that there was a history of violence committed by Mr Knowles against Mrs Bourke, there is no evidence to suggest he took any action to bring about Mrs Bourke's death.'

There are some, including local police, who hold a different view.

Ray was an innocent victim and Cashmore is greatly missed in the tiny community he tried to protect. Knowles will never hurt anyone again.

LEGAL EAGLE'S WINGS CLIPPED BY GREED

Norman O'Bryan was born to be a barrister. His grandfather, Sir Norman, and his father, Norman, were towering legal figures who sat with distinction on the Victorian Supreme Court bench.

Not that the youngest O'Bryan was given an easy ride because of his bloodlines. He possessed a brilliant legal mind, the required work ethic and an unshakable self-belief that would lead him to the top of the family trade.

At Melbourne University, he won the Supreme Court Prize for top student (his grandfather had won it in 1914) then a Rhodes Scholarship to Oxford. His name is on academic honour boards next to those of prime ministers, US presidents, High Court judges, Law Lords, governors-general and premiers.

Yet this legal jet crashed in a fireball of greed, deception and intimidation, shredded in the very court where his family had built a spotless reputation.

Mark Elliott was a respected partner in the prestigious Melbourne law firm Minter Ellison until he decided to strike out on his own to take on big companies in lucrative class actions. There was plenty of money to be made but for Elliott, it was never enough. He had a plan, not so much a get-rich-quick scheme but a get-even-richer one. It would cost him his reputation and his fortune before his mysterious death.

Elliott, O'Bryan and others embarked on a legal deception worth millions – and they would have got away with it if it wasn't for a retired Adelaide nurse and a former bus driver from Ballarat. They saw what a succession of courts couldn't – that something wasn't quite right in the $64 million case – and refused to be silenced.

'They wanted to charge ridiculous amounts just to distribute funds,' former nurse Wendy Botsman says. But when these legal big guns turned on her, she had someone on her side prepared to fire back.

To understand what happened over eight years, we first need to understand the nature of class-action litigation. In many cases, individuals wronged by big companies do not have the money for a prolonged legal battle. But when there are thousands of victims, they can band together in one action under a lead plaintiff. They can get justice without financial risk.

Such cases can be spectacular. Power company SP Ausnet agreed to pay $496 million in compensation to 5000 victims of the 2009 Black Saturday fire in Kilmore.

These actions can take years and require a third-party funder – financiers (punters in pinstripe suits) who pour in millions to pay the legal costs in exchange for a slice of the final settlement. Where there are big piles of money, there are those with even bigger appetites and some of the funders started to gouge, taking more than was reasonable. In one case, the funders and lawyers wanted $11 million of a $12 million settlement. Then the courts stepped in. A judge would decide what was a reasonable cut (usually between 20 and 30 per cent) of the final pot, taking into account monies spent and risks taken.

When done right, class actions mean victims are compensated, unethical or lax corporations punished, funders rewarded and justice served.

Enter Mark Elliott, smart, charismatic and with a nose for an opportunity. He had already made a fortune as an investor and executive at Computershare and saw class actions as another business opportunity. Elliott wanted to redefine these big cases with a business model that was clever, unique and – as we will see – completely unlawful.

He set up Elliott Legal, described as 'a boutique law firm specialising in . . . the conduct of complex class-action litigation'. In the beginning, Elliott bought small packages of shares in 165 publicly listed companies and lay in wait to launch actions.

Under this model, Elliott, as a shareholder, would be a plaintiff (payment one), his firm would run the action (payment two) and he would act as the funder, entitled to a settlement percentage (payment three). He would tell potential clients he was driven by a sense of justice and felt like he was 'swimming with sharks' in the deadly sea of class-action litigation.

As some of his cases bounced around the courts, judge after judge pointed out there were significant conflicts of interest. So Elliott refined his model. He would move much of the grunt legal work to another firm and finance the process through Australian Funding Partners Limited (AFPL), of which he owned 76 per cent. The remainder was owned by the wife of Norman O'Bryan, SC.

Elliott launched 18 class actions but one that appeared particularly juicy was Banksia Securities, a Kyabram company that funded property and development projects. It had raised $663 million from 15,622 investors (mostly country retirees) when, in 2012, it sank like the *Titanic*.

Within months, Elliott began proceedings against Banksia on behalf of the investors. One was former nurse Wendy Botsman, who had invested about $24,000. Another was former bus driver Keith Pitman who, even in his late 70s, would stand in the main streets of Ballarat for hours to sell RSL badges for the Anzac Day Appeal.

O'Bryan was the senior counsel and stood to make millions through the Banksia claim. When Chief Justice Anne Ferguson said

O'Bryan could not act as the lead barrister while his family owned shares in the funding company, he promised to divest that interest.

The broader issue was whether there was actually a need for a class action because receivers had been appointed to recover as much money as possible, funds that would be reduced once Elliott took a giant bite.

The case rolled on and there was finally a settlement of $64 million (after the receivers took their fees). Then it was up to a court to decide what was a fair slice for Elliott's funding company. In such a case, the court can appoint a contradictor – a person to examine all the bills.

In January 2018, AFPL argued in the Supreme Court that as they had done everything by the book, appointing a contradictor would waste the money of the poor victims and delay payment.

Justice Clyde Croft, believing that O'Bryan and Elliott were telling the truth, found a contradictor would be a 'waste of limited resources'. On 30 January 2018, he approved the $64 million settlement and ordered Elliott's company be paid $12.8 million (plus GST) and the legal team $4.75 million (plus GST).

Except Pitman smelt a rat. During subsequent hearings, he would rise early, pack a lunch and take a train to the Supreme Court to make sure he wasn't railroaded. Now 84, he had $20,000 invested in Banksia. As one of 10 victims on a committee to oversee the return of investors' money, he saw receivers take $11 million, leaving $64 million. When Elliott's team wanted at least $20 million: 'I felt this was too steep. It was too much. Elliott had barged his way into this case and then wanted a lot of money for doing very little,' Pitman says.

'When Banksia went under, it was devastating but then to find out about conflicts of interest and lawyers looking after themselves, instead of the people they're supposed to be helping, has been unbelievable.'

Botsman wasn't comfortable either. Unfortunately for Elliott and O'Bryan, her son, Chris, was a lawyer, then living in Sydney, who specialised in white-collar crime. He was also a heavyweight, having worked for the Financial Conduct Authority and the Australian Securities and Investments Commission. He thought the settlement of $64 million was too low and the amount given to the funders and lawyers outrageously high.

Chris asked questions on behalf of his mother and received rubbery responses. So he did what good lawyers do: he went to court, arguing that a contradictor should be appointed.

Here, Elliott and O'Bryan made a fatal miscalculation, deciding to bully their way to victory. They went to court to stop Wendy Botsman, threatening her with financial ruin through inflated court costs, saying she could be forced to pay $5289 a day if her action failed.

Even though they were told to send any documents to her lawyer and son, Chris, they had a process server turn up at her house, an act clearly designed to intimidate. It was the legal version of a horse's head in the bed.

She was asked to provide details on the value of her house and her assets. And so the Banksia class-action lawyers – her lawyers – were using the precise tactics class actions were meant to stop: threatening individual victims with financial ruin if they took on the big guys.

'It was very stressful,' says Botsman. 'But Chris was very reassuring.'

She says if her son and his colleagues had not worked for nothing, no one would have stopped the class-action lawyers' scandalous payment.

The bullies failed and the Court of Appeal ordered a contradictor be appointed. The appointment of Peter Jopling, QC as the contradictor would prove to be a masterstroke.

Like O'Bryan, Jopling had been a brilliant Melbourne University law student, becoming an associate to High Court judges. Like O'Bryan, he was a senior barrister at the Bar and an Order of Australia recipient.

The two senior lawyers had contrasting styles. O'Bryan was a bulldozer. His approach was to set out his version of the facts, suggest his view was the only viable version and that anyone who thought differently was an idiot. Jopling used the 'helicopter view', explaining his case in broad terms before returning to forensic detail.

Elliott, O'Bryan and junior barrister Michael Symons tried to thwart Jopling's investigation by threatening him with costs, providing vague answers and delaying the production of documents.

'If O'Bryan was ever challenged, he would always double down,' a colleague says.

Jopling was exactly the wrong type of person to bully. Behind the scenes, some legal heavyweights tried to persuade Jopling not to rock the boat, but he would not be deterred.

For smart lawyers, the Elliott team was particularly dumb. They could have negotiated a compromise. They could have said that because Botsman was being so stubborn with her court action, they would take a smaller slice of the pie to allow their clients to get their money. Instead, it was the courtroom version of the Gunfight at the O.K. Corral.

But one key player was not there. The architect of the whole dodgy scheme had died unexpectedly. On 13 February, Mark Elliott was found dead on a property in Flinders. A police report found there was no foul play. The family went to great lengths to suggest Elliott died in an off-road single vehicle accident. In fact, he had taken his own life.

Coroner Caitlin English found the 58-year-old shot himself in the neck with a shotgun. The family refused to cooperate with the coronial inquest.

'I am satisfied that at the time of his death, Mr Elliott's mental health was affected by ongoing legal proceedings regarding his conduct in the Banksia Securities class action, which may have led to a recognition or suspicion that he would likely lose his career and be liable for significant damages. The same litigation was a significant factor in the death of another lawyer involved with the case.'

Over the previous month he had stockpiled sleeping pills, first gaining a prescription and a repeat by saying he was travelling to the US and wanted them for jet lag. Then he returned to the same doctor saying he had lost the prescription to gain another.

On 12 February he was taken to hospital with symptoms of an overdose. The following day he was released, drove to his Flinders property and he shot himself.

Coroner English also found another lawyer sucked into the Elliott get-rich(er)-quick scheme Peter Trimbos took his own life by lying down on railway tracks.

'I am satisfied that at the time of his death, Mr Trimbos's mental health was affected by ongoing proceedings regarding his conduct in the Banksia Securities proceeding, which may have included a recognition or suspicion that his career and reputation would suffer irreparable damage and the possibility that he would be liable to pay significant damage,' she found.

On 27 July, in front of Supreme Court Justice John Dixon, the final act in this legal tragedy began. There were 13 lawyers, including five silks, representing all parties. Legal fees were likely to run at more than $100,000 a day.

In one document, O'Bryan quipped he charged less than Jopling. The difference was Jopling was earning his fee. When Jopling took the stage (it was a remote hearing due to lockdown), he told Justice Dixon he would provide a helicopter view. In reality, he took a flame-thrower to O'Bryan, Symons and the late Elliott. He told the court the team had spent years deceiving courts and had misled seven Supreme Court judges.

'It was Mr Elliott's idea. Mr O'Bryan joined him as an equal co-venturer and Mr Symons was their willing and active recruit,' Jopling said.

'The most striking feature of the course of conduct they pursued was that it involved each of them as lawyers acting dishonestly and without any regard to their duties, to their clients or their paramount duty to this court.

'The business model of AFPL and the lawyer parties was to make demands for costs that had no basis in fact and then to come up with bills to support these demands . . . This was a party like no other.'

In his clipped and cultured voice, Jopling explained how Elliott wanted to charge $20 million and how legal bills were fabricated. He even read a text from Elliott of plans to 'double-cross' the receivers who had done the bulk of the work.

'Whenever anybody got in the way of the $20 million that they were trying to seize for themselves from this litigation, Elliott, O'Bryan and Symons turned to threats and intimidation.'

Jopling said that far from getting nearly $20 million, they should get nothing, pay compensation to their clients and shoulder the legal costs.

The question was how would the brilliant bare-knuckle O'Bryan, the dux of every class, the lawyer who always doubled down, respond?

No one saw it coming. Trapped in Jopling's vice-like grip, O'Bryan 'tapped the mat' and conceded. O'Bryan's lawyer, David Batt, QC, told the court his client would not dispute the claims against him, would accept any financial punishment and would not pursue any fees for the Banksia claim. He also accepted he could no longer practise as a barrister. A few days later, he returned his Order of Australia.

Symons followed, issuing a similar statement accepting that he was finished as a barrister.

Why did O'Bryan surrender? Perhaps, he finally saw that, blinded by greed, he had failed to act in the interest of his clients. Perhaps he saw a legal bill of more than $3 million at the end of a trial that he was bound to lose. Or perhaps he knew that to try to maintain the Elliott-inspired fantasy would require him to give perjured evidence in the court where his father and grandfather had presided with such distinction.

Elliott, the man who believed he had all the answers until he didn't, was not alive to hear how Justice Dixon described him.

'Mark Elliott held in contemptuous disregard his clients, the Court, his colleagues, and the administration of justice. He was driven by greed and prepared to do anything to obtain financial reward for himself, without concern as to whether his actions were lawful.

'He was an odious individual who heaped shame on the legal profession, and the exposure of his conduct should act as a lesson to all lawyers that conduct of this kind will be found out, and will not be countenanced.

'As will emerge through these reasons, this strong language was warranted. Mark Elliott was the architect of one of the darkest chapters in the legal history of this State.

'He fraudulently inflated his claim for fees at the time of the Partial Settlement, and encouraged O'Bryan and Symons to do the same in respect of their fees in the Trust Co Settlement.

'He destroyed relevant documents to avoid disclosure of his conduct. He swore false affidavits. He attempted to intimidate litigants, unrepresented group members and other officers of the court, to pursue his own financial interests and conceal his wrongdoing. He provided false information and instructions to AFPL's solicitors, intending to hamper the Contradictor's investigations.'

He ordered the main offenders pay $11 million in compensation and $10 million in costs.

O'Bryan and Symons immediately filed for bankruptcy.

VICELAND: LIFE AND DEATH IN SIN CITY

The rivalry between Australia's two great cities is friendly, often passionate and never-ending.

Melbourne wins on sport. The AFL grand final and Melbourne Cup beats the City to Surf and the Golden Slipper by some distance. In fairness, the Gay and Lesbian Mardi Gras just shades Moomba as a spectacle (although dressing as a chicken to jump into the Yarra as part of the Birdman Rally must surely soon become an Olympic sport).

Sydney has a better bridge, a better harbour and better oysters. Melbourne has better bars, better coffee and better laneways. But there is one area where Sydney traditionally has Melbourne well and truly covered — corruption. At its worst there was not an area of power in that great city not influenced by colourful people who should inhabit prison rather than the celebrity pages of certain toadying newspapers.

The intriguing three-part ABC documentary *Exposed: The Ghost Train Fire* is a detailed analysis of the 1979 Sydney Luna Park fire which killed six children and a young father. It also shows a justice system utterly bankrupt.

Exposed goes into the sort of forensic detail you would expect of police. Instead, within hours, the actual police (wrongly) concluded the fire was due to an electrical fault and then deliberately ignored or concealed evidence that didn't fit their theory. They bulldozed the site, destroying the crime scene and any clues that could point to the truth.

As *Exposed* reveals, photos of the ghost train ablaze show the lights and electric sign operating.

It is inconceivable senior NSW Police botched this investigation so badly. The alternative is obvious – whoever ordered the arson was on the protected list, and back then, there was no one more protected than Abraham Gilbert Saffron, the man they called Mr Sin.

The policeman put in charge of the Luna Park investigation was Detective Inspector Doug Knight, who was neither an arson nor homicide expert. Five years earlier a royal commission found him to be a liar and in business with a Saffron associate. The only cop who apparently didn't know Knight was a crook was Commissioner Cec Abbott, who said in 1982: 'In my own personal opinion (he) is a highly intellectual person and one who performs most efficiently.' (More on Cec later.)

Can there be a worse crime than covering up the murder of seven people, including six children? After his pathetic investigation Knight was twice promoted, retiring a superintendent.

Years later the National Crime Authority reviewed the Luna Park investigation. It found: 'Luna Park, it was alleged, had been coveted by Saffron for over 20 years and the fire in the ghost train had been lit as a trigger to evict the incumbent tenants and gain control of the park lease for himself.'

It found insufficient evidence to charge but did pinch him for tax evasion, finally sending Abe to jail where he belonged.

Saffron built a vice empire on a triangular business model – the three points were bribery, blackmail and arson. He organised sex, often with underage boys and girls, secretly photographing patrons for later use against them. He paid bribes to police – $750 per club for local police and $5000 a week for senior police – and was so brazen he repeatedly visited the bent NSW Deputy Commissioner Bill Allen at headquarters.

Victoria Police mounted a secret surveillance operation (without telling NSW cops) after being tipped off Allen would leave his office at the same time each week to take a slice of the bribe money (Saffron was only one of many contributors) to be distributed to key politicians. As predicted he left police HQ at the exact nominated time and was followed as he wandered with lunchtime crowds in Macquarie Street on his way to Parliament House. Allen was part of the Luna Park cover-up.

The third point of the triangle was arson. Seven Saffron properties, bars, massage parlours and nightclubs caught fire between 1980 and 1982. At inquest he was implicated in four and – surprise, surprise – the authorities failed to prosecute.

Instead of trying to conceal his smouldering reputation, he used it to make even more money. One honest (and tough) Melbourne businessman bought a two-star hotel in Sydney for $2 million, unaware it was a Saffron property. Three days before settlement, Saffron reached out to him, saying the new price was $2.25 million. When the Melbourne man mentioned the iron-clad contract, Saffron responded: 'What if there was a fire? What if one of your hotels burnt down? Or more than one? People could be hurt, businesses closed, insurance premiums could go through the roof. It would be a tragedy.' The Melbourne man paid the extra $225,000.

Here is just a small personal example of how the Sydney System worked.

A group of NSW Criminal Intelligence police, sick of the fix, started an illegal bugging campaign to gather information on protected crooks. One was drug boss Robert 'Aussie Bob' Trimbole, a likely target of a proposed royal commission. The tapes picked up chatty conversations with a NSW Police officer Trimbole called 'The Gardener'. Trimbole was fishing. In multiple conversations to multiple sources, he asked if there would be a commission.

He fled Australia in 1981. Three weeks later, a royal commission was established under the gun barrel-straight Justice Donald Stewart, a former NSW policeman who saw the corruption first-hand.

On 23 June 1983, I published a story highlighting the questionable relationship between Trimbole and The Gardener. It was not a big story in Melbourne but in Sydney, they went nuts. I was accused in Parliament of having a pathological hatred of NSW Police. Assistant Commissioner Cec Abbott was livid, saying it was an outrageous lie but, in the interests of justice, he would order an exhaustive investigation.

On 27 June 1983, I was interviewed by two stern-looking NSW Internal Affairs detectives who flew all the way from Sydney. They walked into the Russell Street press rooms just after 2 pm. They managed to ask a total of seven related questions – four regarding the source of the story and three the identity of the alleged corrupt leak. What I did tell them was Trimbole had been tipped off by a second source. 'This information, plus the evidence about The Gardener, was given to a senior NSW policeman who destroyed this evidence,' I told them.

They asked his name and I declined to give it, although it was obviously someone in Criminal Intelligence. They looked at each other, put their pens away, closed their government-issue folders, packed up their portable typewriter, made their excuses and left.

The typed record of interview went just over one page.

Here was not one but two bombshells: a middle-ranking cop had buddied up to Australia's number one drug boss and a senior officer had covered it up. They could have checked files, seized diaries, looked for whistleblowers, identified witnesses at a bar used for secret meetings and run a comprehensive investigation.

What did they do? They closed the file in three days.

On 1 July, Abbott released a statement that after receiving a report (they interviewed me for 20 minutes on the Monday, he got the report on Thursday) the matter was closed: 'In summary no evidence of a substantive nature was produced which would prove such an allegation.'

Abbott may have considered the matter closed but Justice Stewart didn't. Less than two weeks later I was in his witness box at a secret session in Sydney. I told him Trimbole had been illegally bugged talking to The Gardener and gave him 27 pages of handwritten notes of the conversations. The police who bugged the buggers gave evidence saying a senior Criminal Intelligence officer had played The Gardener the tapes and showed him the transcripts, blowing the secret bugging operation.

The Gardener gave evidence to the commission on Monday 26 November 1984. He entered as a high-flyer (NSW Police had wanted him to be the liaison officer for the Stewart commission). He left the witness box with his reputation in tatters. He retired on the Friday. He told Justice Stewart his relationship with Trimbole was perfectly professional and conducted with the knowledge of then Assistant Commissioner Abbott.

The Gardener produced his typewritten notes, all signed Sergeant First Class. The trouble was that, at the time, he was Sergeant Second Class. 'He could offer no explanation as to why he would misrepresent his rank on the notes,' Stewart found. But I can: he faked them.

No charges were ever laid against anyone for accepting bribes from Aussie Bob. Trimbole, Australia's most wanted fugitive, died of natural causes in Spain in 1987, a free man.

Saffron, meanwhile, had senior police, premiers, federal politicians and judges on his payroll. As an old man he tried to use his power to rewrite history. He started to donate dirty money to charity and sue anyone who called him Mr Sin, including me.

At the same time court records started to 'disappear' from official holdings. It was as if it never happened. But it did.

Saffron died in 2006 a gangster, a parasite and a killer. The world is a better place with his passing.

THE BUSH PLOT THAT COST A MAN HIS COUNTRY

When this reporter met his future wife we were both in high school. I was the new boy, having transferred from the sort of northern suburban institution that offered drug trafficking, identity fraud and car re-birthing as elective subjects. She was the popular type, a goody-goody who played softball and still had friends from church group – God knows why.

Think James Dean and Doris Day and you're on the money.

It was the first Year 12 class of the year (actually Form Six) and we had never spoken when I slipped her a note, proposing marriage. She threw it in the bin. She has always been neat.

This to me was a temporary setback and I took on a Pepe Le Pew-type pursuit which lasted several years. Eventually she found the combination of brooding good looks, raw sensuality, rapier wit and humility irresistible and retrospectively accepted the original proposal. Not before time she realised she had stumbled on the equivalent of the Hope Diamond in a Two Dollar Shop.

The wedding reception cost $20 a head, which included a three-course meal, the band, sherry (dry and sweet) and generous cheese platters.

The police reporters were assigned a room without carpet so it could be hosed out at the end of proceedings.

Some use a more direct path to impress a lady. Like the drug dealer who asked his girlfriend if she fancied some chilli crab for tea. When she said the idea sounded 'grouse' he booked two first-class tickets to Singapore so they could have the real thing.

Which brings us to the curious case of Julian Mathias Buchwald, a young man so desperate to make his younger girlfriend fall in love, he orchestrated a bizarre kidnap plot that left her traumatised and him with a criminal record – and without a home.

Back in 2008, Buchwald was a 22-year-old Gippsland timber logger besotted with his girlfriend, then aged just 17. They met at their local church with the overly excitable Buchwald pressuring her to marry as soon as she turned 18.

Not unreasonably, the object of his affection was keen to finish high school. Wisely, the local pastor suggested the couple take a time-out and they stepped back for about a month.

Clearly, this jacked off the lumberjack who hatched a plan he hoped would leave the teenager (who we will call Holly) so much in love she would swoon for this loon near Nar Nar Goon.

In March he asked her parents if he could take Holly on a picnic to his folks' sprawling rural property. The plan, he told them, was to plant trees and walk to a waterfall. Harmless enough, you would think.

Ever the romantic, he later claimed he had planned a treasure hunt, with the prize a handmade wooden platter she would find near the waterfall where they would have yummy sandwiches he had prepared.

What he didn't say was that on the morning of the date, he went to the property to hide gloves, a balaclava, a jacket, a yellow blanket, ropes, duct tape and military pants.

He left her in his four-wheel drive on a pretext (he had planted a deer skin near the track and said he was going to look for the 'startled' wildlife). He returned wearing fresh clothes and a balaclava, pretending to be a crazy bush-bound kidnapper. She was hog-tied, blindfolded with duct tape, chucked in the back seat and driven six hours to the Alpine National Park.

When he reached the Buchan Headwaters Wilderness area, he dumped her on the ground then he hid the car about 20 metres away. He did not know the area well, which meant in more ways than one, he had no Buchan idea.

This poor girl listened as her kidnapper dug holes to bury evidence. She thought she was to be raped and buried alive, a reasonable fear when the man in the balaclava used his knife to cut off her clothes.

Buchwald then cut off his clothes and lay down two metres away. He called out in a weak voice, pretending he was also a victim of the kidnapping, before untying her. He had scratched his head when he dumped the car and decided to leave the blood on his face to support his story. When she saw him she thought he looked like Dracula.

He urged her to grab what she could and run, shoving a sleeping bag into her arms. They plunged into a freezing river and kept going. She soon found she was carrying a sleeping bag cover containing a toothbrush and half a pillowcase filled with desiccated coconut.

The bizarre Buchwald had a knife, a shovel and one jar each of peanut butter and tahini – a condiment made of ground sesame seeds. (While such an exotic spread may be valued in a well-stocked pantry, it is hardly a priority pick for a Bear Grylls's Survival Pack.)

Buchwald told Holly he bravely fought two kidnappers until they smashed him in the head with a metal rod, then stuffed him in the boot, leaving him unconscious and vomiting blood.

For the next week, they stumbled barefoot and naked around the bush to avoid their 'kidnappers'. It rained as they repeatedly criss-crossed a freezing creek, sheltering at night in the sleeping bag he said was dropped by their tormentors.

The fleeing couple took the most rugged routes to deter the non-existent pursuers. One night he suggested they have sex to keep warm. She refused. On night four, he said as they were likely to perish in the cold they should marry 'in the eyes of God' before they died. Again she refused, saying her parents would not approve.

Realising his plan was now as damp as the sleeping bag, he returned to the dumping point, dug up their damaged clothes after claiming he had stumbled on the kidnappers' hidey-hole.

Now semi-dressed, they walked out of the bush to be picked up by a passing farmer in a utility. Naturally it didn't take police long to break down this ridiculous story and Buchwald was charged with kidnapping and making a false report.

While on bail he decided to disappear. So where would an Australian resident of German descent decide to hide? India, of course.

Buchwald, a blue-eyed blond, obtained a false passport, dyed his hair jet black and covered himself in more fake tan than an Oaks Day starlet before boarding a Chennai-bound flight. Indian authorities saw through his disguise – not surprising – and he had to return to Australia.

At his plea, the County Court heard he suffered a pervasive developmental disorder, which meant he struggled to empathise with others. He was sentenced to five years and three months, for kidnap, making false report and jumping bail.

In 2014 the Immigration and Border Protection Department told Buchwald his Permanent Residency Visa was under review. Buchwald responded by showing he had job offers on release, a spotless record before his crazy kidnap ploy and his life, friends and family were Australian. His only knowledge of German history, it would appear, came from re-runs of *Hogan's Heroes*.

His pleas were rejected and in October that year, immigration minister Scott Morrison cancelled his visa.

Buchwald appealed to the Federal Court before Justice Mordy Bromberg (a fair man awarded three Brownlow Medal votes in his days as a St Kilda footballer).

But there was no case as the minister acted within the law.

If Buchwald had applied for citizenship before his hare-brained love scheme, it would have been granted and then residency would not be an issue.

But he didn't and [in 2017] he was chucked on a plane and dumped in Germany. He speaks only English, has no German friends, limited career prospects and a seemingly bleak future.

Buchwald was rightly sentenced to a long stint in jail for a crime that was stupid, callous and brutal. Having served his time, he is now being punished again by being stripped of his true nationality.

Buchwald is as Australian as an emu and this would be officially recognised if not for a quirk of timing. His family settled in Australia years earlier but he was born in Germany in 1985 when they returned for an extended visit. His sister, who was born two years earlier, is an Australian citizen yet Julian is treated as a foreigner. Same parents, same home, same upbringing – different nationality. How can that be?

While it is certainly legal, is it fair?

TERROR IN THE HEART OF FRANKSTON

It was the rain that dark winter that chilled your soul. Not that you were caught in the storm – it was worse than that. It was the rain that transported you more than 20 kilometres away to Frankston, where homicide detectives were in a race against time to find the man who turned killer whenever the weather turned nasty.

Paul Charles Denyer, 21, selected those days, believing the rain would wash away clues and keep potential witnesses indoors.

He had already struck twice in the weeks before the storm hit the verandah that Friday. No one knew he had already set a trap for his third victim. He had cut two holes in a cyclone fence along a track between golf courses off Skye Road. Then he sat in his car and waited. It was Year 12 student Natalie Russell who walked down the track, just 250 metres from home when she was grabbed. Her body was discovered in one of Denyer's lairs. It seemed the killer had escaped again to hunt more victims.

Early that Sunday, the phone rang. The person on the other end didn't introduce himself. He didn't need to. All he said was: 'We've got him.'

Denyer killed Elizabeth Stevens, 18, on Friday, 11 June; Deborah Fream, 22, on Thursday, 8 July; and Natalie Russell, 17, on Friday, 30 July.

In seven weeks he terrorised Frankston. Then premier Jeff Kennett recalls: 'You could have thrown a match and the place would've exploded. There was outrage, but more importantly there was this genuine, genuine fear.'

For the last year [2022] or so award-winning documentary maker Terry Carlyon and I have retraced the events of 30 years ago, talking to the police who found him, the pathologists who discovered key evidence and the judge who sentenced him, for the program *No Mercy, No Remorse*. We haven't attempted to reconstruct the crimes or speculate on Denyer's motives. We look at the investigation, from the moment detectives saw the first victim until the killer's sentencing.

It was seven weeks in Frankston that won't leave anyone connected with the case. As Natalie Russell's best friend, Karen, said: 'There isn't a woman in Frankston who doesn't check her back seat before getting into a car.'

Some police involved I consider close friends, and yet I was unaware how affected they remain by Denyer and his crimes. Perhaps because they had to remain clinical they weren't able to release their emotions or maybe, as trial judge Justice Frank Vincent says: 'I don't believe that those who work in that area for any length of time emerge undamaged.'

Most of us from time to time work under pressure. Most of us from time to time are under professional stress. Now think of the Homicide Squad detectives trained to be methodical, to take their time, to collate everything with an eye to presenting a watertight case to a jury.

Then there was the winter of 1993, when every hour, every day without an arrest took them closer to the next murder. They were dealing with families in grief and a community in fear. There were no mobile phones to check, no CCTV footage to scan. They reviewed hundreds of suspects and thousands of tip-offs.

And then it would rain.

It began when Peter Halloran, then head of the Homicide Squad, viewed the body of the first victim, Elizabeth Stevens. The fatal wounds made him fear the worst.

He told his superiors he suspected the killer would strike again, and soon. Some thought he'd watched too many movies. But Halloran was right.

Rod Wilson was then the senior sergeant in charge of Homicide Squad crew seven. There may have been murder detectives as good as Wilson but none better, and he knew the stakes couldn't be higher. The discovery of Natalie Russell's body was the lowest point of the investigation. 'I couldn't sleep a wink. The reality was he had gone again and we had missed our opportunity. It was gut-wrenching.'

Then, the breakthrough, from an unlikely source.

At about 2.50 pm on 30 July, Russell had left school on the last day of term; about the same time, postie Vikki Collins saw a battered yellow Toyota sedan parked in Skye Road with a missing rear numberplate. When she passed she glanced in her rear mirror and saw a driver with a chubby face slinking down in the driver's seat, trying to hide.

Collins noticed a student walking towards her. It was Russell, who was about to turn down a track between two golf courses into the trap Denyer had already set. Those were the days before mobile phones and if Collins had waited until she had finished her round to ring police, it would have been too late. Instead she drove into a private driveway, knocked on the door and asked a woman if she could use the phone to call police.

Within 15 minutes, two marked units arrived. When Denyer saw police while returning to his car after killing Russell, he put his bloodied hands under his jumper and walked home. This was the first time Denyer was placed at a crime scene. 'It was the golden nugget of information,' Wilson recalls.

The day after Russell's murder Denyer was again on the hunt, parking next to a woman napping in her car in a shopping centre. He was only foiled when her friends returned.

When Wilson knocked on the suspect's door and was invited in, he had a 'gut feel' Denyer was the killer. He was happy to go to the station to answer questions without asking why he was a person of interest.

'He was so enthusiastic to play the game, to be important,' Wilson recalls.

Scooped into the investigation was local detective Darren O'Loughlin, part of the most famous police family in Melbourne, with 18 members who have served as sworn or unsworn members. When O'Loughlin, a practising Christian, silently prayed for the truth to be found, Denyer looked at him and said: 'That man is trying to get into my head.'

He said the expression on Denyer's face was darkly distorted. 'I saw the evil those girls must have seen.'

Wilson led the interview and Denyer answered questions easily – too easily. He knew where he was at the exact time of every shooting, leading Wilson to believe Denyer rehearsed his alibis.

After 1500 questions, Wilson asked about fresh and healing cuts on Denyer's hands. Denyer rolled out his prepared version of events. For the first time Wilson called him out as a liar.

At the autopsy they found a piece of skin that would match the fresh wound on Denyer's hand.

During a break Denyer asked O'Loughlin about his faith and then, according to the Frankston detective: 'He said, "I did it," and I said, "Did what?" And he said, "I committed the murders, I committed all three of them".'

I asked Rod how he listened to the worst humanity has to offer without betraying the slightest emotion. (During the interview he occasionally stopped to flick imaginary lint from his suit jacket, giving him a pause to gather for the next question. It was like a boxer who moves away from an opponent before re-engaging.)

'If we were to blow that investigation because we felt frustrated or did something that would jeopardise that in any way, then you couldn't live with yourself. The end game is the only thing that matters. Getting this guy to court. Getting him convicted and getting him off the streets is the only goal we have.'

Denyer pleaded guilty, and Justice Vincent sentenced him to life with no minimum. As a defence lawyer and later Supreme Court judge, Vincent has seen more killers than just about anyone in Victoria. In sentencing Denyer, he thought of the victims: 'There were the young women who were killed, and their families and those around their families and those involved in the hunt for the killer, but there were many thousands of women and others who had to live with this fear.' The Court of Appeal overturned the sentence and gave Denyer a minimum of 30 years. In April 2023 he became eligible for parole, his application was knocked back but he is free to apply again.

David Limbrick is a Liberal Democrat state MP with a strong civil libertarian philosophy. He was also Natalie Russell's boyfriend. The crime and the aftermath made him drop out of university and lose his way. More than a year later he decided not to let Denyer ruin another life and returned to study, married and had three children. Natalie's death has never left him, which is why he sponsored a petition asking the government to pass legislation to keep Denyer in jail, reflecting Vincent's original sentence.

As Bernie Rankin, then a Frankston detective senior sergeant and later head of the Homicide Squad, says: '[Denyer] will never not be a risk to the community. Never.'

FROM RUSSIA WITH LOVE

There is a quaint BBC television program called *Antiques Roadshow* where snoozers produce various artefacts accompanied by stories on how they became family heirlooms.

Sometimes the owner is told they have just arrived on easy street (like the bloke with a metal detector who found a Roman helmet worth more than $4 million), while others are informed their Ming vase was actually made by Frank Ming, the retired stationmaster from Scunthorpe.

We all have yarns that become part of family folklore (indeed, my own father nearly started a war in Pakistan over a wayward soccer ball, but that is an entirely different story).

Which brings us to the most unfortunate John William Henderson, a gentleman formerly known as William Marijancevic, who appears to have been duped by a fantastic fable told around the kitchen table.

Hendo had the misfortune of being caught up in a raid by Cairns police on room 241 of the Reef Palm Motel way back in April 2002. Police were busy arresting a woman with two plastic bags containing about 60 grams of cocaine when Henderson poked his head around the corner.

Police found he was carrying a bum bag containing $5320. The curious cops checked his hire car outside and found 23.3 grams of cannabis plus a sports bag with $592,600 in $50 and $100 bills. For some reason they jumped to the conclusion he was a drug dealer and seized the lot.

Henderson argued that while he had an extensive rap-sheet, this time he was an innocent bystander with a perfectly good explanation for the cash.

And this is it.

While he is a colourful crook, with 56 convictions in Queensland and Victoria for violence, drugs, theft and receiving stolen property dating from 1963, his family history is even more intriguing.

A couple of relatives are known to police and have entertained detectives with improbable alibis over the years. One was caught tunnelling into a Melbourne bank where a policeman (accidentally) stood on his nose as the suspect peeked through the broken floor – a painful example of a Rozzer on your Schnozzer. The accused later argued he was a good Samaritan who entered the tunnel to persuade a friend not to break into the bank.

He was acquitted.

According to Marijancevic legend, their forefathers were Croatian gypsies who became confidantes of Russian nobility during the 1917 Revolution.

'My mother and father told me stories when I was growing up about how my great-grandfather helped transport members of the Russian royal family across borders and received the jewellery as a reward,' Henderson explained. In other words, it was a case of the Tsar saying Ta to his Grandpa.

Around December 1996, while visiting his father in the Victorian hamlet of Picola, Dad produced a box from under his bed containing earrings, a bracelet, a necklace and a brooch – all gold and diamond-encrusted. Then Franjo Marijancevic instructed 'Look after your family.'

Knowing the history of gypsies, tramps and thieves, the dutiful son placed the antique jewellery in an ANZ Collins Street bank safety deposit box in his wife's name. He did not tell his sister or his two brothers he was holding the family fortune to be distributed at a later date. He reasoned that silence, like a rare royal Russian bracelet, is only valuable when it is golden.

After his father's death five years later he showed his siblings the hidden treasure and they decided it should be valued for sale. They chose a city jeweller because, Henderson would later claim, his shop was the nearest to the Collins Street bank where the gear was held.

In December 2001, the jeweller sketched the items, estimating a wholesale value between $600,000 and $700,000 with a retail price of $1 million. This was a pleasant surprise, as Henderson assumed the price was between $10,000 and $20,000.

Within weeks a man called Daniel, who Henderson says he didn't know, rang about the jewellery. How he knew it was for sale or found the phone number is one of those mysteries within a mystery but let's not get bogged down in details.

Meanwhile, Henderson and his siblings decided to invest in the Queensland real estate market, choosing a Kuranda property. He travelled to Queensland several times to negotiate with a local who stood firm on the price.

In February 2002, Henderson and his wife flew to Cairns for further discussions and fortuitously it coincided with Daniel re-emerging to buy the jewels for $620,000.

When the man-without-a-surname produced his chequebook, Henderson demanded cash. On 12 March 2002, Daniel fronted with the money in a fruit box (naturally).

Henderson and his wife counted the cash and wrote a receipt but unfortunately didn't keep a copy. He jotted Daniel's surname and telephone number on the nearest piece of paper, which happened to be a $50 note. Sadly, the details were lost when police seized the money.

So while Henderson remembers the date of the deal, the name of the dealer, like some members of the Russian royal family, managed to escape.

The Hendersons wandered to banks and a casino to exchange many of Daniel's $50 notes for $100 ones before placing the loot in the safety deposit box.

Cynics would claim this was a laundering operation but he explained he found the cash 'far too bulky'.

He had a fair point as the fruit box had to be filled with 12,400 notes, or a single stack 135 centimetres high.

Flush with funds, Henderson wanted to seal the deal over the Kuranda property and set up a meeting with the local seller in a Cairns shopping centre coffee shop just weeks after Daniel delivered. He planned to produce the cash to negotiate a discount on the property price.

This may seem a strange way to do business but Henderson was never big on paperwork, which may explain his failure to file a tax return for nearly 10 years.

He would tell the tax authorities that while he was on a social security pension, he enjoyed a remarkable run at the track, the casino and even won about $70,000 on Powerball. He supplemented this income by investing in the apparently lucrative bric-a-brac market, although the only proof he could produce was for the $8500 sale of an antique clock.

He was eventually hit with a back tax bill of more than $1 million, a judgement he found most unfair.

While he was explaining himself to the tax department his lawyers were arguing their way through a series of hearings all the way to the High Court that the seizure of the Cairns cash was a wicked injustice.

It would take four hearings, 12 years and thousands of words but Henderson's argument was simple: the money was not tainted and not even taxable, as it came from 'long-standing family heirlooms'. The trouble is that judges tend to be pedants when it comes to pendants, particularly those of a supposed antique Russian variety.

It quickly became clear there were as many holes in Henderson's story as there were in Nicholas II post-Revolution.

First, you might remember, Henderson said when he received the jewellery in 1996 he placed it in an ANZ bank safety deposit box. He also said he chose a nearby jeweller because it was around the corner from the bank.

Bank records showed his wife rented the safety deposit box well after that date. Indeed, they had sourced such a box on 13 March 2002 – the day after the mysterious Daniel turned up with his mysterious fruit box with the mysterious $620,000 in cash.

It was also months after they had the long-standing family heirlooms valued, which knocks down the claim they picked the closest jeweller available.

The jeweller gave evidence in an early hearing that he remembered the Henderson jewels because it is 'rare to see items of such quality'. He opined they were of 'central European origin'. The jewellery, he recalled, was in a red velvet bag inside a red box.

Very royal indeed.

As the case dragged on through different courts, the jeweller could not be cross-examined due to alcohol-related brain damage. Sadly, he could no longer tell the Crown Jewels from a Crown Lager. Luckily he still had the sketches of the jewellery he valued back in 2001.

The state gave the sketches to Brisbane valuer and jeweller Kenneth Penfold for a second opinion. Mr Penfold concluded that, far from being antique contraband, the booty was manufactured after 1950. So unless the Tsar stumbled on a time machine, the romantic gypsy Marijancevic yarn was a fabrication.

Eventually the High Court ruled Queensland authorities were right to seize the cash as an asset of crime and awarded costs against Henderson. Which left him madder than Rasputin when the final answer to his appeal was – *nyet*.

A MILLION REASONS TO FIND A SERIAL KILLER

By the time Homicide arrived at the unmade road it was already a cold trail – but now, 37 years later, police have a million reasons to believe they may catch a serial killer suspected of murdering six women taken from Melbourne streets.

It is perhaps Victoria's most baffling murder mystery – six females, aged from 14 to 73, all grabbed seemingly at random in an 18-month period and dumped in scrub. All were on foot when abducted from or near main roads; all but one in broad daylight.

In each case experts could not establish a cause of death and personal items had been removed from the victims, either to conceal identity or to be kept as trophies by the killer.

By the time the first body was found at Tynong North, on 6 December 1980, the killer had struck five times – if, that is, there was only one murderer.

There were several homicide investigations, followed by a taskforce probe, Canadian and US crime profile examinations and two Criminal Intelligence reviews. More than 2000 people were interviewed, 11,400 pages of notes taken and detailed coronial inquests held. But no charges were laid.

Now police will offer a $1 million reward ($6 million in total) for information they hope will lead to the person or persons responsible for the murders of two women whose bodies were found in Frankston and four found in Tynong North.

The head of the Homicide Squad's Cold Case Team, Detective Senior Sergeant Peter Trichias, knows that rewards work in seemingly dead-end cases. He says cold cases can be solved when alibi witnesses recant, witnesses decide to come forward or offenders slip up and incriminate themselves. And there is always the chance of an accomplice who may have helped in the cover-up.

But first, the facts.

Bertha Miller, 73, the aunt of then chief commissioner Mick Miller, left for church on Sunday, 10 August 1980, intending to take a tram along High Street, Glen Iris. Her body was found off Brew Road, Tynong North, in December 1980.

Eighteen days later Catherine Linda Headland, 14, was heading to catch the bus to the Fountain Gate shopping complex. Her body was found at Tynong North, near Miller's.

Ann-Marie Sargent, 18, disappeared after intending to catch a bus to the Dandenong office of the Commonwealth Employment Service and then visit the Clyde post office on 6 October 1980. Her body was found with the remains of Miller and Headland in December 1980.

Police believe the dumping ground was selected by someone who knew the area well.

Allison Rooke, 59, left her Frankston home to go shopping on 30 May 1980, walking to the nearby Frankston-Dandenong Road to catch a bus. Her body was found on 5 July 1980, hidden in scrub near Skye Road, Frankston. Joy Carmel Summers, 55, was to have caught a bus on the Frankston-Dandenong Road on 9 October 1981. On 22 November 1981, her body was found in scrub beside Skye Road.

Narumol Stephenson, 34, disappeared from her car outside a Brunswick flat on 29 November 1980. Her body was found about 100 metres off the Princes Highway, near Brew Road, on 3 February 1983.

A 1985 review by the Bureau of Criminal Intelligence suggested there were three killers – the sand quarry murderer, the Skye Road offender and another who killed Stephenson.

For this to be correct there had to be two serial killers targeting women on foot who removed personal items before dumping bodies in scrub and then stopped killing at around the same time.

And then, just by fluke, seven weeks after the last sand quarry victim was killed, Stephenson was murdered and dumped off Brew Road.

A 1990 re-examination by the same agency rejected the 'three killers' theory. 'On the balance of probabilities, the same person or persons were responsible for the murders of Allison Rooke, Bertha Miller, Catherine Linda Headland, Ann-Marie Sargent and Joy Carmel Summers.' It did not have enough facts to draw conclusions regarding Stephenson's murder.

The review examined several suspects but declared the 'best nominated' was Harold John Janman, a former projectionist with a propensity for offering women lifts in his car and with links to both Tynong North and Frankston.

But interesting links are not evidence and Janman, now aged 85, has always declared his innocence.

So what do we know about Janman?

He presents as a deeply religious family man and a prude who would turn 'girlie' photos to the wall in the small city projection room where he worked, and yet he had been charged with soliciting for the purposes of prostitution the year before the murders commenced. It was also around that time, he would later tell police, that 'My wife was going to leave me.'

He freely admitted that he often offered women lifts on the Frankston-Dandenong Road, where Rooke and Summers disappeared in 1980 and 1981. He agreed to drive with police down the busy road and identify where he invited women into his van.

He indicated nine stops, including the two where Rooke and Summers would have been waiting for a bus.

But he was not so forthcoming on every question.

Detective: 'Do you know where Skye Road is?'

Janman: 'Where, sir?'

Detective: 'Skye Road.'

Janman: 'No sir, I have never heard of it.'

And yet for years he had worked as a projectionist at the local drive-in just off Skye Road, near where the bodies were found.

Police took him to where the bodies were found. '[He] became nervous and sweated a lot. He walked around the sites as asked, but at no time did he walk in the immediate vicinity of where the bodies had been lying.

'Extensive areas around the sites had been cleared of bush and scrub by the police crime scene searchers and the investigators stated that without some prior knowledge it would not have been possible to tell exactly where the two bodies had been lying,' according to a police analysis.

Three days after the interview and on the anniversary of the discovery of the first body at Tynong, Janman turned up unannounced at the Frankston police station to ask Senior Constable Michael White: 'You know I was brought in about two murders in Frankston, well why haven't I been asked about five murders instead of two?'

White: 'Which other ones are you talking about?'

Janman: 'The ones in Tynong . . . I'm just saying, why haven't they asked about that?'

The trouble was no one, at least publicly, had at that time linked the two murder scenes. No one, that is, except Janman.

According to FBI crime profiler Robert Ressler, serial killers often reach out to investigators. 'Some offenders attempt to inject themselves into the investigation of the murder, or otherwise keep in touch with the crime in order to continue the fantasy that started it.'

It is a matter of fact that after Janman was interviewed on 3 December 1981, the murders stopped.

Fifteen years after the last body was found, Janman was nabbed in St Kilda when he approached an undercover policewoman and asked for sex. He immediately told police he was 'the prime suspect in the Tynong North killings'.

Homicide investigators try to find links between where bodies are discovered and the offender, as in most cases killers return to areas they know.

Janman had lived in Garfield, the area adjoining the killer's dumping ground. He had worked at a nearby hotel and was a truck driver whose route took him to the Brew Road sand quarry where three of the victims' bodies were dumped.

In a subsequent taskforce investigation, codenamed Lyndhurst, Janman agreed to two polygraph tests. He failed both.

Janman was not the only suspect in the case. Raymond 'Mr Stinky' Edmunds murdered Shepparton teenagers Abina Madill and Garry Heywood in 1966 and is suspected in a series of unsolved rapes and murders but as he moved to NSW in 1980, he has all but been written off in this case.

Distant relatives of Bertha Miller were nominated but investigators from the Lyndhurst Taskforce discounted them. And there is a new (if unlikely) name: Bandali Debs, who was convicted of the 1998 murders of Sergeant Gary Silk and Senior Constable Rod Miller in Moorabbin.

Debs murdered sex workers Donna Hicks (Sydney) and Kristy Harty (Melbourne), taking both from the street. But he was nominated not by a new witness but by his former crime partner, as part of his rejected submission for a retrial.

Police say the abrupt Debs would not have had the cunning to persuade women to voluntarily accept lifts, and other claims made by the former partner against Debs have been proven false.

Trichias says cold-case investigators will not just review but reconstruct the investigation. He says his team is keeping an open mind and not concentrating on one suspect: 'We hope that someone has information that will help us find the answers.'

The million-dollar question is whether that someone will now make the call.

HORRORS LURK BEHIND CLOSED DOORS

Troy Andrews and Phil Goodburn have spent most of their careers chasing drug traffickers, armed robbers and wannabe gangsters. With a combined 55 years' experience, they believed they had seen the worst society had to offer.

That is until they started working in Croydon's Family Violence Unit (FVU), where they see cases that leave them shaking their heads.

The FVU doesn't deal with the causes of domestic violence and they don't analyse trends or try to educate the community on gender respect. They work in the here and now, when minutes can add up to murders. It is an investigative team trained to act immediately when the victim is in imminent danger of death or serious injury.

This is the life-and-death battle fought every day in every Melbourne suburb and every country town. The grim reality in some of these cases is that if they cannot find a solution, the victim will die.

The almost unimaginable fact is that more women are murdered than gangsters, prisoners, bikies and drug dealers combined, with a woman killed by a partner or ex-partner every week in Australia.

Detective Senior Sergeant Andrews and Detective Sergeant Goodburn were trained that the successful outcome in a traditional investigation is to find and prosecute the offenders. In family violence they need to move before the final crime and often when the victim will not make an official complaint. 'Some of the people that we are dealing with here are movie stuff,' says Andrews.

They are working on up to 190 extreme-risk cases a month. And this is in just one police district. It is the same in every FVU around the state.

There is the woman who arrives home to find her ex-partner waiting in her house, armed with a knife. A neighbour hears the noise as the woman fights for her life and calls the police, who luckily arrive almost immediately.

In the man's borrowed car is a bag with gaffer tape, underwear and another knife. In his phone are detailed notes of his plan to abduct, rape and murder the woman. 'The boot was lined with a tarp,' says Andrews.

He says no matter the circumstances these cases are 'always about power and control. They think: "I own her, she is my property, I can do what I like with her."'

With traditional crooks, police have a fair idea of the likely profile, but on the dark end of domestic violence there is no 'type'. It happens in nice suburbs and nice streets. We think of Julie Ramage, who was strangled to death in 2003 inside the family home by her brute of a husband, James. They were a handsome couple with kids in private school, double income and nice friends. No one knew she was trapped in a violent prison. 'Name an industry and it will be there,' says Andrews. 'They can hold down jobs and appear to live normal, respectable lives.

'People are being tortured. They are in living hell and we don't see it. There are people who have been in these relationships for 25 years and you shake your head as to how they survive. Pound for pound they are the most dangerous offenders we have to deal with.'

For a number of reasons, many of the victims refuse to sign complaints, which means police have to find other methods.

There is a woman who couldn't understand how her ex-partner always knew her movements. Eventually when she walked into a police station to ask for help, the offender's car was spotted outside. 'In the car was a balaclava and a pair of night goggles,' says Andrews.

When police checked her car, they found it had been secretly fitted with tracking devices.

One victim was stalked for 11 years – the only relief was when her stalker was in jail or a psychiatric unit. When she moved to Victoria he chose to become homeless, then walked or took trains more than 1000 kilometres with the sole aim of finding her. A psychologist contacted police with a blunt warning: 'He is going to murder her.'

This is the sort of case where the criminal code alone cannot provide a solution and requires welfare, medical, prison and police authorities to work together. When this man was released from jail he was involuntarily committed and the woman moved to a new location.

An office worker would pour water on his wife's head every time he walked past her in a bizarre act of habitual humiliation. When she finally left he destroyed the house.

A woman moved to Tasmania to get away from a stalker while he was in jail. 'He walked out of prison, went to the airport, flew to Tasmania and was arrested in her house that night. He has since been banned from Tasmania,' Andrews says.

When a woman moved on and started a new relationship, her stalker broke into her house and sent her photos from inside. Later he took photos inside her new boyfriend's home. When she visited a friend he sent a photo standing outside carrying a gun.

A later police raid found he had four firearms. They also found a virtual shrine to her and her hacked computer passwords. A check of his records showed he had created a false identity and was talking to her through a dating site.

There are thousands of women working in Melbourne and around the state who know they will be humiliated, beaten and sexually assaulted on a weekly basis and who feel they can't speak out – often because they fear they will be killed.

One woman is choked every night by her son but won't sign a complaint because she doesn't want him jailed. 'When some come to police, they are beyond critical risk,' Andrews says.

A woman suffered an acquired brain injury after her partner repeatedly threw her through a plaster wall. Despite her injuries he convinced the doctor the victim was mentally ill and self-harming. To add insult to serious injury, the offender then began a relationship with the doctor. Yet the woman refused to sign a complaint because her tormentor is now her principal carer.

A teenager who escaped her violent family was abducted, forced back and tortured. Her crime? 'She went on social media like any other kid,' says Andrews.

The traditional police response to family violence has varied from apathetic to illegal. When the woman did not want to go to court, the police would try to separate the victim and offender at the time – to cool down – and then leave them to it. On occasions the bully might cop a belting as a warning but there was no follow-up.

There were no specialists and it was never treated as a real crime – a practice that continued well after the extent of family violence became obvious.

Joy Maree Rowley was strangled to death in her Rye home in 2011 by her former partner, James Martin Mulhall, despite a string of family violence reports that showed she was in imminent danger. She was one of many whose lives could and should have been saved.

Now there is a serious commitment. A detective senior sergeant, three detective sergeants and 12 senior detectives will staff the Croydon FVU.

'We are really being supported by the courts – not many of our offenders get bail,' says Andrews.

If police can charge, they will, but if they can't, they have developed other tactics. They will move victims, help them conceal their identities, use anti-bikie disruption methods, turn the perpetrators from the hunters to the hunted.

'Some of the people we have looked at would have been murdered. We have saved them,' says Andrews. 'Our message is simple: you do not have to live with this. There are people here to help you.'

Importantly, other key areas in the police force that are difficult to access have bought in. Recently a bully who gets a kick out of terrorising his ex-partner got a different sort of buzz — at the end of a Special Operations Group electric stun gun during a high-end raid. And Victoria's elite surveillance squad (known as 'The Dogs') roll out to follow the type that like to follow their victims.

For police there is tremendous satisfaction in not so much as solving crimes as stopping them. A veteran homicide investigator told me his best day in the job came when his team foiled a murder plot where a retail executive tried to hire a hitman to kill his wife. They slipped in an undercover agent to pose as a hitman and recorded the details as the businessman briefed the supposed killer. They even bugged him as he practised his grief-stricken response to being told of his wife's demise.

The homicide detective eventually knocked on his door to say: 'I have terrible news. Your wife is alive and you are under arrest.'

It doesn't get much better than that.

WHEN ACQUITTAL DOES NOT BRING PEACE

Everyone likes Roger and Joy Membrey for who they are, what they have done and how they have reacted under unbearable strain since their daughter Elisabeth was murdered in 1994.

There was initial shock, fading hope, a sense of loss, followed by false dawns when police found a new lead, a peek of hope when a suspect was charged and then a crushing wave of depression when a Supreme Court jury voted for an acquittal.

Like many crime reporters I have covered the Membrey case for years, and like many crime reporters I have come to know and respect the shattered parents. Now every few months Roger rings for a chat, always inquiring about my health and the changing state of newspapers before we turn to Elisabeth. He is looking for anything that would give them hope even when there is none. It is clear that as time moves on the pain grows deeper.

There is grief, of course, but you suspect a sense of guilt that despite all their efforts they are no closer to the answer.

'I am 76 years old and we desperately want to find the truth for Elisabeth. We will not be on this earth forever,' he says. 'There is a sense that we have failed her. We are caught in this sort of half-life.'

Once they travelled and were able to find some respite but now they dwell on the tragedy every day.

For years their gut-aching sense of loss was tempered by hope of a breakthrough but now police have closed the case and the Membreys can only look back at what went wrong. 'It could have been solved and it should have been solved,' he says.

Elisabeth was 22 when she disappeared. She had finished a shift at the nearby Manhattan Hotel on 6 December 1994, when she was attacked in her Ringwood home. Police subsequently established the killer tried to clean the bloodied crime scene, bundled the body into the boot of her red Mazda wrapped in her doona and took her to an unknown location. The body has never been found.

Homicide detectives soon started to look at regular drinkers at the Manhattan, including Shane Andrew Bond. He was one of many interviewed back then and he claimed that while he recognised Elisabeth as one of the pub's bar staff, he didn't know her. Although this would later be found to be a lie, police accepted it at the time and moved on to three stronger suspects.

Perhaps if they had dug deeper they would have found his flatmate saw Bond covered in blood around the time Elisabeth disappeared. Much later Bond would confirm the bloody incident but would declare he had bitten his tongue while having a fit.

It would take 16 years for the original suspects to be cleared. Indeed, one fitted the case so well he was close to being charged until a sophisticated undercover operation effectively proved he was not the man. Another review of the file showed Bond was nominated as the killer six times but as he had been interviewed at the time and there were stronger suspects, he was discounted.

This time cold-case detectives thought he was worth a closer look.

Eventually police found at least 10 witnesses who claimed Bond had implicated himself in the death, the flatmate who said he found him covered in blood hours later and a female patron at the Manhattan who said Elisabeth told her Bond was 'hassling her'.

Two days after the murder Bond mysteriously flew to Queensland for medical attention. He drove a car that fitted the description of the suspect's vehicle and he had a limp, the same as a man seen arguing with the victim on the same day.

And so in 2010 Bond was charged with the murder, giving Roger and Joy the hope they would finally learn the truth.

But there were no eyewitnesses and no DNA, plus Bond steadfastly maintained his innocence. His defence team argued the witnesses were mistaken or that some were motivated by the $1 million reward.

Roger and Joy sat through the eight-week trial and heard the 76 witnesses who testified before a jury that deliberated for a marathon eight days before acquitting Bond.

The Elisabeth Membrey case shows the best and worst of homicide investigations.

We are one of only a handful of regions in the world with the will and the competence to actively investigate cold-case murders. Throughout the world unsolved cases are closed and forgotten in months – and only reopened if fresh evidence falls out of the sky.

Here detectives devote thousands of hours reviewing such cases looking for the slightest leads.

The April 2012 jury decision left the Membreys devastated but also, it would appear, left Bond deeply wounded. This month he again appeared in court this time on driving and dishonesty charges. According to the *Herald Sun*, his lawyer, Effy Lagos, told the Dandenong Magistrates Court that Bond's life had descended into chaos because of the Membrey case, due at least partially to 'overwhelming and relentless' media attention. She said he moved around the country trying to find anonymity, began using ice and couldn't hold a job.

While the Membreys were shocked at the verdict, a relative of Bond's who also sat through the trial was not. 'Shane is a dickhead and if he was the killer I would have no problem with him being convicted. But when you listen to all the evidence there is no way he did it.

'Witnesses changed their stories and some of them were there for the million-dollar reward. The prosecution put a case at the start of the trial but had totally changed by the closing address.

'The Membreys are decent people but we couldn't approach them during the trial to express our sympathy. The police charged the wrong man, which means the real killer is still free,' the relative says. 'Cold-case detectives should have another objective look and try to arrest the offender, for the sake of the Membreys. We would urge anyone with information about the case to contact the police.'

Roger and Joy are still looking for miracles. They dream of new evidence that could force a retrial (this will never happen) or a fresh inquest (which also won't happen).

Police declare a homicide case solved when charges are laid, so while Bond was acquitted detectives still consider the Membrey case resolved.

It is natural as you age to look back at your life and the Membreys are increasingly consumed by their daughter's murder, distraught they haven't been able to find her body and bruised by a court process they think has more interest in procedure than the truth.

'We just want to give her some dignity,' Roger says. 'We feel someone has power over us.'

DNA LINKS NEW SUSPECT TO MEMBREY

A five-year reinvestigation into the murder of Elisabeth Membrey has unearthed fresh evidence identifying the likely killer and found police previously charged the wrong man.

A DNA match to samples collected in the victim's car has now been linked to the brother of Membrey's housemate, a Melbourne man convicted of rape in Queensland.

Another man, Shane Bond, was charged with the murder in 2010 and acquitted two years later by a Supreme Court jury. He has always maintained his innocence and said that while he drank at the pub where Membrey worked, he did not know her. There was no forensic evidence linking him to the Ringwood unit or Membrey's car.

The new suspect, who cannot be named because of a Supreme Court suppression order, was a witness at the trial. He testified that he had been to the Bedford Road unit to visit his older sister (who owned the property) 'five or six times, maybe not even that'.

Police say someone Membrey knew entered the home between midnight and 3 am and killed her in the hallway. Detectives concluded the killer must have known she was home alone at the time of the attack, despite the cars of both housemates visibly parked side by side in the driveway.

Membrey's housemate had broken her ankle days earlier in a horse-riding accident and was staying at her boyfriend's home, a fact known by only a handful of people, including the suspect's parents. The brother was living with his parents at the time of the murder.

The suspect told police he once moved Membrey's car when it was blocking his sister's vehicle.

But the sister told police he had not driven either car and she would never have asked him to move the vehicles, which were always parked side by side. The unit had parking for three cars with direct street access.

Forensic tests established the dust and soil found in the wheel trims and doors came when the car was driven on a dirt road at speeds between 60 and 70 km/h for at least four kilometres.

There were traces of Membrey's blood in the car and witness sightings of the vehicle driven in Bedford Road between 3.30 am and 4 am on 7 December.

As Membrey didn't drive her car off bitumen, police reasoned it was the killer. Tests showed the soil was consistent with the Kinglake and Silvan areas, leaving detectives to conclude the body was left less than 100 kilometres from the unit.

Police found a bucket filled with wet rags, no toilet paper in the house and the toilet roll and holder missing.

Witnesses told police the suspect would refer to the Membrey case, saying: 'Liz is in a safe place' and 'They won't find the body, there is a lot of bush around there.' A relative said when the suspect was asked about the missing woman, he said: 'She's in a river.'

In one of several accounts he gave to police he claimed to have been at the Bedford Road shops on 6 December to visit a woman working at the hairdresser's but she was too busy to see him. Police checked with the hairdressing staff from the time, and no one recognised him.

Detectives were told that three days before the murder he turned up unannounced and Membrey refused to let him in.

He denied he had been there on that date, saying he went there 'one or two weeks before Elisabeth disappeared . . . to say hello to my sister', who was not home. He said Membrey had allowed him to use the toilet. Detectives surmise that with the toilet paper and holder missing, he wanted to produce a credible reason why his fingerprints or DNA might have been at the crime scene.

Witnesses told police they saw a blue Holden parked in the driveway around the time Membrey was attacked. The suspect told police when he visited he drove a gold/brown V8 Commodore but others said he drove a blue Torana to the unit.

The suspect left Melbourne with a mate, days after the murder, without explanation, cutting off many friends and family. He appeared to have suffered an arm injury that required medical attention. When he left Victoria, he had his arm in a cast.

The suspect told a friend just before he left he needed to use a backhoe to fill in a hole for his boss. He was on WorkCover at the time.

As they left for Queensland the man insisted on driving past the Bedford Road unit where Membrey had been killed 10 days earlier, although it was a detour from their planned route.

During his testimony at Bond's trial he was asked about a woman's wallet found in the glove box of his car after he left Melbourne. Under questioning, he denied telling another woman it belonged to a friend: 'Liz'. The suspect would later say he handed it in at a Caloundra roadhouse next to the police station. The woman who found the wallet in the car said it was black leather. Membrey's wallet and keys were missing from her unit and have never been found. Her wallet was black leather.

More than six times concerned relatives and friends of the suspect contacted police to nominate him as Membrey's killer, saying he was obsessed with her, had a history of stalking and had made incriminating admissions.

Membrey and the housemate were friends for years and members of a dance club. The brother said: 'We used to go and watch them dance.'

A woman who lived in the same street as the suspect found him knocking on her window, asking to be let in. Another time she woke to find him standing in the bedroom doorway. He was also blamed for a series of small burglaries in the area, suggesting he was accomplished at breaking into homes.

Twenty years after the murder he was convicted of a Queensland rape of a woman he knew. His DNA was put on the national database and matched a sample from Membrey's car – the vehicle driven by the killer into bushland to hide the body.

Police interviewed more than 3000 people as part of the Membrey investigation. The man was one of four main suspects in the murder. Bond was acquitted by a jury and two others were subject to elaborate undercover operations that led them to being cleared by investigators.

Without additional information the new suspect will not be charged. There remains a $1 million reward for information that leads to the arrest and conviction of the killer.

Elisabeth Membrey, a La Trobe University politics graduate, had been offered a job as a trainee journalist with Channel Ten. She was a regular letter writer to *The Age* on subjects that remain current, such as US trade relations and the treatment of the mentally ill.

Legal sources say the Coroner is considering holding a fresh inquest to examine the new evidence.

ELISABETH MEMBREY

You aren't supposed to write a story as a favour but this time I bent the rules. Roger and Joy Membrey, two wonderful people tinged with a bone-aching sadness, approached me hoping some publicity could reopen the case of the murder of their daughter, Elisabeth, killed in her Ringwood unit back in 1994.

A man had been charged and acquitted. Others had been investigated and cleared. I unwittingly helped clear one suspect. Convinced by an investigator he was the one, I named him on radio predicting he would be arrested. Later he was the subject of an elaborate undercover operation that culminated with him meeting a so-called Mr Big who was a corrupt cop. Under the sting he needed to tell the boss about his involvement in the Membrey case so he could be written off. He said he was innocent even though 'that bastard Silvester gives it to me every anniversary'. It convinced police he was not involved.

It was over, although the Membreys couldn't face reality. In the end, I agreed. They were too nice and too decent to refuse.

But I was wrong. There was hope.

Suspicious Missing Persons police began a reinvestigation and found a suspect – one who was on the books from the beginning. When I found that police had a new lead, I rang Roger and he was conflicted. He had been told by police to keep quiet but over the years we had developed a mutual respect. He couldn't lie and he couldn't tell the truth.

I told him not to say anything he would regret and the next time I rang him, it would be with news, not questions. Later I found he was becoming ill with dementia and was drifting away. Joy had to park her sadness to care and protect him.

By the time I rang with news of the breakthrough, Joy said Roger was in care and close to death. In those twilight months he would walk his ward carrying a picture of his daughter and weeping.

He died three days after my call.

Joy said: 'I just hope he is up there and is reunited with our daughter.

'He couldn't have loved anyone any more than he did Elisabeth.'

PART 5
THE IMPACT

The crime scene can be cleaned and the file assigned to the archives but for many involved in the case it never leaves them.

Talk to retired cops, and many have that case – the unsolved one – that late at night takes them back. Did I do enough? Was there another, better way? What happened to the family? Is the offender still out there?

Sometimes there is a knock at the door. It is cold-case detectives wanting to talk. A DNA match, a new confession, the chance of a breakthrough.

But often they are just left with their thoughts and their doubts.

Here, we look at the cop who fought back after being shot, suffered from PTSD and was saved by his support dog who had been trained by an inmate in Bathurst Prison.

The police hostage negotiator who saw so much death he considered taking his own life, then with help, rebuilt himself and now works in another field of the emergency services.

There's also the son fighting to keep his mother's killer in jail, and the man who had his childhood stolen by an evil cult but refuses to see himself as a victim.

These are stories of resilience, of people who have been dealt terrible cards in life and who refuse to surrender.

THE SERGEANT WITH NINE LIVES

It was a fairly typical police wake. A suburban pub, open-neck shirts, stick-on name tags and a speech from the brass. The difference was that the man they came to eulogise was not yet horizontal.

Being given up for dead is nothing new for Ron Fenton, for it was nearly 37 years ago police first planned his funeral. He was given hours to live when he was shot in the head, was touch and go when he broke 37 bones in a motorbike accident, came close to ending it at his own hand while in the depth of depression, was a couple of gasps away from drowning in a raging river and had twice been diagnosed with terminal cancer.

Fenton's life has been truly remarkable. But he is not ready for it to be told posthumously – not yet.

At 65, he knows he is dying – the cancer has enveloped his liver, the chemo knocks him around and only morphine gives him enough relief to function. Yet he turned up, with nearly 200 friends and former colleagues, at a Point Cook pub to celebrate a life filled with tragedy, love and a steely resolve to survive. It was a living wake, where the guest of honour was still about to enjoy the chat, the memories and the plates of sausage rolls.

'This is a chance for me to thank all the people who have helped me get through my life,' he says. 'I have had an amazing life and feel blessed. I'm humbled to see so many people here. I thought we couldn't fill a shoebox.'

From the moment Ron walked into the Police Academy in 1972 as a 16-year-old cadet, he was a star. He graduated in 1974 dux of the class and was the youngest recruit to join Search and Rescue and dux of the sub officers' course.

And then he was shot.

The gunman was Kai 'Matty' Korhonen, a former army reservist trained in high-powered weapons and mentally wired to use them. On 21 November 1984, armed with a military-grade semi-automatic assault rifle and 200 rounds of ammunition, he ambushed security guard Peter Poole, who was sitting in his car.

Sergeant Fenton and his partner, Senior Constable Paul Gilbert, headed to Fairbanks Road in Clayton and were second on the scene. 'It was pretty obvious he was dead,' says Fenton.

When police tried to stop Korhonen's car at Rickett's Point, unaware he was a murderer, he blasted them with 20 shots, injuring one officer.

'He's shooting the shit out of the car,' one told D24, the force's communications centre.

Fenton and Gilbert immediately responded to the call, knowing the offender was almost certainly Poole's killer.

They went to a park near his abandoned car, hoping to corral him away from houses. But Korhonen emerged from behind a fence and opened fire, hitting the police car 27 times.

Fenton, the driver, opened the door to make a dash for cover. Illuminated by the internal light, he was shot in the back of the head with a military-grade bullet. The car was riddled, including eight bullet holes in the windscreen and seven in the driver's seat backrest.

(The transport branch later sent Fenton a letter to say he was not liable for the damage.)

The homicide report states both police were 'miraculously spared by chance'.

Gilbert, bloodied and blinded by shattered glass, huddled on the passenger-seat floor and radioed D24.

Police were ordered to remain stationary as 'We don't know that it's safe to go in.' Gilbert pleaded: 'Get an ambulance for my mate. I can hear him but I can't move.'

Sometimes heroism arrives without a brass band. In the radio chatter there is a quiet voice – Sergeant Mick Romeril. He chooses to disobey the order. 'We're in a plain car and we might head up to the injured member and put him in the car.'

And they did just that. Two units with four officers went in to rescue the trapped police.

Gilbert cradled his partner's skull after they were dragged out. In the ambulance, the paramedics said: 'Look, he's not going to make it.'

At the hospital, his family was told he wouldn't last three days. Then, after nearly two weeks in a coma, they were told he wouldn't recover his brain function.

They were wrong.

Gilbert, who was at the living wake, recalls the shooting, saying they took up a secure position but moved out to warn another unit to douse their lights.

'We were reversing back when all hell broke loose. Shot after shot went into the car. It was a nightmare. The car was full of smoke and I reached out and couldn't feel Ron. I couldn't see because of blood in my eyes.'

Gilbert remains amazed at Fenton's recovery. 'The inner strength of the man remains an inspiration to me.'

Fenton left hospital with more than 30 pieces of shrapnel in his skull. He was told he would never return to even light police duties.

Again, they were wrong. He became a respected Police Academy instructor and an inspiration to a generation of police.

(Korhonen, who fired 132 shots in the end, was sentenced to a maximum term of life for the Poole murder plus 88 years for shooting police. He served 15 years, meaning he didn't do one day's jail for the attempted police murders.)

Fenton wanted to be fully operational and over 11 years worked his way back, learning to write and shoot with his non-dominant hand.

Back in the job he loved, he hid the gathering dark clouds, ignoring the signs of building post-traumatic stress. The dam burst after a violent arrest where the offender gloated that he had served time with Korhonen and wanted to get the same gun to finish the job.

'I hit the booze, the pokies and the drugs. I did everything,' Fenton says.

The worst were the night terrors, a recurring nightmare that he was trapped underwater in a fast-flowing river, a flashback to a near-death experience in Search and Rescue.

In 2012, he retired due to ill-health, destined to be another dreadful police statistic, one who took his own life due to PTSD: 'I've tried to top myself five times.'

He was barely surviving with the aid of 17 psychotropic drugs when his life was saved by a crook he'd never met and a dog trained in a jail.

In Bathurst Prison, Benni, an inmate serving time for drugs, was training an American Hunting Labrador as a trauma dog. Yogi, a rescue dog, would have been put down if he couldn't find a home. Fenton and Yogi saved each other's life.

Benni was briefed on Fenton's condition and every night in his cell would mimic the policeman's impairments to train the dog how to intervene.

Yogi now sleeps in the same room with Fenton. If the former policeman's breathing becomes stressed, the dog will use a paw to turn on a night light and jump on the bed to stop night terrors.

Benni and Ron are now friends. They keep in touch and Benni now owns his own business.

'As far as I know, no inmate involved in the dog program has reoffended,' Fenton says. 'I really hope it is introduced in Victoria. Benni is an amazing man. He came to see me last year and Yogi loves him. You can see the bond between them.'

For Fenton, that bond is vital. 'When I shuffle off this mortal coil, Benni will take Yogi back. It is important I know Yogi will go to someone who loves him. He has taken care of me and he deserves to have someone look after him.

'When I was told I had months to live, the black dog, the suicide dog, jumped off my shoulder and started barking in my face. Yogi stood between us and said, "Bugger off, he's mine". So the brown lab beat the black dog.'

At Fenton's lowest, when he thought he couldn't get off the couch, Yogi would grab their ball and demand they play. 'He wouldn't take no for an answer.'

Yogi and Fenton may have saved each other, but they have done more than that. When Fenton applied to have Yogi's expenses paid under WorkCover, the claim was knocked back, even though the rescue dog saved money as Fenton no longer needs weekly therapy and to fill himself with drugs to survive.

Fenton took them on ... and won. 'Yogi is now considered a legitimate medical expense. I know five cases of first responders with assistance dogs who can now claim. Everyone wants to leave their mark on life and getting Yogi's Law passed is one of the crowning achievements of mine.'

When they thought Ron was about to die from gunshot wounds 37 years ago, they planned his funeral with full police honours. When he finally goes – and knowing him, it will be at a time of his own choosing – does he not deserve that same mark of respect?

*

[Ron was given a police funeral with full honours. Chief Commissioner Shane Patton delivered one of the eulogies.

Ron asked Benni to care for Yogi in retirement. Benni agreed and was a mourner at the funeral, sitting with the police top brass in the chapel of the Police Academy.

Ron had been told he was to be awarded the Order of Australia for services to mental health. He died in April 2021 before the Queen's Birthday honours were announced. His friends and family took his ashes to the presentation.

Ron would have liked that.]

LIFE, DEATH AND FINALLY REDEMPTION

There is no one road to breaking point and often no signposts. For many, it is a journey that takes thousands of steps and for others, it just arrives – an unexpected destination reached in one giant leap.

In the case of police officer and hostage negotiator Anthony McLean, the surprise is not that he suffered from post-traumatic stress disorder, but that it took so long for him to reach the point where his life imploded.

The harsh realities of policing shouldn't have been a shock to the idealistic teenager who joined up within a year of leaving school. His father, Alan, was a policeman for 32 years and his brother is still in the force. Anthony served for 31 years, mostly in country NSW.

Many of us think of the hard edge of policing as an urban problem and that the work of country cops is a little more gentle. The truth is, in the city there are specialists. In the bush, you just have to find the answers yourself.

Just months after his 1988 graduation and posting to Albury, McLean was called to an accident where two motorcycles had collided head-on. Both riders suffered fatal injuries, but he still tried CPR on one who had a giant hole in his chest.

The next year he was at the scene where three young men died after their car slammed into a parked tray truck. He dragged the 17-year-old driver free, hoping he was still alive. 'I'm sure he took his last breath in my arms.'

The distance from Sydney meant regional centres needed their own hostage negotiators, a position handed on internally. There was a tradition that when a hostage negotiator moved on they would recommend a local officer as the replacement. 'When the local man retired, he passed the baton to me,' McLean says.

The training took three years, including full-time study blocks and part-time fieldwork while remaining a general duties officer. It is not just one cop with a bullhorn, but small teams trained as experts in judging risk with the strategic flexibility to adapt to changing emotional triggers while relying on access to psychiatrists' expert advice. The negotiator has to be able to win the trust of mentally and emotionally stressed offenders who threaten violence on others or themselves. The wrong move or the wrong call could be fatal.

Not that McLean felt the pressure at first. 'I always felt calm because we had been trained so well,' he says. That was in the beginning.

His first case was a man armed with a knife holding his former partner hostage. Talking on the phone, the offender would say he was tired and needed a break. Eventually, he surrendered, but any sense of satisfaction soon dissolved when investigators later told McLean: 'Every time he got off the phone, he raped her.'

He was called to a crisis about once a month, including suicide interventions, sieges and hostage stand-offs. Most ended well. Some didn't go to plan.

Such as the man on a roof threatening to leap onto a spiked fence. McLean felt he had the situation under control until a chaplain took it upon himself to climb on the roof to take charge. 'Then I had to talk two people down.'

There was the man under his house threatening self-harm. McLean tried to persuade him to come out to receive help. Instead, he drank an arsenic-based weed killer. At the hospital, they were told there was no antidote and it was only a matter of time. 'He died two hours later.'

Not that general duties policing was a respite. In 1996 a burglar he was chasing stabbed him with a syringe, claiming he was infected with hepatitis B. It took three months for McLean to be cleared. The same year he was called to the suicide of a retired doctor who had disembowelled himself with a cut-throat razor.

A keen AFL centre-half forward in 2001, he went to a team function at the Tumbarumba Bowling Club but didn't drink because he was on night shift. At 4 am, he was called back to a car accident. His friend and teammate had hit a tree and was lying dead at the base. A few hours later, he had to inform the victim's pregnant girlfriend he was dead.

Most of McLean's grim jobs didn't make the headlines, but one did – big time.

It began on 23 February 2001, when two officers arrived at the Snowy Mountains shack of troubled local Jim 'Hank' Hallinan, 57, to arrest him on a warrant for failing to attend court on minor charges.

Hallinan, who didn't like police and was suffering a psychotic episode, threatened them with a rifle, and they fled. When police returned, it began a siege that lasted 33 hours.

'I was working in the watchhouse at Tumbarumba when I got the call about the siege. We went as the relieving [hostage negotiation] team.'

Police tactics that remain open to question were based on the fear that Hallinan could escape a cordon of up to 100 police and head to Tumut armed with his rifle. The tactical head was not at the scene and didn't know the distance from the cover to the shack.

At one point, the negotiators used what is known as third-party intervention – broadcasting, via a bullhorn, a taped plea from a friend of Hallinan to surrender.

The response was immediate and unwelcome. 'He came out and fired shots at us while we were behind a tree. I could hear the bullets whizz past. We looked at each other and said: "Well that didn't work."'

The negotiators were told by a consulting psychologist: 'This will not end well unless you take immediate action.'

After 33 hours, police planned to break the deadlock by luring the gunman out where there would be police dogs on either side, ready to take him down. A sniper positioned to protect the negotiators was ordered to move to cover an arrest team.

'My job was to draw him out by abusing him. I called him every name I could think of.'

He was lured out, but the dogs did not have a line of sight and didn't attack.

Meanwhile, the Alpha arrest team had broken cover from a line of trees and were trying to get close enough to disable him with non-lethal bean bag shots fired at close range from a shotgun.

'The Alpha team was firing distraction devices onto his roof. It was like a movie,' McLean says.

Then Hallinan turned, raised his gun and began to take aim at the arrest team.

'He was about to fire on them. A sniper then shot him in the head. He didn't just fall – he flew into the air and was flung back.'

The scene fell into chaos. McLean was told to remain at the scene while others were interviewed. The hostage negotiator was forced to remain for five hours metres from the body of the man he had tried to save.

Later, when the sniper rang his parents to say he was unharmed, the NSW Police department billed him for the call.

McLean feels he was treated as a criminal rather than a victim. He says all the main players in the siege left policing.

'I had a career that was surrounded by death and more death,' McLean says. He started to have mood swings, flashbacks, broken sleep and nightmares, often with him being chased by stormtroopers.

'I tried to hide it because if it became known, they would take your gun away and you are finished.'

But it was not an incident on the road but behind a desk that proved the tipping point. As a chief inspector, he worked in strategy and actively argued against a restructure that would force officers to relocate. When in 2018 a fellow chief inspector and McLean's good friend was notified he was to be transferred, he went home and hanged himself under the house.

'After that, I was a dribbling mess. I felt I was responsible. I considered suicide and had the noose around my neck. I also thought about driving into trees.

'My family remained rock solid even though I gave them hell.'

When he sought help, his psychiatrist told him that while suicide may be an option for him, he would leave behind his family that would need counselling for years. 'He said it was a long-term solution for a short-term problem.'

Medically discharged from the NSW Police Force in 2019, meditation and a PTSD recovery course brought McLean back from the brink.

In late 2020 he applied for a job as a regional manager in the Victorian SES. 'When I was offered the job before I accepted, I told the boss about my PTSD. The response was: "So?" They have been so supportive, from management to the volunteers. I'm not broken to them.'

HOOKING ONE THAT ALMOST GOT AWAY

It is to be the last roll of the dice in a murder investigation that looks destined to remain unsolved. Thousands of hours, hundreds of interviews and dozens of leads have led to nothing, so it is time to pony up with a giant reward offer.

The victim, James Russouw, 24, was a young man with an impish grin, a wide social network, a warm personality and a secret life selling cannabis to friends. In the scheme of things, his crimes were minor but the consequences deadly.

Eight years after the March 2008 drug-related ambush, police announced a $1 million reward in the hope of finally finding the truth. For Senior Detective Simon Hunt, this was more than a cold case he inherited from an ageing file. He joined Homicide just weeks after Russouw's body was found in his burnt-out Jeep Cherokee at the East Burwood Reserve, his throat pierced in a planned execution. This was not a crime of passion or a one-punch explosion but a cold-blooded murder where the victim was lured to his death.

Friends and family told police Russouw would never let a stranger into the car, so investigators always believed the killer was someone he knew and trusted. Hunt (who became lead investigator in the case in 2010) came to know the Russouw family — decent, hard-working, close and devastated by the brutal death of their son and brother.

The cold-case detectives knew the reward would be their last chance to generate new information and decided to release some grainy CCTV images taken of a man making a call at 10.54 pm to Russouw from a public phone at the Burwood East Kmart complex, just one kilometre from the murder scene.

While police concluded that the man was the likely killer, the footage was so poor it was seen as having little evidentiary value. The decision to release the footage was to make the reward announcement a little more newsworthy.

'We wanted something fresh to attract media attention,' says Hunt.

It did more than that; it led them to the killer.

Within a few days a call to Crime Stoppers nominates Christopher John Lavery, who — like James — is a former Whitefriars College student.

The caller, also an ex-student, recognised Lavery's slightly rolling gait and saw the figure was wearing long, ill-fitting pants bunched at the bottom in a way favoured by his former friend.

Lavery was on the periphery of James's social group, a few years younger and not a close mate but, as phone records show that they talked on the day of the murder, he was interviewed by police. It turned out the two had more than a school in common — both were of South African heritage and had taken to dabbling in the lucrative cannabis market. Lavery told detectives he was at the movies at Forest Hill Chase shopping centre at the time of the murder and had a witness to prove it. Sure enough, his mate confirmed they watched the late screening of *Rambo III*.

The movie started around 9 pm and finished just after 11 pm. As James was captured on CCTV driving into the reserve at 11.03 pm with a passenger who must have been his killer, that cleared Lavery. That is, if the alibi witness was telling the truth. And so cold-case detectives, armed with the Crime Stoppers tip, knocked on the witness's door without warning, before he could rehearse his answers. 'He was vague at first but he soon said that he'd been holding onto some information for years that he wanted to tell us,' says Hunt.

The man, later to be known as 'Witness A', said Lavery paid him $150 to lie and later threatened that if he ever told the truth, he and his family would be murdered.

In his latest version of events he said they went to the movies but Lavery slipped out 30 minutes later.

Phone records showed the alibi witness rang Lavery at 10.59 pm and the call went unanswered. So why ring the bloke sitting next to you at the movies in the last five minutes of the film?

Police would allege he could not answer because he was about to hop into Russouw's Jeep on the way to the reserve. Lavery would counter he dropped his phone in the cinema and asked his friend to ring so he could locate it.

This new statement made Lavery the key suspect but it was hardly a compelling case, as it relied on a shifting story. And with a new $1 million reward it would be easy to argue Witness A was motivated not by conscience but greed. (However, he did not approach the police after the reward announcement – they went to him.)

The real key was the one solid piece of forensic evidence police had kept secret for years. The killer sprayed petrol on the body and the car from a Decor drink bottle, then left a five-metre fuel trail to set alight. He would have assumed the bottle would melt in the fire but it survived, revealing an unidentified palm print. Lavery had moved to Cairns, where he was fingerprinted after a drugs caution – and it would prove to be a match. And so in April 2016, just over one month after the $1 million reward was offered, the arrest was made.

At the five-week trial, the background of victim and accused are ruthlessly examined, although Russouw is not there to defend himself. The jury is told that he was heavily involved in the music industry, took to selling cannabis to friends and, as he became more active, used a St Albans couple to satisfy his demand for kilos rather than grams.

When they were busted Russouw was not savvy enough to quit while ahead. The drug dealing had become his major source of income and he broke his own rule of only dealing with people in his circle of trust.

The police case is Lavery was also a dealer (although not as big as Russouw) who promised a new supply link. And so they were to meet on the night of 7 March, with Lavery to introduce a new supplier who would sell Russouw more than two kilos on the spot for around $13,000.

They say Lavery made the phone call from Kmart at 10.54 pm and that his distinctive white Honda Legend was caught on camera leaving the shopping centre two minutes later.

They met, the jury was told, in a nearby street and drove into the reserve. Lavery then hopped into the back seat of the Jeep, leaving the passenger seat empty for the non-existent supplier to make the exchange. Then, from behind, Lavery produced a Wiltshire StaySharp knife and stabbed Russouw in the neck 'without the slightest warning'.

The jury deliberated for nearly four days before returning a guilty verdict.

It is hard to comprehend that this young man, brought up in a comfortable middle-class environment and with no criminal record, was prepared to kill another young man for the price of a second-hand car.

On the day of sentence, two families are present. They sit metres away from each other in padded green seats in the wood-panelled court, perfectly decent people brought together by life-altering violence. Years earlier they may have passed each other in the corridors of Whitefriars, not knowing their worlds would one day collide.

Just before 11 am Chris Lavery, 31, enters the court and is escorted to the dock. He has put on weight in the 18 months since his arrest, but still has the same distinctive rolling gait identified by a former friend on the CCTV from the night of the murder. He smiles, mouths a greeting and blows a kiss to his family.

As Justice Mark Weinberg enters the court, Lavery – now attuned to court protocol – rises, buttons his grey suit jacket and bows respectfully. Justice Weinberg covers the details of the case, weighing the cold-blooded nature of the crime against the offender's lack of criminal history and his chances of rehabilitation. He sentences him to 25 years, with a minimum of 21.

Later, in their comfortable eastern suburbs home with their grey nomad caravan in the drive, Lorna and Cecil Russouw reflect on the horrible nine-year journey from the day they learnt of their son's murder, which exposed his double life, to the ultimate conviction of his killer.

'There is no closure. We hate that word, there is no such thing. It never leaves you,' Lorna says.

'Every birthday, every family gathering is always tinged with sadness,' says Cecil.

They say they have learnt that Lavery went to their son's funeral, apparently crying inconsolably in the car on the way (they believe it was an act in front of witnesses to strengthen his alibi).

'This was all done for the dollar. I can't get my head around that,' Lorna says.

A member of the Lavery family says the jury has convicted an innocent man: 'We honestly feel for the Russouws, but the trial threw up more questions than answers. He was convicted on inference and not firm evidence. Why would you do this for $13,000? It doesn't make sense.'

SON'S FIGHT FOR MURDERED MOTHER

The boy was 12 days old when his mother nipped out to the nearby milk bar to grab some groceries for a quick omelette. She would never return.

For more than 10 years he believed she had abandoned him for a new life. That was a lie. 'I just believed she had left when I was very young and had never loved me,' the boy, who is now a man, says.

In primary school when kids asked Jake Blair why his mother didn't take him to school or pick him up, he would make up stories to satisfy their curiosity. After a teacher overheard a particularly graphic one, he was hauled to the principal's office and his father, Garry, summoned to explain.

They returned home and Garry chose that moment to reveal the truth – or at least part of it – taking him to her simple grave at Casterton. He was in Year 3.

Sometime later, when Jake asked more questions, Garry handed him some newspaper and magazine articles that would tell him what really happened. She had been the victim of a serial killer.

'Dad explained it the best he could,' says Jake.

For the boy, there was no initial horror. After all, he didn't know his mother or comprehend the circumstances of her death. It was a little like reading about a stranger. He says he developed a form of detachment to cope.

But as the years rolled on, the crime and its impact on his life 'just got bigger and bigger'.

On Thursday 8 July 1993, Debbie Fream, 22, was at home at 27 Kananook Avenue with Jake (only days out of hospital) and a friend when she realised she needed more milk for the omelette. Her partner, Garry, was at work. At 7.20 pm she drove 600 metres to the local milk bar to buy a half-dozen eggs, two litres of milk and a chocolate bar as a treat.

As she jumped out of the car, serial killer Paul Charles Denyer, who a short time earlier had tried and failed to abduct another woman, slipped into the back seat, hiding next to the baby capsule.

When she started to drive he stuck a knife to her neck. Shocked, she lost control and clipped a building. He shoved a fake gun in her side and threatened to blow her head off if she didn't cooperate. He ordered her to drive down a number of local streets, repeatedly threatening to kill her.

She swerved onto the wrong side of the road, flashing her lights to try to get help, but Denyer grabbed the wheel, forcing the car to straighten. He ordered her to stop, marched her into the scrub, strangled and then stabbed her to death.

Over seven weeks Denyer, who had stalked hundreds of women over four years, killed Elizabeth Stevens, 18, Fream and Natalie Russell, 17.

Originally sentenced to life with no minimum, on appeal he was given a minimum of 30 years, meaning he will be eligible to apply for parole. At a meeting of 350 people in the St Kilda Town Hall, friends and family of Russell rallied support for a petition to keep Denyer in jail. In an act of solidarity, Jake Blair took to the stage to support them.

Liberal Democrat state MP David Limbrick, who was Natalie's boyfriend, has been pushing the state government to amend the law to basically reinstate Justice Frank Vincent's original life sentence. Despite his passion, he is unlikely to succeed.

The friends and family shared stories and memories of Natalie. Jake stood there silently, for he had no stories. Denyer stole them when he slipped into the rear seat of his mother's Nissan Pulsar outside the milk bar.

Denyer killed three people but he left hundreds of victims — those who knew and loved Elizabeth, Debbie and Natalie, and many others who learnt to fear the footsteps of strangers.

At a business function, a man said to me that he went to the same school as Natalie Russell. They weren't in the same year and he remembers her as a friendly teenager he would pass in the corridor. As we spoke he burst into tears. Some things never leave you.

The story of Jake's life is both tragic and inspirational. He was robbed of a loving childhood and adult opportunities, yet he has dragged himself from the brink of alcohol and drug abuse: 'I think I was trying to self-destruct.'

One reason he re-evaluated his wayward lifestyle was to make sure 'I didn't end up in a cell like Denyer.'

Jake says his mother's killer stole his future. A good student, he lost his way and moved from job to job, including car detailing, lawn mowing, planting pines, landscaping and working as a roustabout. He would do the research on possible careers, then lose interest. 'I think I could have been a doctor or a lawyer and not fallen into the life I have had.'

In some ways baby Jake lost two parents that night. There are pictures of his father, Garry Blair, days after Denyer killed Debbie showing a devastated and bewildered young man, consumed with sadness and shock. He would not be allowed the time to grieve as he had a tiny baby to raise.

It would prove too great a burden.

They moved to Yeppoon in Queensland, Warrnambool and then to Mount Gambier. Garry became more absent, using drugs and booze to deaden the pain.

'He just wasn't able to cope, and for him, it just got harder and harder,' says Jake.

One day, Garry took his trail bike out on a dirt track and plummeted down a 10-metre embankment, leaving him a quadriplegic. He was told that with years of therapy there was a chance he could walk again.

Beaten down by life and scarred by death, he no longer had the will to try. 'He just gave up,' says Jake. He died in August 2012, aged 53.

Aged care nurse Gail Ak lived in Frankston during the seven weeks when Denyer killed and saw the police in Skye Road the day Natalie Russell's body was discovered. She has followed the case ever since. 'I can remember the fear that everyone felt.'

When a political promise of help for Jake wasn't delivered, she offered him her spare room. 'I made a promise to take him in,' she says. She introduced him to a balanced diet and a stable lifestyle. Painfully thin at 60 kilograms when he arrived, he has put on nearly 10 kilograms in three months. Within days of returning to Melbourne, he found a job.

After the St Kilda meeting, he went out with Russell's friends and family. 'They are really good people,' he says.

He has joined their campaign to stop Denyer being granted parole. 'He has done nothing to deserve it. He will never change, and they must keep him inside.'

Denyer was 21 when he murdered. One of the appeal judges who overturned his original sentence to never be released privately said that perhaps a medical breakthrough in the future would change him. It hasn't.

Under the law he is entitled to apply for parole. That doesn't mean it should be granted. The onus is on the prisoner to establish they are no longer a risk to reoffend. His application would be reviewed by a panel at the Adult Parole Board that would have access to quarterly reports on his prison behaviour. Then they study psychiatric reports. Denyer would be interviewed on video from prison.

The families of his victims are also entitled to make written submissions.

Denyer has at different times expressed a desire to transition to being a female and be called Paula. The gender issue would also be analysed by the parole board.

As a serious, violent offender, if parole was tentatively approved it would be sent to a second panel for review. Denyer could then be told to reapply in two years or parole could be granted. He would certainly be banned from the Frankston area.

The notoriety of the applicant is not supposed to be an issue for the parole board but a successful application would result in public outrage.

It is hardly surprising those who knew the victims oppose Denyer's parole but I have spoken with many of the police who dealt with him, homicide detectives who dealt with dozens of murderers and have sympathy for many of them, yet not one who investigated Denyer believes he is an acceptable risk. They remember a man who stalked hundreds of women, killed to satisfy a bubbling hatred, loved the notoriety, would not have stopped until caught, was getting better at killing and has never shown any remorse for his crimes.

[In 2023, Denyer became eligible for parole and applied for release, his application was denied.]

DAVID'S CHILDHOOD IN A LOCKED BOX

David Freeman couldn't choose his early path in life, but he could choose his name – by flicking through the phone book until his finger found his future.

'I picked it because that is what I had become: a free man,' he says.

For 12 years, David was held prisoner by a cult and from the age of two was hidden with a group of children in a remote country house – described as a school – that was actually a prison.

This is the sort of story that doesn't happen here. You occasionally read a snippet about a weird cult in the United States or some fiefdom in Europe, not in a peaceful rural setting 90 minutes from Melbourne.

Perhaps that is why police were slow to react, and the cult was able to survive for 20 years, led by the charismatic and seriously loopy Anne Hamilton-Byrne.

David spent most of his adult life trying to forget, moving to Iceland, marrying, fathering children and working outdoors as a roofing contractor until he finally understood he needed to deal with his past.

He has reconnected with one of the original detectives Julie Cochrane, now a clinical psychologist, and finally feels he can tell his story.

Hamilton-Byrne, a Melbourne yoga teacher in the 1960s, convinced her followers she was the latter-day Jesus and, through fake adoptions and gifts, controlled more than 20 children between 1967 and 1987. They were the chosen ones who would guide Mother Earth into peace after the inevitable Doomsday.

David was kept at Kai Lama, a secluded, sprawling house at Eildon's Bolte Bay, from 1975 until 1987. He was rescued by police after one of the children escaped and convinced a local policeman they were being held captive.

David has no recollection of life before the cult: 'My first memory is crying at Eildon, missing my mother. I would cry myself to sleep.'

Imagine a childhood where there was no laughter, no affection and a life infected with fear. 'There was nothing to look forward to.'

When David suffered an asthma attack, he would either be locked in a cold bathroom to sleep or taken to a small shed. 'I was tiny, it was dark, and you could hear animals outside. I was terrified.'

They were tended by two female cult members at a time, residents of Melbourne, instructed to oversee the students/inmates (up to 12 lived at the property) on two-week shifts.

Occasionally, the cult leader would arrive at Eildon. 'She would tell us she was our mother, but there was no love. She was frolicking from house to house, saying she would be back for Christmas but would never deliver,' David says.

'Anne was obsessed with education and the standard was quite high. She wanted a smarter "race" of children.'

Hamilton-Byrne travelled the world, developed a taste for designer fashions and cosmetic surgery and amassed a fortune estimated by police to be at least $50 million thanks to donations from her followers. (In a later class action, David and five of the other children received a paltry $21,000 each as compensation.)

The children had their hair dyed platinum blond and styled in identical bobs. Life was bleak. 'We were brought up by robots ... There was no love, no compassion,' says David, who recalls crying for so long he ran out of tears.

When one of the carers uncharacteristically gave him a peck on the head, tucked him in and said goodnight, he thought: 'What was that? It was weird.'

Hamilton-Byrne told the children they had been chosen to lead the world. One boy was selected to be overall world leader, but when he fell out of favour, a girl was picked as a replacement.

Julie Cochrane, a senior detective at the Tactical Investigation Group when she was moved to the Operation Forest investigation into The Family, says: 'I was shocked at what happened to those children.'

Back in 1987, the initial head of the taskforce, a wide-eyed Peter Spence, told me what he had found. I thought he was exaggerating. He wasn't.

Cochrane says Hamilton-Byrne was not a misguided spiritual figure but a sadist who savagely beat a young girl with a stiletto shoe. She took a jar of bull ants and threatened to pour them down the back of one terrified boy. The full-time Eildon kids were assaulted, with one receiving up to 10 beatings a day. There were allegations of rape. Many were given LSD.

'I found their allegations credible, and I remain disturbed as to why some of those people were not interviewed over serious assaults, including rape,' says Cochrane. 'Looking back, I think we could have done more and people like David didn't get the help they needed.'

Despite an investigation that lasted six years, clear evidence of child abuse, allegations of rape, fake adoptions and criminal activity, Hamilton-Byrne and her stooge husband, Bill, were fined $5000 each for falsifying statutory declarations after they were caught and extradited from the US.

It's a bit like criticising Hannibal Lecter for poor table manners.

David remembers constant hunger and having to survive on a strict vegetarian diet. Withholding food was a regular punishment. To survive, David stole pet food and stale bread left for birds.

When he was finally rescued: 'I was 14 but so small I looked nine.' He needed human growth therapy for years.

David was a smart and curious boy, and his only respite from this hell was in books. By the age of 11, the stories he read showed him life wasn't supposed to be like this. 'I started to put the pieces of the puzzle together. I knew this wasn't normal.'

Stories such as Enid Blyton's Faraway Tree series showed him children were supposed to have fun and adults were supposed to be protective. An illustrated book on camping became his favourite. There were pictures of a dad with two smiling kids going fishing. 'I would thumb through it all the time.'

Every day, he prayed for freedom, but when that day arrived, his nightmare was far from over. The children were housed at the St John's Home for Boys and Girls before eventually being reallocated to family homes – all except David, who remained in government care.

The children became a little famous for a time. David hated the notoriety and at the age of 15, he made himself a promise: he would never speak a word about his childhood.

At the age of 18, he was released from government care with little support – accommodation in a halfway house. He worked for a while and started travelling the world. At a kibbutz in Israel, he met a girl and followed her to Iceland. 'I just wanted a normal life.'

To try to achieve that, he put his terrible childhood in a locked box. 'For 25 years, I didn't tell my partner, my children or my best friend.'

He invented a past that wouldn't raise questions, saying he was brought up in Melbourne with a mum, a dad and a couple of siblings. 'I wore a mask 24 hours a day.'

He tried to give his children what he never had. If they cried, he picked them up, kissed them and was determined to make them feel safe and loved.

By the age of 40, he could no longer suppress the past. There were unexplained flashes of anger, mood swings, depression and suicidal thoughts. He took to alcohol and self-medicated with drugs.

'I was on a downward spiral and drove around with a noose under the front seat,' he recalls. At a two-storey car park, he had the noose around his neck and was about to jump when his phone rang. It was his daughter. 'She pulled me back from the brink.'

He sought help in Iceland and reached out to Julie Cochrane. 'I was so lucky to find her again.'

Cochrane says David is thoughtful, sensitive and remarkably resilient.

When asked about the 'Auntie' helpers who brutalised the children, David says they were forced to go to Eildon. When asked about Hamilton-Byrne, he says: 'She was a sick woman, I feel sorry for her.' She died in 2019, aged 98.

While living in Iceland and fighting for his mental health, David let his Australian residency lapse. In early March 2023, after a twelve-month wait, he was granted a one-year working visa to stay in Australia. He could then apply for a second year with the expectation it would flow on to an Australian citizen application.

While coming to terms with his past, certain events take David back. 'The smell of eucalyptus and Australian bird noises can give me the chills. There remains a shadow there, ready to pounce.' There is one big difference: 'I'm not scared anymore.'

THE FOUR-DECADE MURDER MYSTERY

As a former federal politician, television commentator, footballer and coach, Phil Cleary is used to having a voice, which is why he is relieved his request to give evidence at the murder inquest of a woman he never met has been approved.

On 6 September [2021], the coroner will open a three-week inquest into the murder of Maria Theresa James, stabbed to death inside her Thornbury bookshop 41 years ago. I covered the case as a young reporter. It was my first murder. It has never left me.

James, 38, owned the modest bookshop in High Street, Thornbury. The front room was filled with hundreds of second-hand paperbacks and magazines wedged in shelves. Behind the small counter was a tiny three-bedroom home where she lived with her two sons.

On 17 June 1980, she was stabbed 68 times in her bedroom. The front and rear doors were locked, and two coffee cups on the counter indicated the killer was known to her.

A couple of years earlier, when I worked up the road at the Croxton Park Hotel, I would pass the bookshop on the tram. The windows were blocked with books and I always planned to stop and explore. I didn't – not then.

When Homicide set up their investigation inside the shop, I was invited in by the then deputy head of the squad.

There was a small kitchen and in the bedroom were the signs of violence: the carpet was stained with blood and fingerprint dust on doors and windows. Within three days the government announced a $50,000 reward – the quickest ever recorded – because police feared the offender could strike again. Today, with shopfront CCTV, phone records and modern forensics, the murder would have been solved in days. Back then it was a case littered with false hope and dead-ends.

Phil Cleary didn't know Maria James but is desperate to know if there is a link to the murder of his sister Vicki, stabbed to death seven years later.

Vicki's murderer, Peter Keogh, was only convicted of manslaughter after claiming he was provoked, an obscene conclusion that blamed the victim for her death. Keogh would serve less than four years.

Keogh had been Vicki's partner and began to stalk her after the relationship ended. At 7 am on 26 August 1987, he went to the Coburg kindergarten in Cameron Street to lay in wait for an hour until Vicki arrived for work.

When she pulled up he attacked, first trying to strangle her, slashing her face then stabbing her repeatedly in the abdomen, leaving her bleeding to death in the gutter.

Eighteen months after the James murder, when police issued an image of the offender, two women rang Crime Stoppers nominating Keogh, adding he attacked their sister with a knife. This victim was Judy McNulty, Keogh's alibi witness for the James murder who now believed he was guilty.

The tip was not passed on to Homicide. If it had been, Cleary contends, Keogh would have been charged with his latest knife attack and become a major focus of the James investigation. Forewarned, he says, Vicki wouldn't have formed a relationship with him.

Keogh is not the only person of interest. There were dozens, with the list now whittled down to less than 10. One is local priest Father Anthony Bongiorno.

Both Bongiorno and Keogh were falsely cleared by DNA tests, only for police to later find the sample was from another crime.

There was the slightest glimmer of hope when the bloodstained quilt, misplaced by police for decades, was found. If the offender left a DNA trace it could be a breakthrough, but for a host of scientific reasons it is a long shot. Like so many leads, it may lead nowhere.

James's son Adam says he told his mother days before the murder that he was molested by the priest. Police have been told James planned to confront Bongiorno on the day of the murder.

More than 30 years after the killing, a witness has come forward to say that on the day of the killing he saw a man matching Bongiorno's description entering the church grounds with blood on his face. Despite the blanket publicity, he didn't at the time connect the bloodied man with the murder less than 100 metres away.

Just hours after the murder, I spoke to Bongiorno, who described how he told James's eldest son, Mark, that his mother was dead. 'We both had a bit of a sob together,' he said.

Bongiorno died of natural causes in 2002.

James remained close to her ex-husband, and they spoke regularly about their children, yet she did not share her suspicions on Bongiorno.

She was bashed three times and her throat cut. Her wrists were bound in front and her body covered by more than 60 nicks and cuts. She was moved three times and a coffee table overturned and broken. Police said she was tortured 'obviously by a maniac'.

The injuries were not consistent with an offender who wanted to silence his victim but one who attacked with venom, determined to hurt and humiliate; a power crime.

On the day of the murder Bongiorno was happy to be photographed by the press – a massive risk if he was seen leaving the bookshop after the murder.

The man believed to be the killer was seen running across High Street but the church is on the same side as the bookshop, which means if it was Bongiorno, he crossed the busy street not once but twice. But by taking that route he would have avoided running past the Catholic school, where he was well known.

The initial police profile of the killer was someone who knew Maria James, lived locally, had an explosive temper and a hatred of women. After interviewing witnesses police released a description of a man seen running across High Street. He was paunchy, about 167 centimetres, with dark hair and wearing light grey trousers. James told friends she was seeing a man named Peter. Police were to find three Peters who knew her. None were Peter Keogh.

Police received four separate tips that Keogh was the murderer. He fitted the description, was 167 centimetres, hated women, had an explosive temper, had a prior for tying up females and an obsession with knives.

Within days of the James murder, a local florist told police an unidentified man bought carnations to be delivered to the bookshop, asking her to write the card. Keogh was borderline illiterate.

Two women who experienced his violence also received flowers from him – always carnations. He lived in the area and was a regular at the Junction Hotel, just up the road from the bookshop. Years earlier he attacked a man in the bar with a broken glass and was sentenced to one month jail.

Interesting but not compelling. In fact, no one confirmed James and Keogh ever met.

Twelve years after the James murder he dated a Junction Hotel bar staffer (he subsequently tried to burn down her house). Three times a regular at the bar warned her, saying Keogh 'killed the girl at the bookshop'. Another said: 'He did Maria James, she was his missus.'

Vicki Cleary confided to a friend that Keogh had threatened 'I will do to you what I did to the woman in the bookshop.'

Even counsellors need counsellors and when psychotherapist Margaret Hobbs needed to talk she turned to her mentor, Dr Jim Goulding. Days after the bookshop murder, she rang to discuss one of her clients: Peter Keogh.

'She said: "I know that bastard did it. He told me he was going to get her",' Goulding recalled. But both Hobbs and Goulding are now dead.

Goulding tipped off police and in August 1980, Keogh was interviewed by homicide detectives. His girlfriend, Judy McNulty, provided an alibi that was later discredited.

Homicide detective Frank Bellesini wasn't part of the bookshop team but when he heard a witness describe a suspect as having a limp, he nominated Keogh. Bellesini knew why Keogh had a distinctive gait. As a young constable 17 years earlier, he had been called to the stabbing of a Northcote railway station porter. Bellesini saw a youth matching the offender's description at Preston Station: it was Keogh.

He pulled a knife and attacked Bellesini, slashing the policeman's palm. Bellesini produced a small Browning .32 pistol – 'a peashooter, really' – and shot his attacker in the kneecap. When told Keogh had an alibi, he wasn't convinced. 'I suspected it was him, but it wasn't my case, and it wasn't my job to stick my nose in.'

On 23 June 2001, Keogh went to the pub and confided to a bouncer: 'I'm going to neck myself.' It was the anniversary of Maria James's funeral.

He drove to his Mansfield Street home and gassed himself, a bottle of bourbon his only companion. Maria James's bookshop was one from the corner of Mansfield Street.

[In 2022 Coroner Caitlin English found insufficient evidence to conclude who killed James but that Keogh and Bongiorno remained persons of 'significant interest'.]

CAN A LEOPARD CHANGE ITS SPOTS?

Criminologists, psychologists, veteran detectives, tea leaf readers and the occasional cross-eyed clairvoyant on the make have all asked themselves the same question when it comes to serious criminals: 'Can a leopard change its spots?'

There are crooks who, while they can't or won't reform, learn to fake the right answers to sentencing judges or stern-faced parole boards. There are also crooks who leave jail filled with noble intentions only to fall back into bad habits somewhere down the track.

And there are those who see the light with varying degrees of clarity. Take Mark Brandon 'Chopper' Read who, after wasting most of his adult life in prison, worked out that it was more lucrative to write about crimes than commit them. For more than 10 years, he became one of Australia's most successful authors and is now the subject of a second biographical film. (We had a sneak preview and it goes pretty well, particularly Aaron Jeffery as Chopper, who will need to press his tuxedo come Logies night. Disclaimer: We had an insignificant consultancy role in the project.)

There is Russell 'Mad Dog' Cox, perhaps Australia's most interesting retired career criminal. Cox spent 11 years on the run after escaping from the maximum-security Katingal facility at Sydney's Long Bay prison.

While on the loose, he organised armed robberies, got away with murder and managed to avoid being shot when arrested in a hail of bullets at Doncaster Shoppingtown. He went back to do his time, married his long-time sweetheart, embraced education and became a model inmate – so much so that prison guards pushed for his release, believing this leopard had changed its spots.

And they were right. When he was released from prison in 2004, he was met by his wife and they quietly disappeared to northern Queensland, refusing all interview offers.

Which brings us to Christopher Dean Binse, an institutionalised prisoner, habitual escapee and master armed robber who well and truly earned the nickname 'Badness'.

Back in the early 1990s he was an elite stick-up man, and while he left dozens of staff and customers traumatised through his acts, he also showed an underworld sense of humour. Having escaped he put a public notice in the paper to announce to the Armed Robbery Squad that 'Badness is Back' and followed up with a Christmas card with the message: 'May all your wishes come true.'

Now 49, he has spent 32 of the last 36 years in prison, has been left in chains and has done more solitary time than any inmate in Australia. Even today he lives in much worse conditions than any animal in the Melbourne Zoo. He is kept in isolation for 22 hours a day, allowed to see only one inmate for the other two. His exercise area is a small patch connected to his cell, he cooks his own meals and has the occasional visit from one relative.

Feeling that he was banging his head against a brick wall, he chose to embark on the ill-conceived strategy of doing exactly that in his cell. 'I'm literally running up like a bull, you know what I mean . . . hitting my head up against the brick wall,' he would later say. He was taken to hospital, treated for cuts and possible concussion before being taken back to the same cell.

Whether he was born bad or the brutality of the system warped him, we will never know. Whatever the reason, judges, police and prison officers would say he was a lost cause.

A prison officer told me: 'I would think he is one of the five most dangerous men in Australia. I would be genuinely frightened if I saw him on the street.'

Certainly his last stint on the outside, in 2012, would seem to indicate he was a hopeless case. Soon he had armed himself to the teeth, hunted down an old prison enemy (only to be thwarted because police got there first), pulled a textbook armed robbery, escaping with $235,000, pulled guns on police and held out for 44 hours in an East Keilor siege. (Indeed, at the time there was a suggestion I was on the list of those he wished to catch up with for a chat – amicable, no doubt.)

Binse dragged out the siege until police hit the house with distraction bombs, blasted it with tear gas and shot him several times with non-lethal beanbag rounds.

In 2014, Justice Terry Forrest in the Supreme Court understandably judged his chances of rehabilitation as poor and sentenced him to a minimum of 14 years.

Then something strange happened. Binse wrote to Ken Ashworth, one of the Armed Robbery Squad detectives who locked him up in the 1990s. He finally wanted to tell the truth. While he had been convicted of four armed robberies back then, police knew he had done several more but lacked the evidence to lay charges.

Ashworth headed to Barwon Prison with few expectations. Binse was a manipulator who often claimed to have changed, once saying: 'I'm a leopard whose spots are fading.' Why would this be any different?

Ashworth already knew which unsolved jobs were likely to be Binse operations. Plus, during one interview more than 20 years ago, Binse had confessed in an off-the-record (and inadmissible) conversation that he had committed those raids.

From Ashworth, 'We had a long chat. He said he had changed and admitted he had wasted his life. He told me things about the robberies that only the crooks would know. He still had a sense of humour and talked about the old days, referring to "Ashie and I" as if we were old mates.'

He put his hand up for seven armed robberies between 1988 and 1991. In one case Binse fired a shot, narrowly missing one of his victims.

Ashworth has dealt with some of the worst of the worst and is no pushover, but he thinks Binse has finally shown real remorse. 'I think he is sincere and he wanted to set the record straight.'

Justice Forrest is another who thinks that if Binse hasn't exactly turned the corner, he has finally found the indicator switch. 'I assess your 2017 prospects for rehabilitation as reasonable. This is a substantial and surprising development since 2014.'

My own dealings with Binse have been sporadic and varied. Back in 1994 he was quite chatty. Knowing I was planning to write a story on him, he wrote from prison, urging me to think again.

'Thank you for your assistance in kindly refraining from such desires in which you have focused upon my adventures.' He then offered the following proverb: 'The trouble with many people who stop to count their blessings is their arithmetic is poor. Regards Chri$ Bin$e.'

By the following year, I was no longer 'Mr Silvester' but 'Slime of the Underworld, The Sewer Dweller . . . You are a gutter low life rodent, who's awash in rubbish, crap and shit . . . It is beyond comprehension how a paper such as *The Age* of high standing quality, persists in attaining [sic] your poor inferior services.' (Several previous editors have expressed similar sentiments, although they rarely carried unlicensed firearms.)

He then suggested he would be delighted if I was to fall foul of the law: 'Be a wonderfull [sic] thought having you in amongst and in the midst of our company, on this side of the fence.'

I have no idea what exactly set him off but I had written of his plan to lead a mass escape from Pentridge. I had also said on radio that after his hair transplant failed, he should change his nickname from 'Badness' to 'Baldness' (a severe case of the pot calling the kettle black).

On another occasion he referred to me as a 'parasitic keyboard jockey'. Now that is just plain silly. You cannot ride a keyboard and if you did, it would just leave nasty indentations on your bottom.

And so with word that he had changed, I reached out to Chris, and to my surprise received the following response, suggesting all has been forgiven.

'To my old nemesis Sly of the Underworld – John Silvester . . . Greetings to you. It's funny how life takes turns and the directions and journeys we make . . . I am misunderstood by the masses and in recent years undertaken [sic] to amend the sinister recalcitrant figure cast by those in the media – you included.'

Chris Binse has more than 10 years to serve and while he should always be treated as a dangerous criminal, there is a duty to try to move him into more humane prison conditions in preparation for his ultimate release.

There can be no doubt that years of solitary have damaged an already damaged individual. By confessing, Binse has taken the first step to reform. Now we have to prepare a path for him to walk away from a wasted life. Whether he makes that journey is a matter for him.

VICTIM OF A FLAWED SYSTEM

Former leading senior constable and accused murderer Tim Baker sits in his sparsely furnished flat, his eyes burning with injustice and his voice quavering with anger. In the corner, his 10-year-old deaf dog, Patsy, sleeps on a mattress, snoring contentedly after a two-hour walk.

Baker's story raises questions about the investigation of police fatal shootings and the treatment of officers with mental illnesses, and exposes a stubborn refusal by police command to change a flawed policy in the face of overwhelming evidence.

Baker always wanted to be a policeman and went to university to fill in time until he was able to join in 1989, aged 18 years and six months. He worked busy suburban stations, transit and the city patrol group until, tired of the endless churn of divisional van shifts, he moved to the Prahran highway patrol.

Baker, like many others, began to buckle under stress and was eventually diagnosed with post-traumatic stress disorder and placed on long-term sick leave.

The treatment of police mental health is never one-size-fits-all. For many the job is an important part of rehabilitation but to be operationally fit means being authorised to carry a firearm. Once there were hundreds of behind-the-line jobs where police, bruised from front-end duties, could withdraw to recover. But the demand for efficiency means most of those duties have been moved to the private sector or public service.

Which means when Baker was cleared to return to duty there was no chance of a slow reintegration. And then someone made a decision that defies logic: they put Baker back on the road as a solo highway patrol unit, one of the most stressful and high-risk jobs in policing.

That was back in 2013 – three years after a coroner recommended such patrols be banned because they were too dangerous.

In April 2005, Senior Constable Tony Clarke was murdered with his own gun while working one-up on traffic duty after he intercepted a car on the Warburton Highway. In the 2010 Clarke inquest, Coroner Kim Parkinson recommended an end to one-up patrols for late-night or remote-area intercepts. In 2015 police finally agreed and banned the patrols but too late for Baker and Vlado Micetic, the man he shot dead in what began as a routine car check.

So, what happened?

Baker says the shift on 25 August 2013 was largely nondescript until he slipped down to St Kilda in the hope of spotting a serial burglar who had been stealing high-powered cars to speed away from police.

Around 10.30 pm he spotted a 'dinged-up Hyundai' that a quick check showed was using stolen registration plates. He followed discreetly along Punt Road and chose to pull the driver up in Union Street, Windsor, a strip he considered low risk because it was wide, well-lit and had regular traffic flow.

According to Baker, when the driver said he found the stolen plates in the rubbish, he decided to take him in for a formal interview.

'I got him out of the car and managed to get one handcuff on. She [female passenger Evelina Niedzwiecki] got out of the car and walked away. He started to struggle. That's when I saw the knife in his hand.

I thought I was going to cop it. I thought I was fucked . . . I let three rounds go. I remember the shots didn't sound that loud, not like on the shooting range. He was lying on his back – there was silence. All I could hear was him gasping. He was dying right in front of me.

'Within 30 seconds the supervising sergeant arrived. I had gone into shock. There was blood and shit everywhere. I went to the side of the road and spewed my guts up a couple of times.'

Baker was taken back to the station and assured he had picked the right spot and conducted a textbook risk assessment. 'I was told I had nothing to worry about.'

On the advice of Police Association lawyers, he refused to make a statement to homicide investigators. 'They were not impressed,' he says.

Driven home near dawn, his driver pulled up silently at a 24-hour bottle shop for him to pick up a six-pack. It would begin a spiral of using alcohol as a prop that would end disastrously.

For the first time in a fatal police shooting there was an electronic record, as the unmarked police car was equipped with a dashcam and Baker was wearing an audio mic.

The tape shows Micetic admitting he has been in trouble with the police and was on bail. He then freely gave his name, address and date of birth. The driver is calm and compliant, the policeman calm and assertive.

It is all routine until the conversation moves to the plates. Micetic either won't or can't give an explanation. The policeman instructs him to get out of the car with the intention of taking him to a police station for interview. Micetic still appears calm. 'I don't know why you are bugging me up for this. I'm not being a smartarse. I'm respecting you.'

Baker responds: 'But you have bodgy plates on your car. Why? They are stolen plates. I'm going to have to interview you about it, so put your hands behind your back for me.'

Micetic responds: 'I think you should talk to your superiors first.'

An increasingly frustrated Baker says: 'I think you should do what I tell you.'

Micetic trots out a series of letters and numbers to suggest he is a registered police informer and should be treated differently. Baker is not impressed. 'Do as you are told, I don't want to use force . . . Do it while I figure out what is going on.'

Micetic is unhappy but both men still appear calm. 'Why are you doing this?' he asks.

'Because you have broken the law.' Baker radios for back-up.

When Ms Niedzwiecki leaves the car and walks away, the situation deteriorates. Micetic falls to the ground. 'What are you doing man? You are going to get into trouble . . . you are going to lose your job.'

They step in front of the Hyundai, blocking the view of the dashcam. There are muffled, urgent words followed by three quick shots and the groaning of the fatally wounded man. Seconds later you hear what sounds like a zip opening, followed by a click. It would later be the key to the prosecution claim that Baker shot Micetic and then planted a knife before calling in the incident.

Baker returned to work two days later but 'life went off the rails pretty quickly. There were flashbacks, it was like a movie playing over and over again. It was always the same. The man lying on the ground bleeding out. My alcohol consumption went through the roof – I was drinking to unconsciousness. I was going batshit crazy.'

Suicidal, he went to a park with his dog, Patsy, and a bottle of pills with the intention of taking his own life. He woke in the Royal Melbourne Hospital in a neck brace with no recollections, later finding he had driven his car into a pole. He was admitted to a psychiatric facility and went through detox but his life continued to deteriorate.

His house was raided by police, looking for receipts to prove he had bought the knife found at the scene and in 2015 – more than two years after the fatal shooting – he was charged with murder.

He spent two weeks in custody, eventually bailed to live with his parents and forced to report at the local station to his former colleagues. He split with his long-term partner. 'He struggled with the police culture,' says Baker.

The Crown case was simple. An audio expert made a statement that a noise 14.5 seconds after the final shot was Baker opening the flick knife he planted on the dying man. This is despite a peer reviewer (a Queensland police forensic recording analyst) disputing the conclusion and the defence having their own specialist who said the knife was opened two seconds before the first shot.

'The prosecution said I had a little hissy fit and that's why I shot him. Then I planted the knife.' Baker, who is gay, says he found the 'hissy fit' expression homophobic and 'just ridiculous'.

Now, let's not be naive. Evidence, including weapons, has been planted on suspects, usually by old-school, heavy-handed detectives. What the Crown failed to explain is why a traffic policeman with no history of planting evidence would be carrying an illegal weapon on the off-chance he might need an alibi. Nor why he would murder someone on a busy street near high-rise buildings where there could be witnesses and when he could not know if incriminating evidence would be caught on the video or audio recordings.

The jury was told Micetic, nicknamed 'Knifeman', had 99 previous convictions, had five knives in the Hyundai and kept a sawn-off shotgun at his house.

It is impossible to know for certain what happened in front of Micetic's car. What is certain is there was insufficient evidence to justify a conviction. Which is why in September 2017 the jury rejected the case against Baker after less than five hours' consideration.

Baker has left policing, his 27-year career destroyed. Despite claims to the contrary, Baker has received no welfare treatment from police since the day of his arrest. 'I have no firm plans for another career. I have been doing this since I was 18. It is all I know. To say I am angry and bitter is an understatement.'

By charging Baker in a case that could not possibly succeed, they also left the Micetic family with no real answers. If this had been a coronial investigation rather than a Supreme Court trial, the question of why police persisted with dangerous single-officer patrols and why a policeman with a history of mental illness was placed under unreasonable stress would have been examined.

The clear conclusion is that if the dinged-up Hyundai had been pulled up by two officers rather than one, the confrontation would not have fatally escalated and Micetic would be alive today. Instead one man is dead and a second may never recover.

Is that justice?

FINALLY, 'IT IS NOW OVER FOR EVERYONE'

After nearly 10 years of confusion and controversy, the families of two police officers murdered on duty believed it would all be over – without the torture of yet another trial.

The Office of Public Prosecutions contacted them to say that Jason Roberts, whose original conviction for murdering Sergeant Gary Silk and Senior Constable Rod Miller had been quashed, was looking at a plea deal.

Under new laws, an accused could seek an indication from the trial judge of the maximum jail sentence they would receive on entering a guilty plea. (Note, seeking such an indication is not an admission of guilt.) Roberts's lawyers had asked Justice Stephen Kaye what sentence he could expect if he pleaded guilty to 10 armed robberies and the murder of Silk. (Under the proposed deal, the charge of murdering Miller would be dropped.)

At the first trial, Roberts and his crime partner, Bandali Debs, were convicted of the murders of Silk and Miller. The prosecution case had always been that the police, on stakeout duty looking for two armed robbers, pulled over the two men in Cochranes Road, Moorabbin, on 16 August 1998, and that Debs had shot Miller and Roberts had shot Silk.

For more than 10 years, Roberts said he was innocent and had been wrongly convicted. In 2020, he was granted a retrial.

During re-investigations and public claims of guilt or innocence, the Silk and Miller families have maintained a dignified silence. Now, with secrecy provisions lifted, they can reveal what happened in the confidential hearings that they hoped would finally resolve the case, which has stretched over four decades.

'We got the call from the OPP to have an urgent meeting with them because something significant had transpired,' says Rod Miller's widow, Carmel Arthur.

A court hearing over several days was held in secret because if there was no deal and it became public, it could prejudice a jury at the later trial.

'It was a very respectful process,' says Arthur. 'We did victim impact statements. It was a closed court, and it was made very clear this was confidential and we had to keep it within the family.'

Eventually, Kaye said the maximum sentence would be 40 years. 'We were quite taken aback with the length of the sentence he indicated,' says Gary Silk's brother Peter, believing it would be closer to 35. 'We were bloody shocked.'

'It was about 10 days between the time the OPP told us this was on the table until we were told that he was going to roll the dice,' says Arthur. 'We went from, "Oh my God this is finally over. If he pleads guilty." . . . It was also right that he didn't have to serve life because it was off the table. It was almost a win-win.

'You think finally this nightmare is over for all of us. No trial, no witnesses retraumatised, [Gary's brothers] Pete, Ian and [mother] Val get the outcome they need, and we can all finally move on with our lives.'

Roberts chose to exercise his legal rights and went to trial. In July, he was acquitted of the murder charges.

Some time ago, Peter and Carmel agreed to talk to me once all legal procedures were completed. Their stories are inspirational, showing how they refuse to be defined as victims and will not allow themselves to be consumed by bitterness.

About eight years after the murders, they married. Arthur served for 18 years on the Sentencing Advisory Council and nine on the Adult Parole Board. She has been awarded an OAM for services to the law and sits on the Victorian Post-Sentence Authority. She is a star. In 2016, when the government changed the law to effectively ban police killers from seeking parole, she felt it was unfair on Roberts, who was originally sentenced to a minimum of 35 years. She believed that if he had reformed, he should be able to seek parole.

On the night he was ambushed and murdered, Rod Miller had only been back at work for a week after six weeks' leave following the birth of their first child, Jimmy.

After an afternoon shift and in the early hours, he signed more than 60 handwritten thankyou letters, which Carmel posted on the Saturday. 'By the time they arrived, Rod was gone,' she says.

After Miller was shot and was losing his battle for life, Arthur's brother took the call and told her that her husband had been injured in an accident at work and she was needed at the hospital.

'When I realised he had been shot I asked, "Where's his sergeant? I want to know what happened", and his brother said: "Carmel, Gary [Silk] is dead."

'The surgeon came out and told me of the injuries and I told him, "Look you just have to save him, I have a little baby. This isn't the way it is supposed to play out, so go back in there and save him."

'About 20 minutes later the doors opened, and it was like one of those movies where they open up to doors of the operating theatre and the doctor walks out really slowly – it was like he was in slow motion, and I knew then he was coming to tell me Rod had died.'

The three Silk boys – Ian, Peter and Gary – grew up in sight of the Glen Waverley Police Academy, and Peter was the one who initially wanted to join. 'I failed the test,' he says. 'I knew I was colour-blind, but I thought I had the system beaten. I was kidding myself.'

Devastated, he went home and his father, Morrie, rang his old friend Chief Commissioner Mick Miller to see if anything could be done. Mick leapt into action. The next day he changed the order, making the colour-blind test the first rather than the last.

The separate funerals of Silk and Miller were conducted at the Police Academy with full honours. For Peter 'It is something that will never leave me.'

The families were unaware of the size of the funerals. 'We were told if we had some friends coming they should get there a little bit early. A little bit early? They should have camped overnight,' says Peter.

For Carmel, it was the long procession outside with the honour guard of police, shoulder to shoulder, stretching more than a kilometre. As she looked out she could see cars moving through traffic and thought: 'Your lives are going along normally and mine has done this unbelievable pivot. You are completely numb. I just thought: "What now?"'

When Debs and Roberts became suspects, Lorimer Taskforce detectives picked up Debs on listening devices considering killing Arthur and her infant son to make investigators think the murder of Miller in Cochranes Road was a targeted killing and not related to the series of armed robberies.

When Arthur was told, she refused to be relocated because she wanted Jimmy to live a normal life. 'One night I went out into the front yard and yelled: "Just come and get me." But I knew we were safe. I just knew Rod wouldn't let anything happen to us.'

As police closed in on the suspects, Morrie was battling terminal cancer. The head of the taskforce, Paul Sheridan, decided to take Morrie Silk into his confidence.

'What a beautiful heart Paul has,' Peter says. 'He came to the family home, and Dad was desperately ill and couldn't get out of bed. Paul said to Mum: "I just want to go upstairs and see Morrie." He went into the bedroom, shut the door, bent down next to him, grabbed his hand and reassured him that they were in control of the investigation and knew who the offenders were.'

Morrie Silk did not live to see the arrests.

Carmel and Peter may have been thrown together by tragedy, but they are connected by much more than grief. Like many comfortable couples, they can finish each other's sentences, share the same sense of humour and look to have fun. They want to honour the past while looking forward.

When Debs and Roberts were convicted in 2002 (and well before Roberts's acquittal on appeal), Arthur hoped that would be the turning point for her. She felt relief and elation, but that night at a function, she burst into tears. 'You think you will be a new person, but I didn't get that feeling. You realise the hard work was to commence in terms of rebuilding my life.'

From 2013 they have lived with a public campaign that Roberts was wrongly convicted. In 2020, his Supreme Court appeal was successful. He won a retrial and ultimately a jury acquittal.

'We are two or three months down the track now [since the acquittal], and it is now over for everyone. We can finally live a life free of legal process. There is no more. It's done.

'These were the cards we were dealt, and we all have to find the best way to play them.'

She refuses to drown in anger and bitterness. 'I think it is the best way to honour Rod. It's not who he was.'

FROM THE THIN BLUE LINE TO A LIFE LINE

Tony and Michelle met in a Melbourne nightclub, which was not unusual for the time. But they did stand out from the usual clientele at that particular establishment.

Casey's nightclub in Hawthorn specialised in the over-35 market, leaving it with a somewhat cynical nickname from younger clubbers.

'We met at Grab-a-Granny's,' says Michelle. She was 19 and Tony was 21. 'Our relationship was based on a lie,' she says. 'He said he was a carpenter, but I was a chippy's daughter and knew more about it than he did.'

Tony Currie, then a promising boxer, had just had a bout at the Braybrook Hotel and stopped for a celebratory drink with mates. He had already applied to join the police force and walked into the Police Academy a few months later.

The couple have been together ever since, including when they received the Citizen Commendation, the highest civilian honour that can be awarded by police, in 2022 for their work in helping police deal with the stresses of a job where one event can be life-changing. The citation, presented to the 'proud and humbled' Curries by Chief

Commissioner Shane Patton, states: 'For providing exemplary service through the support of current and former members of Victoria Police and their families where members have been involved in critical and life-changing incidents.'

For years the Curries have invested their money, time and passion to present seminars, conferences and small gatherings for cops and their partners, designed to turn victims into survivors.

The Critical Incident Forums involve police who have survived dealing with death and who share their battles to recover from trauma. The stress can come from one or a hundred incidents, from shootings, car accidents, sex crimes or domestic abuse. From dealing with evil to looking for answers where there are none.

Those who knew 'Kid' Currie when he was in the force would have bet he was more likely to be rapped on the knuckles by a chief commissioner than presented with an award by one.

His tendency to test the rules began early. At the strictly live-in academy he would scale the perimeter fence and race off to Michelle, waiting in her car, before returning in the morning. He was convinced he had them fooled, but some instructors chose to turn a blind eye.

An instinctively brave and practical cop, Tony was, he admits, hopeless at paperwork, which is why Michelle, a savvy law clerk, buffed and polished many of his assignments.

Again, the instructors knew, and marked him down. This annoyed Michelle more than Tony. 'I would think: "That introduction was really good, why didn't it get top marks?".'

From that night at Casey's, she was attracted by his smile and sense of fun – then watched as it drained from him over nearly 12 years in policing.

'My father said for 10 years he didn't know Tony could smile,' she says.

There are police who have a career without seeing an offender with a firearm. From the time Currie marched out of the academy, trouble seemed to be looking for him. Within weeks of graduation, a man pulled a knife on him. Within months a troubled Vietnam veteran lured police to his house and pulled a gun in a planned 'suicide by cop'. Currie drew his service revolver: 'We were in a Mexican stand-off.'

The Special Operations Group (SOG) was called and one of them shot and wounded the veteran.

Soon Currie would join the SOG. The welterweight boxer was at that time the lightest and smallest applicant to be accepted, but he soon built a reputation as one of the toughest.

If policing is seen as a brotherhood, the SOG was almost a cult. 'They were so insular, they were like the mafia,' says Michelle. 'They worked together, had social trips, went to the movies and even went to have their haircuts together.'

Currie became so obsessed he would sleep in the office to make sure he wouldn't miss a job. Hyperalert and always on guard, he became disengaged and distant at family or non-police gatherings. His job as an assault team member and explosives technician consumed him.

So, why did Michelle stick with him? 'There was always a glimmer [of what he had been] there.'

In November 1988 the SOG went to arrest Jedd Houghton (a suspect in the Walsh Street murders of constables Steven Tynan and Damian Eyre) in a Bendigo caravan park. When Houghton pointed a handgun at the police, Currie and Paul 'Possum' Carr fired, killing him instantly.

To have shot dead a suspected double cop killer gave Currie and Carr (who would die 15 years later, climbing a mountain in the Himalayas to raise money for the Make a Wish Foundation) celebrity status within policing, but behind closed doors it was different.

The terrible Houghton shooting scene stayed with Currie. 'I couldn't get it out of my head. There were night sweats and broken sleep. No matter how busy I was during the day, at night the images [inside the Bendigo caravan] would come back.'

Two months later Currie shot and wounded another armed man during a raid on a cannabis plantation. It was made clear to him there couldn't be a third.

When he tried to talk a man out of shooting himself, the man stuck his gun in the side of Currie's head. Currie would have been justified in using lethal force, but instead he and others wrestled the gun from the man's hand.

Yet, it wasn't the workload or the danger that led Currie to think it was time to leave, but exactly the opposite. Back in uniform, he hated the mundane and was addicted to the adrenalin surge from the life-and-death raids.

In 1996, he resigned. It is fair to say Michelle and many in the police hierarchy were relieved.

'The week after I left I went for a run and did my best time ever. It was as if the weight of policing had been lifted from my shoulders,' Currie says.

'For me, it was like he had left and then come back,' says Michelle.

The Curries built a successful window glazing business and were bought-out for a lucrative sum.

They had a son, who only knew his father as a professional type, not a law enforcement action man. When a police helicopter appeared on the TV news, Michelle told their young son: 'Dad used to abseil out of that.' The boy responded: 'Yeah, in his dreams.'

They retired in 2011. Three years later Tony's good mate, former armed robbery detective Mark Wylie, took his own life. Wylie had been shot and wounded in 1986 during an arrest raid on a Russell Street bombing suspect.

'I was aware of his struggles, but like others, I believed he would battle on through as he had in the past,' says Currie. Then a second police officer killed herself.

Tony and Michelle decided to use their experience to reach out to police and families who were suffering similar pressures after critical incidents. The first forum was in 2015, and they have been holding them ever since.

Tony enlists a group of police involved in previous fatal shootings to reach out to present police involved in similar incidents. They talk of the broken sleep, the mood swings but also of the truth that there is a way back. Usually, the new members of that dreadful club are just relieved to know their feelings are shared.

'Some will say: "I thought it was just me." It is about letting them know they are not alone,' Currie says.

The Curries' Critical Incident Forums allow cops and their families to share stories that many have locked away for years. Organised outside the formal police structure, they encourage many to open up in a way they would not within a departmental program. Rank doesn't matter, and nothing ends up on a personnel file.

'It is an informal approach where no one is judging you,' says Michelle. 'There are people who thought they would never recover who are now helping others. It takes time to heal, and everyone recovers at their own pace.'

Tony says: 'Policing is one of the greatest and most rewarding jobs. Some of the friendships you make last forever.'

But he has a message to those who are struggling: 'There is life after policing.'